x8.95X

AMERICAN POLITICAL THOUGHT

AMERICAN POLITICAL THOUGHT

MAX J. SKIDMORE

St. Martin's Press
New York

To Charl

Library of Congress Catalog Card Number: 77-086296
Copyright © 1978 by St. Martin's Press, Inc.
All Rights Reserved.
Manufactured in the United States of America.
0
fedc
For information, write St. Martin's Press, Inc.,
175 Fifth Avenue, New York, N.Y. 10010

cover design by Karen Shein-Kull

cloth ISBN: 0-312-02894-6
paper ISBN: 0-312-02895-4

Preface

Although this book is not lengthy, it discusses, in addition to the major influences on American political thought, those strains that run counter to the "main currents." These crosscurrents are often ignored despite the influence they may have had, if only through the reactions they provoked. *American Political Thought* is designed to provide a coherent introduction to political thought in this country, yet remain sufficiently brief to permit examination of original writings and secondary materials. Its purpose, in other words, is to serve as a core around which instructors can organize a variety of works to suit a wide range of approaches. Such a treatment can combine the flexibility of a thematic study based on primary sources with the consistency and continuity of a course centered on a traditional text.

The citations in the footnotes and the text itself include the key original and secondary readings that expand upon the themes of each chapter and may well suggest directions for further study. Beyond these, additonal readings that would be of value are listed at the end of each chapter. These listings, of course, are highly selective and represent only a small portion of the vast amount of worthwhile material available.

I should like to thank Professor Mulford Q. Sibley for his invaluable comments upon the manuscript, Pauline Williams for typing and clerical services above and beyond the call of duty, and Carolyn Eggleston of St. Martin's Press for her always cheerful and helpful assistance. I alone am responsible for any inadequacies that remain.

Max J. Skidmore

Contents

	Introduction	**xi**
1	**Theoretical Backgrounds**	**1**
	Greek and Roman Thought	1
	Judeo-Christian Thought	3
	Protestant Reformation Thought	6
	English and French Post-Reformation Thought	11
	Additional Readings	16
2	**Religious Roots**	**17**
	Democratic Tendencies in Colonial New England	17
	Dissent in the New England Colonies	26
	Colonial Attitudes Toward Indians	29
	Politics and Religion in the Middle and Southern Colonies	30
	The Secularization of Politics	31
	Additional Readings	34
3	**American Consciousness and the Revolution**	**36**
	Prerevolutionary Political Writers	39
	The Arguments of Thomas Paine	43
	Principles of the Declaration of Independence	46
	Additional Readings	49
4	**The Constitution and Its Critics**	**51**
	Precedents for a Written Constitution	52
	The Articles of Confederation	55

The Constitutional Convention and Ensuing Debate   58
Is the Constitution Reactionary?   62
Additional Readings   65

5 The Early Republic   67

The Political Philosophy of Thomas Jefferson   70
The Political Philosophy of Alexander Hamilton   75
Federalists Versus Republicans: Political Developments   76
Other Exponents of Jeffersonian Philosophy   80
Additional Readings   85

6 Jacksonian America   87

Jacksonianism: Extension of Suffrage and
    Rising Black Consciousness   87
Worker Agitation: Thomas Skidmore and Frances Wright   90
Andrew Jackson's Thought   96
Interpreters of Jacksonian America   98
Additional Readings   102

7 Romantic Response   104

The Brook Farm Community   107
Ralph Waldo Emerson and Margaret Fuller   109
Walt Whitman and Orestes Brownson   112
Henry David Thoreau   114
Additional Readings   119

8 National Power and Nationalism   121

The Growth of National Power   121
The Growth of Nationalism   127
Additional Readings   132

9 The Rights of Man Reconsidered   133

Background of the Debate over Slavery   134
The Southern Position   139
The Position of Moderates   147
The Abolitionist Position   149
Additional Readings   155

10 Industrialism: The Age of Individualism   156

Social Darwinism and Its Advocates   157
Wealth and Social Darwinism   163

\

Meliorist Social Darwinism   166
Reform Movements and Reformers
   in the Late Nineteenth Century   167
Additional Readings   172

11 Into the Progressive Era   **174**

American Socialists and Anarchists   175
Rise of the Social Gospel   177
Black Civil Rights: The Debate over Direction   179
Progressive Thought   184
The Progressives' Impact on Politics   187
Additional Readings   193

12 Postwar Malaise   **195**

Bigotry in the Postwar Years   196
Political Statements in Literature in the 1920s   199
Protest Before the Depression   202
Additional Readings   206

13 The Great Depression and Its Aftermath   **208**

The Thought of Herbert Hoover   209
A Conservative Critique of the American System   211
New Deal Pragmatism   213
Critiques of the New Deal   218
Additional Readings   224

**14 Currents and Crosscurrents in
      Contemporary America**   **226**

Political Thought from Nonpolitical Writers   227
The Conservative Critique of
   Modern Political Assumptions   231
Leftist Thought and Movements for Reform   237
Additional Readings   248

Index   **251**

Introduction

One of the more obvious functions of political science is to provide descriptions of political processes and institutions and, under certain carefully prescribed conditions, to assist in predicting political trends and developments. Another function, though one that may be less obvious in modern times because it is often ignored, is to aid in achieving the purposes of politics, the most important of which is to establish and maintain good government. This latter function not only provided the initial justification for a science of politics but even today justifies its existence more fully than anything else.

The American political tradition stresses that good government is that which insures justice and protects freedom. Although governmental activities have expanded tremendously in recent decades and the demands of good government are considerably more complex than in earlier times, the principles of freedom and justice remain fundamental. Because government has become so complex and complexity vastly increases the likelihood that freedom and justice will be compromised, even unwittingly, every political action takes on new importance. These and other factors, such as the awesome power now available to rulers resulting from the burgeoning of science and technology, make it more essential than ever before to engage in political studies and evaluation. Now that the issues at stake include for the first time the very survival of life on earth, political science is even more vital than when Aristotle described it as the "architechtonic science."

The terms "political theory" and "political philosophy" are often used in confusing fashion. "Theory" may be defined so narrowly as to apply, for example, only to empirical generalizations, or so broadly that it includes virtually any thought about politics; "philosophy" usually implies some attention to judgments of value. For our purposes the broadest definition is the most serviceable, remembering that it is difficult to engage in political thought without making some value judgments. In studying American political thought we will reject the view that it is separate from political science; however formal or informal the political scientist may be, and however one defines political science, broadly or narrowly, political thought is at its core. The greatest benefits from studying political thought come from the insights that such study may provide into the actual functioning of politics, and these lead directly to evaluation of political actions and political systems. In this very real sense, therefore, the study of political thought may be among the most concrete and least abstract activities in the entire study of politics. Much more so than many people recognize, political theories and philosophies direct political action; in too many cases, unfortunately, the philosophies that lead to certain actions may be unrecognized even by the persons taking those actions. The study of political thought could possibly lead to more rational political actions as well as to more effective evaluations of those actions.

Because of the scarcity of formal political philosophers in the American tradition—figures such as Plato, Aristotle, Hobbes, Locke, or Rousseau, who stood apart from their societies in order to examine them from a detached point of view—there are those who contend that America has no political theory to speak of, that what guides to action exist are purely pragmatic or expediential. Such a view ignores centuries of vigorous political thought and fails to recognize that much of the speculation that historically has come from political philosophers has, in America, come instead from statesmen, actors on the political scene. This fact itself has no doubt affected the character of American political thought and therefore of American politics and political institutions.

The basic questions in the American stream of thought are not unique to America. What are the boundaries between human rights and property rights? What are the duties and the rights of the community and the individual? What obligations exist between the people, collectively, and their government? Such questions are fundamental issues everywhere and have been throughout much of human history. In attempting to deal with them, America has produced something unique. The traditions of American political thought, some inherited and some having arisen in response to native conditions, together form the key to the development of the institutions of American politics. Even more important, American political thought can provide the necessary understanding of the operations of those institutions, and therefore of American politics. Perhaps most important of all, the study of American political thought can provide insights into what America should be and what it is likely to become.

AMERICAN POLITICAL THOUGHT

1

Theoretical Backgrounds

As a nation, the United States was the result of conscious action by a group of dedicated human beings. Rather than evolving gradually through the ages, it came into being clearly defined and with visible origins. American political thought, however, did not spring into existence fully matured with the signing of the Declaration of Independence. Its theoretical sources are numerous, and its roots reach far back in history.

Greek and Roman Thought

As early as Plato and Aristotle we find the idea that an ethical government must operate according to law, or with regard to certain consistent rules. These philosophers differed upon many things; in fact, Aristotle, who most authorities conclude had studied with Plato, was severely critical of his teacher.[1] Nevertheless they both accepted human beings as social animals who cannot exist naturally apart from some society, they viewed humankind as essentially rational, and they agreed that "the end of the state is the good life," as Aristotle put it.[2] They were concerned with justice and virtue, not with rights, and had no conception of individual rights against the state because they considered the interests of the state and the citizen to be identical. The major end of the state and the citizen was the common good. Moreover, Plato and Aristotle both assumed that politics and ethics are inseparable. Plato's *Republic* and Aristotle's *Politics*, two of the most notable classics in all of political literature, formed the foundation for much of the subsequent riches of the Western world's political ideas.

There were, however, other strains of Greek thought that had more immediate and direct influence upon the emerging political traditions in the West. Stoicism, in particular, was the principal medium by which Greek thought was introduced into the Roman world. The Stoics developed the idea of worldwide brotherhood, and they formulated the conception of natural law (*jus naturale*), an idea that was to dominate political thought for centuries. The best known of the Stoic writers was actually a Roman, Cicero, who had studied in Greece. His works synthesized the ideas of the late Stoic school and had considerable impact upon the development of Roman law, which is still the foundation for many of the world's legal systems.

Cicero, in his *Republic*, defined natural law as right reason consonant with nature.[3] In essence natural law consists of moral principles discoverable by reason that form the basis for human laws and other actions. In later times natural law came to be inseparable from natural rights. Not until the last 150 years or so has there been a serious challenge to the notion that there is a law of reason which is eternal, absolute, and universal and that man-made law is valid only when it conforms to this law of right reason.[4] Such an assumption would influence the development, centuries later, of the ideas of constitutionalism and even of judicial review.

In addition to formulating the idea of natural law, the Stoics went beyond earlier Greek thought in still another way. Despite the extraordinary scope of their minds, neither Plato nor Aristotle saw beyond the confines of the Greek city-state, or polis. Each distinguished the Greek from the non-Greek world, which he viewed as peopled by barbarians, and neither was troubled by the existence of slavery. Each considered a state larger than the polis to be ungovernable. The Stoics, however, concluding that there was one natural law that was the same for all persons, Greek or non-Greek, assumed also that all humanity shared a common rationality and a common inheritance from God. Just as natural law governed all peoples, so should all peoples become subject to a world law (*jus gentium*), devised as a product of human reason to interpret natural law; both would be universal. To accommodate local and cultural differences, there would be a local law (*jus civile*), based upon custom, that would be subordinate to world law.

As Roman political thought developed, it departed from the Greek conception of the citizen as one with the state. The Romans considered the individual to be prior to the state and the state to be constructed by citizens who consented mutually. Theories of the formation of the state by contract were centuries away, but the Romans did sow the seeds for a doctrine of consent that, together with the idea of universal law, made possible the later development of the notion of individual rights, something essentially foreign to Greek thought. It is doubtful that doctrines either of individual rights or of the right of revolution could have developed as they did had Roman thought not modified Greek thought in this fashion.[5]

Judeo-Christian Thought

Roman and Greek thought would come to us by way of their impact upon Christianity, which was to dominate the Western world for centuries. But Christianity was also influenced by another strain of thought, that of the Hebrews.

The dominant themes of Hebrew thought were the Law and the Covenant. The Law was a rigid code of conduct prescribed by God, not by human beings. The Covenant, on the other hand, was an agreement between God and men, providing an element of consent. Violating the Law was therefore sinful not only because it was counter to God's will, but also because it was a failure to live up to the agreement of the Covenant.

Christianity is built upon Jewish law and prophecy, Greek philosophy, and Roman law. It took from the Stoics, by way of the Roman jurists, the idea of natural law and identified it as a part of the law of God, or divine law. When St. Augustine, a towering figure in early Church history, spoke of law, for example, he did not limit it to the law of reason as described by Cicero but expanded it to include God's will.

In *The City of God* he distinguished between two cities, that of God and that of man. Since human nature is dual, both body and spirit, human beings are simultaneously citizens of the two cities, but only in the City of God can there truly be peace. Augustine did not precisely identify human institutions with the City of Man nor the Church with the City of God. He contended that in order to achieve justice, a state must teach belief in Christianity. It is the sinfulness of human beings that made the City of Man a necessity and with it human institutions such as property. Property, the consequence of sin, would have no place in the City of God, but it, along with coercive functions of the state, is essential on earth directly because of human evil.

Augustine was careful to stress the requirement of obedience to secular, or state, authority. Again, there is duality. The Church too is necessary as the embodiment of God's will on earth and as such also demands obedience. Here, early in the fifth century, he anticipated

the doctrine of the "two swords," which was made official by Pope
Gelasius I at the century's end.⁶ The doctrine demanded submission
to the power of the state in temporal matters, and submission to the
power of the Church in matters spiritual; both church and state were
supreme within their respective spheres. The actual dividing line
between the two authorities was tenuous, foreshadowing the questions of jurisdiction and the struggle for power between the "two
swords" that plagued the Middle Ages.

Essentially, society in the Middle Ages was static. The most
prominent characteristics of the era were social—and even
geographic—immobility, an emphasis upon status and hierarchy, and
a strong sense of all portions of reality as interdependent. This
interdependence could be seen not only in the meshings of individuals' activities within society but also in the interlocking of man-made
and divine law, which extended to the fundamental workings of
nature and the universe.

Medieval thought is amply captured in the writings of St.
Thomas Aquinas, who lived in the thirteenth century. Aristotle's
works had been lost to the West prior to the beginning of the
Christian era. However, Muslim scholars had translated and pre-
served his writings, which were discovered by the Spanish and made
available in Europe shortly before Thomas's birth. The exposure to
Aristotelian philosophy revitalized Christian thought, with consequent implications not only for theology but also for theories of
government. Scholasticism, the effort to produce a synthesis between the philosophy of Aristotle and the theology of Christianity,
reached its apex with Thomas.

Thomas accepted Aristotle's ideas of the state with some modifications. He agreed that the state was natural and that it was to
further the common good, but argued that its purposes were subordinate to the goal of spiritual salvation. Thus, although he accepted
Aristotle's justification for the state as deriving directly from human
nature, he did not consider the state to be the reflection of ultimate
value, which could only come from a higher realm. In following
Aristotle's view of the state as resulting from the social nature of
human beings, Thomas rejected Augustine's notions that it resulted
from the evil in mankind and that its functions were to control that
evil. He therefore interpreted its role more favorably than had his
predecessors among the Church Fathers as providing for mutual aid
and comfort, that is, as a cooperative human venture.

St. Thomas's thought is unusually valuable for the insights that
it gives into the medieval mind, but he produced no one systematic
work that gives a complete picture of his political thought. The best

representation of his political ideas is found in his major work, the *Summa Theologica*; portions of his *De Regimine Principum* and his commentaries upon the works of Aristotle are also valuable.

Political theory owes most to his conception of law, which, in tune with most medieval thought, involved a hierarchy of types related in a complex way. Thomas identified four categories of law. Eternal law is the will of God, which humanity can never fully understand, an emanation from the Prime Intellect, which is unchanging through time and space. Natural law results from the exercise of reason; when human beings apply reason to attempt to understand the eternal law, they discover certain moral truths and self-evident propositions. These may be used as standards by which to judge human actions. There have been thinkers who associated natural law with divine law. As Thomas conceived it, however, divine law is clearly distinguishable as a third type. Divine law is the same as revelation—word that comes directly from God. The Ten Commandments, for example, represent divine law. The remaining category is human law, that is, man-made, or positive, law. In a sense, human law may be related to expressions of natural law, since to be valid all human enactments must be consistent with the principles of natural law. Natural law cannot vary, but human laws must because they exist to give expression to natural law in widely varied circumstances such as different cultural, economic, and social conditions. Practical considerations demand that human laws must differ to accommodate different situations, but in every case they must reflect principles of the unchanging natural law.[7] Thus, the state was to enforce man-made law derived from natural law, which, in turn, was a part of the eternal law.

Along with the Thomist treatment of law went the attitude, again characteristic of the Middle Ages, that the ruler who fails to abide by the law is not a true ruler but a tyrant. Many medieval thinkers saw the universe as so tightly ordered that they viewed a tyrant not only as one who wrongs human beings, but even more important, as one who violates the whole system ordained by God for the ordering of the world. Nevertheless, there was no notion of individual rights against the state. Duty was paramount in Thomist thought. A tyrant was one who ruled in his own interest, not for the common good. He could be and should be deposed, but only by a legitimate public authority. Any other course Thomas believed to be too dangerous to the community. Even a tyrant was to be obeyed while he held office, unless he commanded actions in violation of the will of God. The Church could then excommunicate a ruler, which would remove all obligation to him from his subjects.[8]

St. Thomas has had immeasurable influence upon the history of philosophy, theology, and political theory. His synthesis of Greek philosophy with Christian theology demonstrated a compatibility that shaped much of the West's intellectual tradition. Although much of what came to be American political thought was generated as a reaction against the Middle Ages as illustrated by Thomistic thought, without St. Thomas those traditions would likely have been vastly different.

Also interesting in terms of later political development are the arguments that resulted from the conciliar movement of the early fifteenth century. The movement stemmed from controversy regarding power within the Church: Should the Pope be supreme or should he share his power with a general council, however constituted? Such struggle, although centered upon Church government, has implications for secular government as well. Many of the arguments developed here were subsequently duplicated when controversies arose over the respective powers of kings and parliaments. The ultimate victory of the advocates of papal power foreshadowed the rise of theories of the divine right of kings.[9]

Protestant Reformation Thought

The ideas discussed thus far have formed the basis for much of Western political thought, of which American political thought is a branch. More vital for the study of political thought in America, however, are ideas that developed during the Protestant Reformation. The Reformation did not begin in England, but the twin continental thrusts of Lutheranism and, especially, Calvinism, together with Anglicanism, its peculiarly English expression, culminated in the English religious and political struggles of the seventeenth century. These struggles, and the theories they generated, formed the basis for much of American political thought and practice.

The two most prominent thinkers in the Reformation were Martin Luther and John Calvin. Although there were evidences earlier of the strains that brought about the Reformation, the incident that marks its beginning occurred when Luther nailed his Ninety-five Theses to the door of the Wittenberg Church in Germany in 1517. The theses criticized the luxury and corruption of the papal court and the sale of indulgences. What began merely as an effort on the part of a priest to reform the Roman Catholic Church soon became a movement that shattered Western Europe's Christian unity, the quality that more than any other had characterized the Middle Ages.

Luther's notion of the priesthood of all true believers simplified the relation between God and humankind. The Christian could communicate directly with God with no need for an intermediary. To the medieval mind the important elements of salvation were good works and the sacraments; Luther substituted the notion of grace through faith. In a period in which many older presuppositions were being rapidly and radically revised, political theory could hardly have escaped being influenced by so striking a view as that which placed the believer into an intimate relationship with God. One consequence of such a view was the elimination of the need for priestly administration of the sacraments, thus removing a major power of the Church over secular rulers. Luther's views also entailed a rejection of the medieval synthesis that had placed politics in a complex and elaborate cosmic ordering of creation directed by God. Instead, Protestantism gave politics a more human setting and related it less to divinely structured nature with layers of law than to human purposes and institutions.

Luther firmly believed in the need for strong secular authority, and he just as strongly rejected any proposition that would grant subjects the right to rebel against their rulers. Although he had himself led a revolt against the authority of the pope, Luther's thought brought about a political quietism that justified virtually unlimited power for the rulers of the state. He believed that the only effective or desirable limits to a ruler's power were the ruler's own virtue and the counsel of his or her spiritual advisers. Luther failed to recognize that the weakening of the church as an institution effectively removed all limits on the ruler's exercise of power. The Lutheran creed therefore encouraged political absolutism in the areas where that faith was dominant. The immediate practical effect of Lutheranism is ironic when it is remembered that Lutheran ideas inherently are intensely individualistic and equalitarian. Part of the paradox results from inconsistency in Luther's thought and part from an inconsistency between his thought and the actions that he supported. Luther provided a new conception of the importance of individual conscience at the same time that other aspects of his doctrines justified political repression. The Middle Ages had very little notion of individual rights because the world was thought to consist of so complex a network of mutually dependent relationships that there was hardly a distinction between the state and society, or even between the private and the public spheres. In helping to destroy the medieval attitude, Lutheran thought contributed to the climate that would later support the notion of individual rights against the state, but this was certainly not Luther's intention and in practice his reforms led to state-dominated churches that were the tools of the princes.[10]

More directly important to the development of American political thought are the teachings of John Calvin, whose ideas are best represented in his *Institutes of the Christian Religion.*[11] Whereas Luther's authoritarianism was softened somewhat by an essentially humanistic temper, Calvin seemed to glory in the need for harsh measures from both secular and spiritual authorities. The Catholic could achieve salvation by submitting to Church doctrine, observing the sacramental rites, and living a life characterized by good works; the Lutheran simply by maintaining faith. Each religion at least granted to the individual believer some role in determining his or her own destiny; not so Calvinism. Calvin conceived of humanity as so evil that no human effort could possibly earn salvation. All human beings deserved to be doomed to everlasting punishment, and all would be except those few whom God in His infinite mercy had elected to save. These few, the elect, were predestined to salvation regardless of anything they might do, and all others were to be damned. There were to be no exceptions to the cold operation of predestination.

Immediately a question arises regarding predestination. If all is foreordained, and if individual effort is inevitably unsatisfactory in God's sight, then why make any effort to live virtuously? Calvinism had no satisfying intellectual answer to this question, but it had a practical response. Calvin held that the elect would experience a sense of salvation directly from God and that this religious experience would lead the convert to practice the true religion, Calvinism, with unimpaired zeal. The elect, of course, were to be the members of the church, a small minority. But even among the majority there might be some who were of the elect, and it would be essential to search every aspect of conduct to help in determining who these might be. These beliefs encouraged extraordinary intolerance and a tendency toward moralizing that would eliminate any consideration of privacy. The congregation of the elect were those who had had genuine religious experiences, and they were to determine the adequacy of the claims presented by those who wanted to become members. Leading a virtuous life, then, might be considered evidence that one was of the elect and hence eligible for church membership. There would be those who fraudulently claimed to have had the experience, and many who would deceive themselves into thinking falsely that they had been chosen. The church had thus been assigned a function of tremendous importance, that of deciding who among the people were saved or damned.

Modern Americans may have difficulty in understanding that Calvinist doctrine called for separation of church and state. Calvin feared that alliance of the two institutions would corrupt the church, and he rejected the Lutheran and Anglican practice of national churches. Nevertheless, this in no way was to lessen the role of religion in secular affairs, for Calvin taught that the secular authorities had the duty to protect the church and its doctrines and to insure the worship of God. The Calvinists thus recognized a separation of church and state, but not a separation of religion and state; the state would be a tool of religion, although the church would have no direct authority over the civil government.[12] The secular rulers, the magistrates, were called by God to perform their tasks and thus should not only be obeyed but venerated by their subjects as agents of God even as were the ministers. The high placement of the magistrate demanded passive obedience as the proper function of the subject.

Calvin recognized that rulers might abuse their powers, but he taught that passive obedience was due even to tyrants, because tyranny was a visitation from God upon the people for their sinfulness and the tyrant, no less than the good ruler, was God's agent. The responsibility of the magistrate was not to his subjects, but to God. Despite this strong emphasis, there were kernels of radicalism implicit in Calvinism, though deeply buried and decidedly minor. These minor implications were emphasized by later generations out of all proportion to Calvin's intent. There were two exceptions to the requirement of passive obedience. If a constitution existed to protect certain liberties, that constitution could be defended against a tyrant because it, too, received its legitimacy from God. More important is the doctrine that a magistrate's commands may be ignored if he orders anything against God's will. Where Calvinists were in the minority, they tended to magnify this provision for passive resistance to serve ultimately as a justification for action. Where Calvinists held power, as in Geneva under Calvin's own rule, the rule was harsh and autocratic, and the stress was upon the major thrust of Calvinism, passive obedience. When they were out of power, Calvinists tended to use whatever rationale might be available to maintain their faith and to convert nonbelievers. In fact their struggles against non-Calvinist rulers were considerably more politically influential than was passive obedience, which continued to be dominant in Calvinist theory.

In England, Calvinism took the form of Puritanism, an effort to "purify" the Anglican Church of its vestiges of Catholicism, and Separatism, a radical movement begun by Robert Browne that advocated total separation from the English church. The Anglicans were largely those supporting the feudal institutions of king and bishop. The Puritans, or Presbyterians, sought to substitute within the church the power of elected leaders for that of the king of England. The Separatists were Congregationalists; that is, they believed that only a particular congregation had the authority to appoint its own minister. So great was the hostility directed toward the Separatists by Anglican and Puritan alike that a group under the leadership of William Brewster and others fled to Holland.

As the power of Calvinism grew in England, so did the power of Parliament. Partly because of the association of the Anglican Church with the monarchist groups, the Presbyterians tended to support the parliamentary forces and became dominant in Parliament. The struggles between Parliament and king resulted in a civil war that began in 1642 and in the beheading of the monarch, Charles I, in 1649. Calvinist leaders were enormously influential in the conflict and from 1649 until 1660 dominated Commonwealth England, the period in which Parliament reigned supreme under the leadership of Oliver Cromwell. In 1660 the monarchy was restored.

Although Parliament had led a revolution, the intent had been to establish the rule of an elite consisting of generally well-to-do Presbyterians. The more radical groups called for a written constitution limiting the power of political institutions and for democratic participation in politics. One faction in particular, the Levellers, who included such figures as Richard Overton and John Lilburne, were responsible for increasingly radical demands; beyond the Levellers were the Diggers and other even more extreme groups. Much of the agitation came from within the army, which pleaded with Parliament to violate tradition completely and establish a rather democratic society. Between 1646 and 1649 the pressures were intense, but the ideas of the Presbyterian moderates generally prevailed throughout Cromwell's Protectorate.

Many of the theoretical issues of centuries to come had arisen within the ranks of the British Calvinists. Among the numerous political pamphlets demanding reforms were the three entitled "An Agreement of the People for a firme and present Peace," the first of which Richard Overton wrote in 1647. This stimulated debates between the officers of the army who sought moderate reform and the soldiers whose demands were more radical.

Each side accepted the validity of higher law, the right of private property, and the notion that government was based upon consent, but their emphases were considerably different. Cromwell and his son-in-law, General Ireton, who spoke for the officers, contended that all rights were based upon irrevocable compact. The spokesman for the soldiers, Colonel Rainboro, emphasized justice instead. When Ireton argued that only the propertied classes should have the vote, Rainboro responded that "the poorest he that is in England has a life to live as the richest he . . . and I do think that the poorest man in England is not at all bound in a strict sense to that Government that he has not had a voice to put himself under."[13] Rainboro, for the soldiers, stressed persons more than property. Although neither side yielded in the debates, the issues concerning the rights of the people, as opposed to those of property or the government, were set forth clearly.

English and French
Post-Reformation Thought

The England into which Calvinism had made its intrusion was also producing some of the world's greatest formal political philosophy as a result of the political and religious ferment of the time. In his classic work *The Leviathan*, Thomas Hobbes broke cleanly with medieval traditions to write one of the earliest works that suggested the principles of liberalism, albeit strongly authoritarian liberalism. The essence of liberalism is its concentration upon the individual. To Hobbes, government was an artificial institution created by human beings for their own security. It was not divinely ordained, nor were there principles of natural or moral law at work. Hobbesian philosophy begins with a darkly pessimistic view of human psychology and postulates a "state of nature" in which the life of man is "solitary, poor, nasty, brutish, and short."[14] Human beings are governed much more by passions than by reason and will, terrorizing one another unless restrained by external force. In order to escape the state of nature, they contract to form a civil society. The government of that society is monarchical, and the monarch must be absolute in order to have the power to fulfill his or her function, the protection of life.

It is important to recognize that although Hobbes stressed the necessity for total power, such power originally came from the people and is to be exercised to protect them from death either at the hands of invaders or other citizens. This, to Hobbes, is the primary function of government. He was consistent and admitted only one circumstance that would justify resistance to a ruler: if the ruler attempts to take a citizen's life, the citizen may rebel because his contract is then broken.[15] Hobbes did not favor absolute power because he desired to have harsh rulers but because a limited ruler would have inadequate power to protect the people from reverting into a state of anarchy, which would again be the state of nature, the war of all against all. Hobbes, one might say, could well be granted the title of the first advocate of "law and order" as the term is now understood.

Writing in the middle of the seventeenth century, at about the same time as Hobbes, was James Harrington, whose political utopia, *Oceana*, recognized the role of property and economic power as central to political power. In his notion of a utopian commonwealth, Harrington anticipated some of the themes of American thought over a century later. He provided for short terms of office with frequent rotation, for election, and for complex forms of representation. His greatest insight, however accurate it may or may not be in detail, was his identification of the power of economics. As political theorist Mulford Sibley remarks, "relative to its times the utopia represents a rather daring vision which will inspire revolutionists of the future." [16]

A figure so influential in the history of American political thought that he may almost be considered to represent its beginning was John Locke, who wrote his *Second Treatise on Government* in 1690. Locke owed many of his ideas to "the judicious Hooker," Richard Hooker, who wrote at the close of the sixteenth century. The first five books of the latter's *Lawes of Ecclesiasticall Politie* were printed from 1594 to 1597, and the remaining three books appeared posthumously in 1648. Hooker argued that government was formed out of a state of nature by consent of the people, although he supported the monarchy and called for passive obedience. He also believed in a natural law that could be rationally interpreted and would accommodate changing conditions. Locke clearly acknowledged his debt to Hooker. [17]

Like Hobbes, Locke began with a consideration of man in a state of nature. Unlike Hobbes, however, his outlook was essentially optimistic; his state of nature was not the grim war of all against all conceived by Hobbes. Locke believed that human beings were essentially rational and in the state of nature had been largely governed by a law of nature that gave rise to morality. To Hobbes, the individual had only one right, the right to self-preservation. To Locke, however, a person had the right not only to life, but also to liberty and property. The right to property, which he defined more broadly than simply material goods, results from mixing one's labor with the products of nature. Because the state of nature contained certain "inconveniences"—that is, no regularized system of law and no common enforcing agent, thus requiring self-enforcement of the principles of reason and law when one happened to be wronged—

people contracted to form a civil society. This was, however, a society considerably different from the fierce authoritarian one envisioned by Hobbes.

Locke's beginning point, like Hobbes's, was the individual, but for Locke the individual was a being with strong rights and with claims against the power of government. Using Locke's notion, American political thought came to embody liberalism. Human beings contracted among themselves to form society and also contracted with their rulers to protect their lives, their liberty, and their property. If the government failed to do this, the people had the right to rebel; they could revolt to prevent the development of a tyranny or to eliminate one. Both law and government existed solely to serve human ends interpreted in the most individualistic of terms. Government was not a leviathan, or monster, that was to dominate citizens, nor was society an organic institution within which everyone fulfilled a designated function directed toward the common good, as in the Aristotelian conception that so greatly influenced the Middle Ages. Lockean society and government existed to permit each person to pursue his or her own goals with a minimum of interference. Government was based upon contract, and law upon consent. These terms, "contract" and "consent," were to become fundamental to much of American political thought.

Locke favored religious toleration, the principle of consent of the governed, the right of revolution, and limitations upon the power of the government; in short, he stressed individual rights in a way that sounds familiar to all Americans. Similarly, he outlined a governmental structure that sounds somewhat similar to that finally adopted by the Founding Fathers. Favoring the separation of government's powers, he divided them into the legislative, the executive, and the "federative," by which he meant essentially international relations. He seemed to place more importance on the legislative power and believed that its separation from the power to execute the laws was a vital limitation. The judicial power, probably because it also dealt with execution of the laws, he assigned to the executive. The heart of his system was majority rule, not at all an accepted principle then or earlier.[18]

Although Locke suggested the separation of powers, the most notable explanation of that doctrine was that of the Baron de Montesquieu in his *Spirit of the Laws*, published in Paris in 1748. Montesquieu favored both monarchy and personal liberty and contended that the English government of the time, although a monarchy, provided for the most freedom for its subjects. In Montesquieu's view, there could be no liberty if the legislative and the executive were exercised by the same agent, or if the judicial power were not separated from the other two. He described the English system as separating the three powers, with the king exercising the executive, Parliament exercising the legislative, and the independent courts exercising the judicial functions. Each power was thus able to check the others. He did not anticipate the great power that the judiciary might develop as it did in the United States, but, as A. T. Mason and Richard Leach remark, "his theory was broad enough to include the courts when they began to exercise judicial review, for judicial review logically forms part of the essence of the separation of powers."[19]

Montesquieu has been subjected to considerable criticism from modern writers as having totally misinterpreted the nature of the British system. That system, far from demonstrating the value of separation of powers, originated the parliamentary form of government in which powers are not separated and the legislature actually exercises the important executive functions. This criticism seems somewhat unfair. It is true that the British system of Montesquieu's day was not exactly as he had described it, but neither was it the parliamentary system of today; it was in a state of flux with parliamentary supremacy developing. The monarch had ceased exercising the royal veto for less than two decades. Whatever the merits of the criticism, the American colonists seized upon Montesquieu's description of the English arrangement and used it as a partial model for their new government.

Other currents in France had some influence on American thinkers, including the Physiocratic school, which disputed the prevailing mercantilistic doctrines of governmental regulation of economic affairs and advocated a "natural" order in which the state restrained its actions and interfered to a minimum extent in the ongoing economy. The Physiocrats were agrarians, believing that all wealth came from the soil.[20] The laissez-faire strain in American thought, the notion advocated by Thomas Jefferson that government should keep clear of the economic sphere, owes much to the ideas of the eighteenth-century French Physiocrats as well as to the work of the Britisher, Adam Smith, whose influential work, *Wealth of Nations*, was published the same year as the American Declaration of Independence.

It is a far cry from the ancient Greeks and Hebrews to the beginnings of modern America. Certainly it would be incorrect to conclude that political thought during the past 2,500 years has been uniformly developing in the direction of American ideas. Nevertheless, all political thought to some extent builds upon the past. America's is no exception. It can be adequately understood only against the background of history.

NOTES

1. Gilbert Ryle, however, contends that Aristotle never studied with Plato; see his *Plato's Progress* (Cambridge: Cambridge University Press, 1966).

2. *Politics* 1281a.

3. Cicero, *Republic* 3. 22.

4. John H. Hallowell, *Main Currents in Modern Political Thought* (New York: Holt, Rinehart and Winston, 1950), p. 18; see also Leo Strauss, *Natural Right and History* (Chicago: University of Chicago Press, 1953), pp. 81–202, for a discussion of natural law.

5. Hallowell, ibid., p. 19.

6. See Anne Fremantle, ed., *The Papal Encyclicals in Their Historical Context* (New York: Putnam's, 1956), pp. 53–54.

7. See A. P. d'Entreves, ed., *Aquinas: Selected Political Writings* (Oxford: Basil Blackwell, 1954), for selections of Thomas's political writings; general secondary treatments include G. K. Chesterton, *St. Thomas Aquinas* (New York: Doubleday, 1956); Martin D'Arcy, *St. Thomas Aquinas* (Westminster, Md.: Newman Press, 1953); and Jacques Maritain, *St. Thomas Aquinas* (Cleveland: World, 1962). For perceptive insights into medieval thought, see Mulford Q. Sibley, *Political Ideas and Ideologies* (New York: Harper & Row, 1970), part II; see especially chap. 10 on Augustine and chap. 13 on Thomas Aquinas.

8. See the selection from *De Regimine Principum* in d'Entreves, ibid., esp. pp. 31–32; and selections from *Summa Theologica* in the same work, esp. pp. 137 and 161.

9. See Brian Tierney, *Foundations of the Conciliar Theory* (Cambridge: Cambridge University Press, 1955); and Sibley, *Political Ideas*, pp. 276–285.

10. See Charles M. Jacobs, ed., *The Works of Martin Luther with Introduction and Notes*, 6 vols. (Philadelphia: Holman, 1915–1932); for an interesting analysis of Luther's thought, see Sheldon S. Wolin, "Politics and Religion: Luther's Simplistic Imperative," *American Political Science Review* 50 (March 1956), 24–42.

11. Benjamin B. Warfield, ed., 2 vols. (Philadelphia: Presbyterian Board of Christian Education, 1936).

12. It is true that the church dominated society and that it received support from taxes; this, of course, is not separation of church and state as we understand it, but there were no ecclesiastical courts and the ministers and the magistrates had separate jurisdictions; the church could expel members, but only the state could exercise physical coercion and force. For interesting insights into these and other issues regarding Calvinism, see Sheldon S. Wolin, "Calvin and the Reformation: The Political Education of Protestantism," *American Political Science Review* 51 (June 1957), 428–453; and Michael Walzer, *The Revolution of the Saints: A Study in the Origin of Radical Politics* (New York: Atheneum, 1973).

13. In A. T. Mason, *Free Government in the Making*, 3rd ed. (New York: Oxford University Press, 1965), p. 13.

14. Thomas Hobbes, *Leviathan* (Oxford: Basil Blackwell, 1957), p. 82.

15. Ibid., pp. 91, 142.

16. *Political Ideas*, p. 364.

17. See, for example, the *Second Treatise*, Peter Laslett, ed. (Cambridge: Cambridge University Press, 1960), chap. 2.

18. See Laslett's "Introduction," ibid., for excellent general background on Locke.

19. *In Quest of Freedom*, 2nd ed. (Englewood Cliffs, N.J.: Prentice-Hall, 1973), pp. 18–19.

20. Sibley, *Political Ideas*, p. 388.

ADDITIONAL READINGS

Corwin, E. S. *The "Higher Law" Background of American Constitutional Law.* Ithaca, N.Y.: Cornell University Press, 1967 [1928].

Curti, Merle. "The Great Mr. Locke: America's Philosopher, 1783–1861." *The Huntington Library Bulletin* XI (April 1937).

d'Entreves, A. P. *The Medieval Contribution to Political Thought.* New York: Humanities Press, 1959.

Gummere, Richard M. "The Classical Ancestry of the United States Constitution." *American Quarterly* XIV (Spring 1962).

Hartz, Louis. *The Liberal Tradition in America.* New York: Harcourt, Brace and World, 1955.

Lewis, Ewart. "The Contribution of Medieval Thought to the American Political Tradition." *American Political Science Review* L (June 1956).

Parrington, Vernon L. *The Colonial Mind, 1620–1800.* Main Currents in American Thought, vol. 1. New York: Harcourt, Brace and World, 1954 [1927], pp. 1–15.

Sigmund, Paul E., ed. *Natural Law in Political Thought.* Cambridge, Mass.: Winthrop, 1971.

Weber, Max. *The Protestant Ethic and the Spirit of Capitalism.* New York: Scribner's, 1958.

2

Religious Roots

Democratic Tendencies
in Colonial New England

The small group of Separatists who fled England to Holland became
famed in American tradition as the Pilgrims who arrived on the new
continent to found the Plymouth Colony in 1620. Although they had
intended to travel to Virginia, they landed in New England. Having
no charter, they concluded the Mayflower Compact, which became
the constitution of the colony and anticipated the subsequent development of written constitutions as basic to governmental systems in
America.

Initially, the Pilgrims owned their land in common following the
inspiration of primitive Christianity, but this experiment was brief,
soon giving way to private ownership. The government of the colony
consisted of a governor elected annually and a Council of Assistants
who were selected by the freemen, a small group consisting of the
"saints," or church members. The first governor, John Carver, died in
1621 to be succeeded by William Bradford, who was to be a power in
the colony for decades and who prepared the "official" history of the
colony, *Of Plymouth Plantation*. Because Plymouth frequently lacked a
minister, the duty of preaching during the early years often fell upon
a nonclergyman, William Brewster. The Pilgrims tended to be less
divided by doctrinal disputes than the Puritans, who, as we saw in the
last chapter, wanted to purge the Anglican Church of Catholic
practices. The colony they founded also received Anglican settlers
more favorably despite its open avowal of separation from the
Church of England.[1]

The Plymouth Colony consisted of a small group of Pilgrims who had fled from two countries and who had little in the way of material resources. By contrast, the Massachusetts Bay Company represented a powerful group of Puritans who had not only ample finances but the security of a royal charter, which specified the government of the company and granted the company the power to govern the colony it founded however it chose, so long as the laws were consistent with those of England. The main group of Puritans arrived in America in 1630 to settle in Boston and the nearby areas, and they brought with them well-known and influential figures.

The "freemen" of the Massachusetts Bay Colony were the stockholders of the company, who met in a General Court to legislate for the company and the colony as well. The court annually chose a governor, deputy governor, and eighteen assistants (all of whom were termed "magistrates") to govern between the meetings of the General Court held four times a year. In 1631 the General Court expanded the definition of "freeman" to include all church members. The previous year the court had transferred legislative power to the assistants, and the freemen no longer participated in legislating directly, although they continued to elect the magistrates. In 1634, however, the freemen of the towns began to appoint "deputies" to represent them in the General Court, which again participated in lawmaking.[2]

Despite their ostensible devotion to the Presbyterian principle, which favored centralization of church authority, the Puritans soon adopted many of the practices of the Congregationalists, who favored local control of church affairs. Rather than being tainted by Plymouth, however, it is likely that they had intended such a development all along, but had concealed their sentiments to avoid offending both their fellow Puritans in England and the English government.[3] Of course the Congregational principle had great implications for secular government. In Virginia, where the Anglican Church was established, the hierarchical system favored the development of strong county units. In New England the tendency toward localism was so strong that by 1691, when Plymouth and the Massachusetts Bay colonies were merged, they had developed similar systems of town government unique to the New World. The New England Calvinists, therefore, had much more in common than not when it came to the actual governing either of church or colony, and in any case the strength and numbers of the Massachusetts Bay Colony quickly overshadowed the small Plymouth settlement.

To some extent, harsh though it was, Calvinism in New England has been unfairly maligned by later generations who failed to recognize that it took a somewhat more humane form in America than it had in Geneva. The Anglicans in Virginia in many ways were at least as "puritanical" in their outlook and their legislation as were their compatriots in New England. Moreover, "while England kept hundreds of capital crimes on its statute books, Plymouth recognized only seven and actually executed only for murder or sodomy."[4]

The Congregational principle explicit in the Mayflower Compact and implicit in Massachusetts Bay had a direct influence upon theories of secular government; also influential was the basis of the compact itself, the notion of contract. Both are related to the idea that the only just government is the one that rules with the consent of those governed. The barest hints of democracy were thus present, though they were no more than hints. The consent involved was only that of the elect, or church members. Although all were required to attend church, only those determined worthy to be members participated in the selection of officers, and only church members could hold office. In the selection of church officers or magistrates participation depended upon church membership. The only democratic element was that those selected were responsible ultimately to the selecting few, but even this was a considerable departure from practices prevailing elsewhere. The Puritans were conscious of England's suspicions that they might be favorable to democracy, and they took great pains to demonstrate that they held no such dangerous ideas. John Winthrop, the Massachusetts Bay Colony's first governor, repeatedly expressed his hostility to democracy, as is indicated by his statement that it was "the meanest and worst of all forms of Government . . . of least continuance and fullest of troubles."[5] His views on equality were similar. In 1630, on the ship *Arbella* (or *Arabella*) that was bringing the saints to Massachusetts, although he was not a clergyman, he delivered a sermon, "A Model of Christian Charity," to the assembled Puritans. In it he declared that God in His wisdom had ordained inequality:

> In all times some must be rich, some poor; some high and eminent in power and dignity, others mean and in subjection. . . . No man is made more honorable than another or more wealthy, etc., out of any particular and singular respect to himself, but for the glory of his creator and the common good of the creature, man.[6]

In this, as in other respects, the magistrates and the clergy were in full agreement. The Bay Colony's great minister, John Cotton, was frequently at pains to justify oligarchy, the rule of the few, and to fend off any moves toward democracy by countering occasional criticisms of the status quo that provided a full veto to the governor and the assistants. In words that Winthrop himself could have uttered, he said:

> Democracy, I do not conceive that ever God did ordain as a fit government either for church or commonwealth. If the people be governors, who shall be governed? As for monarchy and aristocracy, they are both of them clearly approved, and directed in scripture, yet so as referreth the sovereignty to himself, and setteth up Theocracy in both, as the best form of government in the commonwealth, as well as in the church.[7]

Thus believing, the Massachusetts Puritans were careful to deny that they were Separatists; at the same time that they accepted the Congregational principle that provided for each church to choose its minister, they retained the Presbyterian practice of influencing if not controlling the local congregations by the synod. The Presbyterian notion involved the formation of groups of churches called presbyteries and groups of presbyteries called synods to supervise the members. Congregationalism in New England modified the practice. Local groups of ministers met in "consociations" to resolve disagreements or, in extreme cases, in synods including all the colony's ministers.[8] The decisions of the synods were not binding, but they wielded enormous influence. The democratic seeds that were in their doctrines were deeply buried and were nurtured not by the Puritans but, against their desires, by elements of opposition to their rule that developed as the years passed.

The degree to which the elite attempted to maintain its power is illustrated by the adoption of the Cambridge Platform by the synod of 1646–1647. Although the platform asserted the principles of Congregationalism, such as the formation of congregations by covenant and the autonomy of local churches, these general principles had little effect in specific cases. "Idolatry, Blasphemy, Heresy, Venting corrupt and pernicious opinions," said the platform, "are to be restrained and punished by civil authority." Further:

> If any church one or more shall grow schismaticall, rending it self from the communion of other churches, or shall walk incorrigibly or obstinately in any corrupt way of their own, contrary to the rule of the word; in such case, the Magistrate is to put forth his coercive power, as the matter shall require.[9]

As Vernon L. Parrington remarks, the adoption of the Cambridge Platform was "the grim prelude to Baptist whippings and Quaker baitings, and the setting-in of the dark days of militant intolerance."[10]

Nevertheless, the community's need for skilled artisans, whether or not they could qualify for church membership, along with other practical considerations made the retention of complete power by a tight oligarchy of the saints ever more difficult. The presence of growing numbers of nonchurch, and therefore nonvoting, members in the community would obviously sooner or later give rise to discontent. Parrington, in agreement with Daniel Webster, notes that the rise of republicanism in New England owed much to the wide distribution of land ownership and contends that the granting of land in fee-simple led to the creation of an independent group of farmers and ultimately resulted in the overthrow of the oligarchy. This, even more than the adoption of the covenant principle of church government on the Plymouth pattern, was responsible for the increasing moves toward democracy and the development of localism and home rule, according to Parrington.[11] Adding to the difficulties of the elite was the possibility for dissenters to flee to the more benignly governed colonies of Pennsylvania or Rhode Island, or even to the wilderness. Thus there were inducements to the growth of equalitarianism. As Parrington notes, "the harsh intolerance of the Cambridge Platform" can be seen as "only the aberration of a passing bigotry."[12]

The results of inroads undercutting complete elite dominance became clear in 1662 with the adoption of the Halfway Covenant. This represented a break with the past in that it permitted the baptism of certain persons who had not had a conversion experience. The result was to open church membership to a wider group and to reduce somewhat the extreme rigidity with which the earlier Puritans had tested those who wanted to affiliate with the church. The extension of church membership, of course, also provided an extension of the franchise and permitted more persons to participate in civil government than had been the case previously. Originally, given the restriction of civil rights to church members, only those who were "certain" to be of the elect could participate in the selection of rulers.

Regardless of other influences, however, one should not underestimate the influence of the notion of the compact or covenant upon American political thought. Even though the only democratic element in the early Puritan polity was the selection of officers, no Puritan would have advocated power without limit for the magistrate or any other earthly authority. Although the people could not restrict the governor, he was in theory limited by scripture and in practice limited by the General Court. John Cotton summed up the Puritan attitude toward limitations of power saying, "there is a strain in a man's heart that will sometime or other run out to excess, unless the Lord restrain it. . . . It is necessary, therefore, that all power that is on earth be limited, church-power or other."[13] Puritan limitations were broad, but they did exist. Cotton's comments also illustrate the Puritan attitude toward power in the family. It was to be limited, but broad and even autocratic:

> So let there be due bonds set—and I may apply it to families: it is good for the wife to acknowledge all power and authority to the husband, and for the husband to acknowledge honor to the wife; but still give them that which God hath given them, and no more nor less.[14]

The notion of a covenant with God and of a covenant among Christians to form a congregation to worship God merged with the developing English belief in the principle of consent of the governed to shape indelibly the direction of political thought in America; nevertheless, in favoring limitations upon power, the Puritan had no thought of expanding liberty, merely of fulfilling God's dictates.

The Mayflower Compact is the most famous, but is only one of many similar documents originating in New England that expressed the notion of covenant. Fundamental to them all is the basic liberal idea that governments are the result of voluntary action on the part of individuals; in other words, they are based upon the principle of consent and they establish the individual as the basic unit of government. Ultimately, therefore, the power of the government stems from the people, not from divine right or any other agency.

Also important is the fact that all such compacts were written, not merely verbal or traditional understandings. But contrary to the assumption underlying later American written constitutions, the early compacts were assumed to be merely human codification of God's will, not exercises of human reason. Nevertheless, the writing itself stimulated considerable thought upon the nature of government and of human rights and duties, and frequently brought about enumerations of the rights of the people. Such lists were narrow and probably resulted more from legalistic desires than from libertarian sentiments, but from these early efforts grew the American emphasis upon written constitutions and bills of rights, both of which were innovations that have been widely copied throughout the world. Even the colonies that did not originate a covenant as their fundamental law relied upon a written document, the trading company charter, as the basis for their governments. Commercial ventures thus influenced the development of written constitutions.

Puritan discussions of the nature of liberty were important as links in a long chain of political thought, but their tone tended to be strikingly different from similar discussions a century or so later. The Puritans' foremost consideration was religious; the descendants of the Puritans in the eighteenth century had become secular. The generalization is also applicable to the Anglicans in the southern colonies, although to a lesser degree. Whereas the lives of the colonists, whether northern, middle Atlantic, or southern, tended in the seventeenth century to be permeated by religious considerations, those of the late eighteenth century reflected a new and very different view of the world. John Winthrop's speech to the General Court[15] sounds strange to the modern ear, as do most seventeenth-century utterances. By the time of the Founding Fathers, something had changed, an American character had developed. The thought of the founders is considerably closer to American thought today than to that of the Puritans, or even the Anglicans of the 1600s, yet they were closer in time to the Puritans than to us. It is significant, nevertheless, different though Puritan thoughts on liberty were, that they concerned themselves to such a degree with the subject.

Winthrop delivered his speech to the General Court in 1645 as a discussion of the true nature of the magistrate's authority and the people's liberty. He compared the relationship between them to that existing between a workman and his employer and concluded that they are very different. The employer hires the skill and the faithfulness of the workman, but the people are entitled only to the faithfulness of the magistrate, who cannot pretend to be a skilled workman in the art of governing. If the magistrate commits an error, assuming that it is in good faith, the people must bear it; he must answer only for failures of faithfulness. As for liberty, Winthrop identified two kinds: natural and civil, or federal. Human beings have natural liberty in common with beasts. "By this, man, as he stands in relation to man simply, hath liberty to do what he lists; it is a liberty to evil as well as to good. This liberty is incompatible and inconsistent with authority."[16]

Civil or federal liberty, Winthrop said, "may also be termed moral, in reference to the covenant between God and man in the moral law, and the politic covenants and constitutions amongst men themselves." He described this liberty as "the proper end and object of authority," and said that it cannot exist without it. "It is a liberty to that only which is good, just, and honest." This liberty, then, can only be exercised in subjection to authority, and it is the "same kind of liberty wherewith Christ hath made us free."[17] He turned to relations between the sexes for an illustration, saying that a woman freely chooses a man to be her husband, "yet being so chosen, he is her lord, and she is to be subject to him, yet in a way of liberty, not of bondage; and a true wife accounts her subjection her honor and freedom, and would not think her condition safe and free but in her subjection to her husband's authority."[18] Winthrop contended that this was the relationship that existed between the church and the authority of Christ, and between the people and the authority of the magistrates:

> If you stand for your natural, corrupt liberties and will do what is good in your own eyes, you will not endure the least weight of authority.... But if you will be satisfied to enjoy such civil and lawful liberties, such as Christ allows you, then will you quietly and cheerfully submit unto that authority which is set over you, in all the administrations of it, for your good.[19]

To Winthrop and to the Puritan elite, liberty was the ability to do that which one should do as determined by the elite.[20]

Winthrop opposed arbitrary government, but he concluded that government limited by rules was regular and not arbitrary. Despite the severity of his remarks to the modern ear, Winthrop frequently was subjected to criticism in his own day as being too lenient, and he favored giving wide latitude to the magistrate to permit him flexibility in adjusting his actions to the needs of a given situation. He was concerned that the elect probably had more to fear from an excessive zeal for purity than from the danger of liberality. In no sense, however, did he see the magistrate as above the law; rather the magistrate merely exercised wide discretion, based upon reason, within the law.

In 1636, shortly after the founding of the Massachusetts Bay Colony, Thomas Hooker, the minister at Newtown, removed his congregation to the Connecticut valley, where they established the community of Hartford. There is little information today as to the reason for the move, and the explanations advanced range from a dispute with the Massachusetts leaders to a desire to obtain more land. In any case, the founders of Connecticut were placed in a situation similar to that in which the Pilgrims had found themselves almost two decades previously. They were outside the boundaries of the original charter, so they formed a civil society and drew up their own compact, the Fundamental Orders of Connecticut. Hooker followed Puritan custom and preached an election sermon at the first election in 1638. Only fragments survive, but they are sufficient to arouse considerable interest and to cause widely differing interpretations as to their meaning.

Parrington, for example, concludes that Hooker was a Puritan liberal whose influence paved the way for the overthrow of the oligarchy. Perry Miller, on the other hand, asserts that Hooker's views were no different from those of the Bay leaders. He demonstrates great similarity between Hooker's thought and that of Winthrop, and contends that the former's sermon, far from being a democratic reaction against Winthrop's autocracy, was a summary of the Puritan position against England's Stuart regime under Charles I and for Parliament.[21] Others have taken various positions, including placing Hooker midway between the two extremes. The truth probably is that Hooker was indeed similar in his thought to the other Puritans, but that there were differences in emphases. The Fundamental Orders, upon which Hooker no doubt had strong influence at the very least, established a more liberal regime than the structure that then existed in the Bay Colony. It based citizenship upon land ownership and community acceptance rather than church membership, thus moving the new community somewhat closer to democracy than its parent, though it can hardly be said to have established a democratic state.

In his election sermon Hooker asserted that the people should choose public magistrates, and that "they who have the power to appoint officers and magistrates, it is in their power also to set the bounds and limitations of power and place unto which they call them."[22] The Fundamental Orders reflected the covenant principle as clearly as had the Mayflower Compact. The document also adopted elements of popular sovereignty and created annual elections in which the freemen (property owners) would choose the governor, the magistrates, and the deputies of the General Court. The court exercised full legislative power with sessions that were independent of the magistrates and the governor, it had the power to censure magistrates, and it could amend the Fundamental Orders. The governor possessed the typical veto power. The governing structure reflected most clearly the devotion to the principles of Congregationalism that motivated the colony and were set forth with rigor in Hooker's "Survey of the Summe of Church Discipline"; as with all New England thinkers of the time, the major concern was religion and the church, not politics and the state.

The tendency among the Puritans to codify their laws is illustrated by the action of the Massachusetts General Court in adopting the Body of Liberties in 1641 and the Laws and Liberties of Massachusetts in 1648. The author of the Body of Liberties was Nathaniel Ward, and his effort in producing the first codification of Massachusetts statutes was the result of his concern as a lawyer for a regularized legal system, not a tender concern for tolerance and civil liberties. In "The Simple Cobler of Aggawam," for example, he wrote: "I dare . . . to proclaim to the world, in the name of our colony, that all Familists, Antinomians, Anabaptists, and other enthusiasts [religious sects] shall have free liberty to keep away from us; and such as will come to be gone as fast as they can, the sooner the better." Furthermore:

He that is willing to tolerate any religion or discrepant way of religion besides his own, unless it be in matters merely indifferent, either doubts his own or is not sincere in it.

He that is willing to tolerate any unsound opinion, that his own may also be tolerated, though never so sound, will for a need hang God's Bible at the devil's girdle.[23]

Nevertheless, the Body of Liberties guaranteed due process of law, described the liberties of various classes of persons, provided freedom from arbitrary arrest and cruel punishments, and went beyond the English guarantees of the day by adopting such provisions as a limited freedom of speech and assembly and by requiring a number of witnesses in order to convict a person of a capital crime. The code of 1648 reenacted and expanded the Body of Liberties. A key point to recognize is that these codes were not solely a reflection of biblical injunctions, although scriptures had a marked influence upon them. Thus even in these early years there had arisen some concern for politics as distinct from religion. The religious concern was still so pervasive, however, that it was a far cry from the secular thought of the Founding Fathers, and it would be an error to consider this budding concern as more than the merest hint of things to come.

Dissent in the New England Colonies

Nathaniel Ward's intolerance was not merely a personal aberration but rather reflected the predominant attitude of the Puritans. Proof of this can be discerned by looking at the fortunes of the two great dissenters who were banished from Massachusetts because of their attitudes, Anne Hutchinson and Roger Williams.

John Winthrop in his *Journal* recounts his bitter campaign to rid the colony of Mrs. Hutchinson's disruptive influence. John Cotton himself had at first encouraged her in her search for the divine light but quickly drew back when her opinions outraged the oligarchy. She denied that the Bible was the sole source of God's revealed will and even contended that she had received direct revelation from God, which convinced the General Court that she had been seduced by Satan. Her inner-light doctrines were based upon the belief that those who were elected were visited personally by the Holy Spirit and that those so visited achieved a status that raised them above all earthly law.

Probably the fact that she was a woman espousing her case brilliantly aroused the fury of the colony as fully as the radical nature of her religious beliefs and the intensity of her followers. Winthrop imparts the Puritan attitude toward women frequently in his writings, as in this passage from the *Journal:*

> Mr. Hopkins, the governor of Hartford upon Connecticut, came to Boston, and brought his wife with him (a godly young woman, and of special parts), who was fallen into a sad infirmity, the loss of her understanding and reason, which had been growing upon her divers years, by occasion of her giving herself wholly to reading and writing, and had written many books. Her husband, being very loving and tender of her, was loath to grieve her; but he saw his error, when it was too late. For if she had attended her household affairs, and such things as belong to women, and not gone out of her way and calling to meddle in such things as are proper for men, whose minds are stronger, etc., she had kept her wits, and might have improved them usefully and honorably in the place God had set her.[24]

Winthrop believed that he had ample reason to proceed against Mrs. Hutchinson with vengeance, but John Cotton's role in her prosecution was even more reprehensible. It does him no credit, especially given his involvement in the development of her ideas, that he, in an ironic touch, pronounced her banishment.[25]

Lest we be smug in condemning the Puritans for their intolerance, though, we should remember just how radical Mrs. Hutchinson was for her day and ask how such persons fare today. It is one thing to abhor the restrictive Puritan society, but the Puritans made no pretense of maintaining freedom for those of diverse opinions. Even modern democracies generally find ways of ridding themselves of those who offend the sensibilities of their leaders too greatly. As A. J. Beitzinger remarks, "it is difficult to imagine such a person escaping conviction in the 1950s under a state criminal anarchy law or the Smith Act."[26]

Vastly more important in the history of American political thought is Roger Williams, who could easily have laid claim to the title of America's first true political philosopher. Despite the brilliance of his political insights, Williams was first and foremost a religious thinker; his political philosophy, like those of his Puritan antagonists, was a by-product of his religious speculation. He was born in England and had been a protégé of Sir Edward Coke, the great jurist. He left legal studies, however, to become an Anglican minister, turning later to Separatism. Williams was a seeker who never felt certain of having found Absolute Truth.

At least two things led to his banishment from Massachusetts: his criticism of the Puritans for not officially separating from the Church of England and for using the state to enforce religious doctrine, and his charge that the Puritan land titles were defective because the land had been stolen from the Indians. Criticism of Puritan religious practices would have been sufficient to have earned him their enmity, but he added economic criticism as well. The Puritan believed in a form of separation between church and state, but held that it was the duty of the state to enforce the true religion. Williams advocated a pure separation, anticipating that recognized in modern American constitutional theory.

The Massachusetts General Court tried Williams, found him guilty of preaching "Newe and dangerous opinions, against the authorities of magistrates," and ordered him out of the colony. He went south in 1636 and purchased land from the Narragansett Indians. There he founded the town of Providence, soon to be expanded into the colony of Rhode Island, and established a government remarkable for its liberalism. Rhode Island was the first of the colonies to be set up on a secular basis. As in Massachusetts, Rhode Island held frequent elections, but contrary to the practice of the Bay Colony, it required no religious test for suffrage. There was a unicameral legislature, the governor had no veto, and the criminal code was less harsh than in Massachusetts. Moreover, there was no imprisonment for debt, divorce laws were liberal for the time, and arbitration was used for dispute settlement, including disputes with the Indians (see p. 52).

The Puritans, of course, were disturbed at such a radical commonwealth's existence, especially in New England. Williams engaged in a long controversy with John Cotton specifically and with the Puritan leaders in general. In 1644, when he was in England after having secured a charter for his colony to protect it from any possible threat by the Puritans, he replied to Cotton's *Keys of the Kingdom of Heaven* with his masterpiece *The Bloudy Tenent of Persecution for Cause of Conscience.* Subsequently he expanded upon his themes in *The Bloody Tenent Yet More Bloody.*[27]

Williams distinguished clearly between the state and the church. He denied that the true church yet existed upon earth and, in any case, contended that coercion could never result in true religion but only in outward conformity not motivated by conscience. Although his views on religion were hardly less aristocratic than those of the Puritans, he stressed true religious liberty and the principle that political power resides with all the people, not merely those adhering to a certain religion. Almost alone in his day, he did not permit his religious views to determine his prescriptions for civil government but based his political thought upon the contract theory, with government by consent to implement his all-important concern, freedom of conscience. Williams took care, however, to separate his views on religious freedom from those on government. He cared about freedom not for its own sake but as a means to reach God. Despite his concern with liberty of conscience, he was interested only in avoiding compulsion in religion, not in encouraging freedom in general.[28] Some writers, therefore, have exaggerated his position. As Williams made clear in a letter to the town of Providence, he thought of the state as a ship that was under the tight control of a captain. Those on the ship should not be forced to attend the ship's worship, nor kept from their own, if any. Nevertheless, the captain not only determines the ship's course, but also enforces rules. In fact, Williams granted the captain the right to suppress speech and writing:

> If any should preach or write that there ought to be no commanders or officers, because all are equal in Christ, therefore no laws nor orders, nor corrections nor punishments;—I say, I never denied, but in such cases, whatever is pretended, the commander or commanders may judge, resist, compel and punish such transgressors, according to their deserts and merits.[29]

In any case, Williams is not only a significant figure in the history of American political philosophy—however small his direct effect may have been—but has earned a place in world political thought as well.

Colonial Attitudes Toward Indians

The Puritan record of dealing with the Indians anticipates much of the murderous approach that dominated the white man's dealings with native Americans for centuries. The Puritan's general attitude is reflected in this passage from John Winthrop's *Journal:*

> There arose a sudden gust at N.W. so violent for half an hour, as it blew down multitudes of trees. It lifted up their meeting house at Newbury, the people being in it. It darkened the air with dust, yet through God's great mercy it did no hurt, but only killed one Indian with the fall of a tree.[30]

Only Williams and John Eliot, among notable figures in New England, dealt consistently with the Indians as human beings, although Samuel Sewall decades later wrote an antislavery tract, "The Selling of Joseph," in which he noted that he, as a magistrate, "tried to prevent Indians and Negros being rated with Horses and Hogs," but was conspicuously unsuccessful.[31]

Eliot was an apostle to the Indians and made a great effort to learn their languages. He was a humanitarian who protested the Puritan enslavement of the Indians after the Pequot War of 1637. To

John Cotton, who urged such enslavement as well as the execution of the son of the Indian leader, King Philip, he said, "to sell soules for money seemeth to me a dangerous merchandize."[32] Eliot's one venture into political thought was a pamphlet of a few pages entitled "The Christian Commonwealth" in which he advocated a stark theocracy with virtually no state except that which would enforce the dictates of Christ as set forth in the scripture. His efforts with the Indians were an attempt to bring them into such a society. It is interesting to note that the Puritans banned the book in 1661 as offensive to the king and the English government.[33]

The Indians themselves prior to the coming of the colonists, had formed a highly sophisticated governmental system, the Iroquois League of the Mohawks, Senecas, Oneidas, Cayugas, and Ononda-gas. The league was formed about 1570 to promote universal peace through brotherhood. The founders, Deganawida and Hiawatha, were believed to have been of miraculous origin. The mothers of the tribe selected the chiefs, who were ratified by popular vote. The confederation used procedures that resemble the initiative, recall, and referendum.[34] Pressures from the white invaders led to internal conflicts and the Pequot War and King Philip's War of 1675, which effectively eliminated organized Indian society in New England. Those Indians who had affiliated with the Puritans were treated in a fashion little different from the others.[35]

Politics and Religion in the Middle and Southern Colonies

Some of the most interesting polities in America were not in New England but in the Middle Atlantic Quaker colonies of Pennsylvania and West Jersey. Along with Rhode Island they were oases of tolerance in a bigoted world. The Quaker practice of arriving at consensus in their meetings, rather than operating on majority rule, was and is a feature that sets them apart from other democratic groups. Unfortunately, the operation of the Quaker "sense of the meeting" has been largely unexamined by political thinkers, who tend to dismiss it as impractical in the political world. The practice nevertheless has stood the test of time for the Quakers. It is true that Quaker societies possess a community of interest that far exceeds any existing in a modern state, but it seems unwise to ignore the possibility that there may be a potential for softening the tension, at least upon occasion, between majority and minority or minorities as they exist in civil societies.

William Penn drew up the Frame of Government as a fundamental law for Pennsylvania in 1682.[36] Pennsylvania practiced an accommodation between freedom of conscience and the need for civil
authority, and formally established separation of church and state.
Pennsylvania was somewhat more restrictive than West Jersey but
each was considerably more benign than most governments elsewhere, though Penn was even more "puritanical" in his moralistic
restriction of entertainments and other activities than were the
Puritans. Penn's thought is interesting, and the Quaker colonies are
worthy of study; by the standards prevailing at the time they were
remarkable and a tribute to Penn and the other Quakers, but Penn
was less consistent in his application of theory to practice than was
Roger Williams in Rhode Island. The most thought-provoking aspect
of Quakerism for the political philosopher appears not to be the
colonial governments themselves nor even Penn's formal ideas so
much as the suggestions that Quaker religious practices may have
for democratic theory.

Further to the south, in Virginia, the Anglican Church dominated society, but its influence was less pervasive than that of the
churches elsewhere in the colonies because of the thinly spread
population. The Vestrymen, chosen by the parishioners, appointed
the ministers and levied taxes for the support of the church. With no
separation of church and state, they were political officers also who
could present to the local governing body, the County Court, cases of
immorality; they appointed church wardens who served before the
court as prosecutors in such cases, and they had the duty of poor
relief. Because there was no bishop in the colony, the Vestrymen
assumed much of the power of the bishops, but ministers had to
travel to England to be ordained. According to Beitzinger, "The
Anglican Church in Virginia was comprised of independent parishes
governed by the assembly in temporal matters of church and state,
with the governor and council having jurisdiction over clergymen in
all civil and ecclesiastical causes."[37] Although this period did not
produce much in Virginia in the way of political speculation, the
political and religious organizations influenced one another and their
functioning was to have considerable impact upon American thought
in years to come.

The Secularization of Politics

As the eighteenth century dawned, the colonies moved toward the
development of what today can be identified as the American

character. Nowhere is the break with the recent past more apparent than in the writings of two New England clergymen, John Wise and Jonathan Mayhew. Wise is notable today for two works, *The Churches Quarrel Espoused* (1710) and *Vindication of the Government of New England Churches* (1717). In these he developed a theory of natural rights that exceeded anything yet seen in America. Wise was minister at Ipswich, Massachusetts, and ostensibly was replying to efforts by the Presbyterian faction, led by minister and noted author Cotton Mather, to restrict the autonomy of the churches in order to halt their liberalizing tendencies. Wise constructed a complete defense of Congregationalism based not upon scripture but upon political arguments. He disposed of biblical precepts quickly and turned to reasoning based upon that of Samuel Pufendorf, the German contemporary of John Locke. He contended that church government should follow that which is best for civil society, and so examined the nature of politics. This is the exact reverse of the Puritan practice.

Wise saw man clothed by God with natural "immunities." The first is that man is the subject of the law of nature, in accordance with which man must live. Second is "an original liberty instamped upon his rational nature," and he who would violate this liberty also violates the law of nature. The third "immunity," is equality. Wise argued that the people are the source of power and that democracy is not only the most ancient form of government but the one that is most natural and most to be preferred.[38] Since the controversy that inspired Wise's works was settled years before he published, it seems clear that he intended to produce a general justification of the principles of democratic government whether in church or state. Although Wise seems to have been ignored during the controversies surrounding the American Revolution, his work certainly points toward 1776 rather than to the absolutist past.

Much further along the line was Jonathan Mayhew, who brought forth a full-fledged theory of revolution in his sermon of 1750, "Discourse Concerning Unlimited Submission and Non-Resistance to the Higher Powers."[39] Mayhew denied that scripture demanded unlimited submission, saying that "nothing can well be imagined more directly contrary to common sense." He argued that rulers who abused their authority were not legitimate rulers, and that it is the people who are to judge. He was not concerned with the fear that the people would overthrow rulers for frivolous reasons because he saw subjects as much more inclined to accept considerable abuse before being willing to revolt. Like Wise, Mayhew argued from a political and rational position. Unlike the Puritans, he construed scripture in the light of common sense.

By the time of the American Revolution, and considerably before, the New England clergy had turned from their preoccupation with the duty to obey and concerned themselves with topics that have a familiar ring today. They were preaching that the people had natural rights, that a government existed to preserve those rights, and that a government that fails to do this not only could be but should be overthrown by the people. Mayhew was not typical, and was far in advance of his day. As a rationalist he anticipated the development of Unitarianism around 1820. But he was dealing with themes that had become current, and he was in the forefront of those who encouraged the tendencies that resulted in the American Revolution.

NOTES

1. Harvey Wish, *Society and Thought in Early America* (New York: Longmans, Green, 1950), pp. 26–29.

2. Edmund S. Morgan, ed., *Puritan Political Ideas* (New York: Bobbs-Merrill, 1965), pp. 94–95.

3. Perry Miller, ed., *The American Puritans* (Garden City, N.Y.: Doubleday/Anchor, 1956), pp. 20–21.

4. Wish, *Society and Thought*, p. 32.

5. From his "Reply to the Answer: Made to the Discourse About the Negative Vote . . . ," as quoted in V. L. Parrington, *Main Currents in American Thought*, vol. 1 (New York: Harcourt Brace Jovanovich, 1954), p. 47.

6. Quoted in Miller, *The American Puritans*, pp. 79–80.

7. John Cotton, "Copy of a Letter to Lord Say and Seal, 1636," in Morgan, *Puritan Political Ideas*, p. 169.

8. See Edmund S. Morgan, *The Puritan Dilemma* (Boston: Little, Brown, 1958), pp. 76–83.

9. Parrington, *Main Currents*, p. 25.

10. Ibid.

11. Ibid., pp. 22–26.

12. Ibid.

13. Quoted in Miller, *The American Puritans*, p. 86.

14. Ibid., p. 87.

15. See the selection reprinted in Miller, ibid., pp. 90–93.

16. Ibid., p. 92.

17. Ibid.

18. Ibid., pp. 92–93.

19. Ibid., p. 93.

20. Ibid., p. 90.

21. See Parrington, *Main Currents*, pp. 53–62, and Miller, *The American Puritans*, p. 88. Probably the best treatment of this subject is Clinton Rossiter, "Thomas Hooker," *New England Quarterly* 25 (December 1952), which concludes that although Hooker religiously was thoroughly orthodox as a Puritan, he was considerably more liberal politically than the Bay leaders.

22. In Miller, ibid., pp. 88–89.
23. In Miller, ibid., pp. 97, 100.
24. Quoted in Miller, ibid., pp. 44–45.
25. Ibid., p. 48.
26. *A History of American Political Thought* (New York: Dodd & Mead, 1972), p. 54.
27. See *The Complete Writings of Roger Williams*, vols. 3 and 4 (New York: Russell & Russell, 1963).
28. See Edmund S. Morgan, *Roger Williams: The Church and the State* (New York: Harcourt Brace Jovanovich, 1967), pp. 140–142.
29. *The Complete Writings of Roger Williams*, pp. 278–279.
30. Quoted in Miller, *The American Puritans*, p. 43.
31. Quoted in Parrington, *Main Currents*, p. 95.
32. Ibid., p. 30.
33. Ibid., pp. 81–84.
34. The initiative is the device that permits voters to place on the ballot proposals for legislation, and the referendum permits voters to accept or reject acts passed by a legislature. The recall allows voters to remove a public official.
35. See Wish, *Society and Thought*, pp. 39–40; see also G. E. Thomas, "Puritans, Indians, and the Concept of Race," *New England Quarterly* 48 (March 1975).
36. For an interesting treatment of the Quaker rule in Pennsylvania and West Jersey, see Beitzinger, *A History of American Political Thought*, chap. 3.
37. Ibid., p. 93.
38. Found in Miller, *The American Puritans*, pp. 121–137.
39. In ibid., pp. 137–142.

ADDITIONAL READINGS

Baldwin, Alice M. "Sowers of Sedition: The Political Theories of Some of the New Light Presbyterian Clergy of Virginia and North Carolina." *William and Mary Quarterly*, 3rd Series, V (January 1948).

———. *The New England Clergy and the American Revolution*. Durham, N.C.: Duke University Press, 1928.

Brockunier, Samuel H. *The Irrepressible Democrat: Roger Williams*. New York: Ronald Press, 1940.

Ernst, James E. *The Political Thought of Roger Williams*. Port Washington, N.Y.: Kennikat, 1966.

Hershberger, Guy F. "Pacifism and the State in Colonial Pennsylvania." *Church History* VIII (1939).

Krinskey, Fred. *The Politics of Religion in America*. Beverly Hills, Calif.: Glencoe Press, 1969.

Miller, Perry. *Orthodoxy in Massachusetts, 1630–1650*. Boston: Beacon Press, 1959.

———. *Roger Williams*. New York: Atheneum, 1962.

———. *The New England Mind: From Colony to Province*. Cambridge, Mass.: Harvard University Press, 1953.

———. *The New England Mind: The Seventeenth Century.* New York: Macmillan, 1939.

———, and Thomas H. Johnson, eds. *The Puritans.* New York: Harper Torchbooks, 1963.

Nash, Gary B. *Quakers and Politics.* Princeton, N.J.: Princeton University Press, 1968.

Osgood, Herbert L. *The American Colonies in the Seventeenth Century.* New York: Macmillan, 1904.

Pearce, Roy Harvey, ed. *Colonial American Writing.* New York: Rinehart, 1956 (a broad variety of collected readings).

Perry, Ralph Barton. *Puritanism and Democracy.* New York: Vanguard, 1944.

Schneider, Herbert W. *The Puritan Mind.* Ann Arbor: University of Michigan Press, 1958.

Wertenbaker, Thomas J. *The Puritan Oligarchy.* New York: Scribner's, 1947.

———. *Virginia Under the Stuarts.* Princeton, N.J.: Princeton University Press, 1914.

Wright, Louis B. *The Cultural Life of the American Colonies.* New York: Harper, 1957.

3

American Consciousness
and the Revolution

John Winthrop is certainly a figure in America's heritage, but then so is the Englishman John Locke. Whether one could call Winthrop, or any colonist of his time, an American depends upon whether the term denotes more than mere residence. White Americans originally were transplanted Europeans who brought with them their European culture. Of course their ideals, outlooks, and practices gradually changed as a result of the distance that separated the settlers from Europe, but of at least equal importance were the modifications that came as reactions to the new and primitive environment. Clearly the early colonists, whether Virginia farmers or Massachusetts Puritans, were Europeans; just as clearly, an American national character had developed by the time of the Revolution. Although one must be cautious in inferring general attitudes from the writings of specific spokesmen, Jonathan Mayhew's works reflect just how much change had occurred.

The growth of a definite American consciousness was gradual, and it would be fruitless to attempt to determine a precise point at which it came into being. What is important is that in the span of a century and a half there emerged an American character that was as different from that of the early colonists as the French character differs from the English. Even the most original and far-seeing political thinker of early America, Roger Williams, a man who anticipated much that was to come, was closer in the tone of his thought to the England of his day than to the America that broke with England.

From the beginning the native Americans, the Indians, were excluded from participation in colonial government and were cut off from any direct participation in the formation of what came to be American patterns of thought. The white immigrants brought with them typically European notions of race that were new to American shores. Thinking in terms of race has become so customary that it may seem puzzling to many that there are societies and peoples that deal with life with no such conception, but the idea of race was foreign to the Indian. The practice of dividing peoples into races came readily to the settlers, however, and it is so ingrained in America that even other European peoples who came to the New World are frequently spoken of as being of different "races" from the earlier English immigrants. The American view of race and the tendency to categorize human beings has had significant influence upon political ideas, an influence that sometimes is overt, sometimes subtle, and always unfortunate.[1]

As the colonists settled into the new environment and established institutions that reflected both their European heritage and the new conditions, they began to conceive of themselves as a very special kind of English subject; though still English, they were Americans. For decades before the Revolution, sermons throughout New England assumed a separate existence as Americans and dealt with basic rights largely as a result, at least initially, of controversies surrounding church government. In the South there were similar tendencies, although the issues were considerably more secular even in the beginning than they were in New England.

The original government of the Virginia Colony was that of a trading company that had sent men as laborers to exploit the resources of the new land. Although religion pervaded all phases of life and was probably as vital to the Virginians as to the New Englanders, the residents of Virginia had not come to the colony primarily for religious reasons; instead, their purposes were largely to seek economic gain. The secular elements in Virginia were strengthened in 1624 when the king dissolved the company and issued a royal charter. Representative institutions had their beginnings five years previously with the creation of a General Assembly consisting of an elected House of Burgesses and a Governor's Council appointed by the company. The initial charter had given full power to the governor, who had lifetime tenure and was answerable only to officials in England, but under the royal charter the General Assembly grew in power. Moreover, the increasingly broad scattering of the population served to encourage toleration and to permit additional individual freedom.

Despite the commercial orientation of the Virginians, the colony was strongly agrarian, and growth of the plantation system and easy access to the sea prevented the early formation of cities. With the absence of cities and the relative self-sufficiency of the plantations, the Virginians grew unaccustomed to the yoke of political authority and irreverent toward English attitudes and laws. When England attempted to tighten its control over the colonies with taxes and other economic measures, and in 1763 tried to halt westward expansion, all of the colonies reacted with hostility, none more so than Virginia. Paradoxically, although the Virginians had developed the institution of human slavery, the white colonists had experienced considerable freedom for themselves and, when they deemed it to be threatened by the British, worked with vigor to maintain it. Generally given more to action and practical affairs than to philosophy and speculation, they easily came to the attitude of "no taxation without representation" and, their practice of human bondage notwithstanding, to the acceptance of the radical arguments of the "rights of man" that exalted human freedom and limited government.

The British actions after 1763 were nothing more than attempts to reassert the nature of the American communities as colonies. The long years of independence, however, along with the great distance from the mother country, the vigorous westward movement, and the presence of thousands of Scotch-Irish and other European immigrants conspired to change the situation. The British actions appeared to the colonists not as the normal course of events between colonies and the mother country but as nothing less than unconscionable attempts to subjugate societies that had become free, regardless of their nominal position as English colonies. In short, it was too late for the British; the colonies had ceased to be English and the colonists had become Americans. Although few Americans as yet were consciously democratic, many accounts indicate to what degree the notions of privilege and respect for authority had weakened. As John Adams remarked, "The revolution was effected before the war commenced. The revolution was in the minds and hearts of the people."[2]

This is not to say that the people unanimously rose to support the Revolution. There was strong support, but as is the case today with most political issues, the majority of the people probably were indifferent to the arguments for and against the Revolution, and no doubt many were opposed to it. It is likely that most politically aware Americans, at least initially, would have favored some scheme that would have gained American objectives while retaining a place for America within the British Empire. Benjamin Franklin had proposed such an arrangement as early as 1754 in his Albany Plan of Union, in which he suggested that the colonies be united, permitted representatives in Parliament, and taxed internally by a Grand Council to be selected by the colonial governments.[3] As British pressure increased, however, many prominent Americans came gradually to advocate more extreme measures, as did Franklin himself, but the early participants in this "pamphlet war" remained moderate.

Prerevolutionary Political Writers

In the period between 1763 and 1775, pamphlets and articles began to appear arguing the issues surrounding America's colonial status. An example is the work of the Boston lawyer James Otis, whose writing exhibits strong Lockean influences. In the best-known of his three pamphlets, "The Rights of the British Colonies Asserted and Proved" (1764), Otis deals with legislative authority and contends that natural law provides rights that limit the powers of government. It is significant that he argued from natural law rather than from colonial charters as the basis for rights. He preferred to remain within the Empire and granted the authority of Parliament over the colonies, but he reasoned that even if the colonists were to be represented in Parliament, such representation still would not justify parliamentary taxation or restrictions of trade because the local legislatures were in a better position to understand local needs. Otis agreed with Locke as to the nature of government: its power derives from the people and its function is to protect their lives, their liberties, and their property.

   He outlined six points regarding the legislative power, including such things as "no legislative . . . has a right to make itself arbitrary," "the supreme legislative . . . is bound to dispense justice by known settled rules, and by duly authorized independent judges," and "the supreme power cannot take from any man any part of his property, without his consent in person, or by representation." He wrote that the "first principles of law and justice" and of the British constitution are:

1. That the people must be governed by stated laws
2. That those laws should have no other end, ultimately, but the good of the people
3. That taxes are not to be laid on the people, but by their consent in person, or by deputation
4. That their whole power is not transferable

Locke's principles are apparent in Otis's argument, as is his essential moderation. In two respects, however, Otis advanced far beyond previous speculation. First, almost alone among the colonists, he consistently wrote of "colonists, black and white," and it is obvious that he considered blacks entitled to the "rights of man" equally with whites. Second, his work anticipates the American practice of judicial review, one of the most innovative principles of the American political system. He wrote that parliaments, when they act unwisely, repeal their acts in response to popular opinion, but if they do not, the courts should declare the acts to be void.[4] In the Writs of Assistance Case of 1761 he was more specific: "An Act against the Constitution is void: an Act against natural Equity is void; and if an Act of Parliament should be made, in the very Words of this Petition, it would be void. The Executive Courts must pass such Acts into disuse."[5] Such arguments did not take hold in the British system, but they led directly to the reasoning in *Marbury* v. *Madison* in 1803 by which the Supreme Court incorporated judicial review as a fundamental principle of the American Constitution.

One of the most widely known political writers of the prerevolutionary period was John Dickinson. Beginning in 1767 he wrote a series of newspaper articles collectively titled *Letters from a Farmer in Pennsylvania*. Always the moderate, Dickinson cautioned against radical action and, like Otis, preferred to remain within the British Empire. The major concern of the *Letters* is parliamentary jurisdiction and the authority to tax the colonies. Dickinson argued against taxation without representation and distinguished between taxes for the purpose of regulation and taxes for the raising of revenue. Because it was necessary for Parliament to regulate trade or other economic activity, regulatory taxes were within its power; taxing unrepresented colonies for revenue, however, was not. Anticipating some of the questions inherent in federalism, Dickinson attempted to distinguish between the jurisdictions of Parliament and of the colonial legislatures.

Dickinson took issue with those who evaluated internal and external taxation differently. All tax measures, he said, that were designed to raise revenue were beyond the power of Parliament to enact if they affected the colonies either internally or externally. Daniel Dulany of Maryland had argued similarly in an earlier pamphlet, "Considerations of the Propriety of Imposing Taxes in the British Colonies," in which he took issue with the British argument that the colonists were "virtually" represented in Parliament even though they elected no representatives, but Dulany's writings were much less widely read than Dickinson's. Like Otis, Dickinson relied upon natural law and stressed the principle of consent. True to his conservatism, however, although he came ultimately to accept the inevitability of independence, he never went so far as to join in the call for revolution.[6]

Dickinson's student, James Wilson, still dealing essentially with the principle of consent, went a step further and denied all parliamentary authority over the colonies because the colonies were not represented. No political authority existed unless granted by consent of the governed. In denying Parliament's power over the colonies, however, Wilson recognized allegiance to the king, thereby advocating a scheme that would provide autonomy for the colonies but still place them within the framework of the Empire.[7] Because Parliament by this time had captured most of the power of the monarchy, the colonists who argued in agreement with Wilson for acceptance of the king and rejection of Parliament would have had little to fear from British dominance had their proposals been accepted, and they were well aware of the fact.

Another major American figure came upon the scene at the time of Wilson's writing. At the age of seventeen Alexander Hamilton, a student at King's College (now Columbia University), produced a pamphlet entitled "A Full Vindication of the Measures of Congress"; the following year, 1775, he brought out another, "The Farmer Refuted," in response to *Letters of a Westchester Farmer*, by Samuel Seabury. Hamilton followed the natural law tradition and stressed the principle of consent as the ultimate authority for government. Added to these strains is an emphasis upon self-interest, an emphasis that would be increasingly apparent in his future work. Hamilton inferred natural rights from the law of nature and stressed the validity of contract theory; he admitted the sovereignty of the English king as king of America but concluded that it resulted from agreement, or contract, between the colonies and the king, not from parliamentary action. Because the colonists had no power to check Parliament, and because Parliament was therefore likely to act in its own interest rather than that of the colonies, there was no power in Parliament to govern the colonies. In other words, legitimate power must be checked; since Parliament's power over the colonies would be unchecked, it was illegitimate.

Seabury had argued that a government must have a locus of sovereignty and that England, or Parliament, must then be sovereign over the colonies. Hamilton responded that the legislative power could not, it is true, be divided within one society but that there could be separate legislatures for different regions within a state under one head. He thus concluded that the king was the only sovereign of the Empire.

In 1775 a series of debates appeared in the Boston *Gazette* between "Massachusettensis" and "Novanglus." John Adams, writing under the pen name Novanglus, was taking issue with the loyalist lawyer Daniel Leonard. Adams's "Novanglus" articles provide an incisive treatment of the nature of the British constitution. He asserted that the English Parliament had no more right to govern America than did the Scottish Parliament. He agreed with Hamilton and Wilson that Americans owed allegiance to the king, and he granted the English Parliament the right to control trade upon the seas, but he concluded that Parliament's power halted at the banks of the ocean. He analyzed the British constitution as providing a mixed form of government, with democratic, aristocratic, and monarchical elements. Parliamentary control over the colonies would violate this constitution, since there could be no democratic element for the unrepresented colonies.[8] Within the colonies each colonial legislature was supreme, even to the extent of altering the colony's constitution; to Parliament he granted no authority whatsoever over any matter within the borders of the colonies.

The loyalist position, for obvious reasons, had little impact upon the development of American political thought. Massachusettensis, or Daniel Leonard, contended that he sought also to affirm the rights of Englishmen, and that if parliamentary power were to be removed from the colonies, the mixed government would be removed, resulting either in absolute monarchy or anarchy.[9] Both he and Seabury in his exchanges with the young Hamilton took a Hobbesian position that power was needed to prevent the turmoil of a state of nature and that power could best be checked and liberties protected with the mixed system provided by the British constitution.

The most extreme and unbending loyalist was an Anglican clergyman of Maryland and Virginia, Jonathan Boucher, who was famous for preaching his sermons with a brace of loaded pistols on the cushions to prevent his being dragged from the pulpit. His congregation finally drove him to England in 1775, where he remained. In 1797 he published a collection of sermons that he had preached between 1763 and 1775, *A View of the Causes and Consequences of the American Revolution*, a vitriolic work that in the words of political scientist J. Mark Jacobson "is probably the best attack upon the revolutionary natural rights philosophy."[10]

Boucher argued from scripture, attacked the contract theory of government, and declared that inequality was the order of nature and the proper order within a state. He turned to Robert Filmer, against whose theories Locke's *Treatises* were directed, to explain the existence of political authority. Government was a positive good and rulers received their power not from the people, not from consent, but from God; as the father rules the family in the order established by God, so do the king and his officers rule the state. To this late advocate of divine right, the most important aspect of politics was the duty of passive obedience to authority.

Essentially the loyalist argument stressed the advantages of the British constitution and tended to reflect a Hobbesian suspicion of human nature and a need for strong power to control the evil in humankind. The loyalists stressed the obligations of the colonists to England and the ties that bound the English-speaking peoples on both sides of the Atlantic. Often they argued in legalistic terms, and they tended to stress continuity of authority and to emphasize duties over rights. In general, they reserved their severest criticisms for anything that they considered to encourage democracy and popular rule.

Those supporting independence tended to owe more to Locke than to Hobbes. They strongly emphasized rights, and they adopted the radical argument that rights were natural and that no government could justly infringe them. They supported their position with a reliance upon contract theory and the notion of government only by consent, either directly given or through elected representatives. In the beginning the concern was for the rights of the colonies; this concern often was stimulated by considerations of property and led to the dictum of no taxation without representation. The orientation then shifted to concern with the rights of Englishmen, and later, at least rhetorically, to the arguments of the rights of man. The stage then was set for one of the most successful pieces of revolutionary literature in world history, which was supplied by the most radical theorist of his age, Thomas Paine.

The Arguments of Thomas Paine

In January 1776 Thomas Paine produced one of the most successful pieces of political propaganda of all time, *Common Sense*. Until then, the tone of England's critics had been moderate. Paine rejected moderation in order to present arguments that, in his view, would appeal to common sense. He took issue with preceding writings that praised the British system even while they called for independence; he had no reverence for the British system, charged the king with manifold abuses of power, and contended that hereditary government had no right to exist.

Like his liberal predecessors, Paine accepted the doctrine of a social contract, but one that bound only citizens with one another, not one that bound citizenry and government. The only defensible government was one that provided representation through elections, preferably frequent elections giving citizens greater opportunity to make their wishes known. Similarly, although most of his references are vague, it is clear that he exhibited a marked preference for local government, the level that is closest to the people.

Paine based his political philosophy upon the existence of natural law that could be made apparent through the exercise of reason. He believed in equality, the possibility of progress, and what we today would call participatory democracy with efficient rule by the citizens themselves. Society to Paine was as natural as it was to the ancient Greeks. Government, on the other hand, was an artificial creation that was necessary, but was a necessary evil. He strongly favored the idea that the best government is one that governs least. But Paine was no anarchist. He granted the government broad functions, though always consistent with the greatest degree of human freedom.

Paine had been born in London, in great poverty. His humanitarianism probably resulted from the influence of his Quaker father, but his early poverty no doubt also was partly responsible for his attitudes, many of which were more than a century ahead of their time. For instance, he advocated many social insurance programs which did not begin in Europe until late in the nineteenth century and in the United States not until the middle twentieth.[11]

Paine proposed a progressive tax on income from estates and a confiscatory tax upon inheritances, from which would be paid an allowance to young persons reaching the age of twenty-one to provide them with an adequate start in life. He also advocated a fund to provide old-age pensions, and he outlined detailed schemes for welfare and the elimination of poverty, which he believed to be caused by bad government. His comprehensive social security programs would also include public education to be supported by tax funds. Almost alone among writers of his day, Paine favored women's rights, asserting that women were subjugated by both laws and public opinion; when he called for equality, he meant for all. Consistent with his emphasis upon government only by consent, he advocated ample public debate upon all issues; the modern penchant for secrecy would have appeared monstrous to him. "How," he would have asked, "can the people rule, can the government be democratic, if the people have no access to complete information and if they are denied even awareness of certain decisions?"

Paine was anything but a conciliator. He was abrasive in tone and tended to view issues in blacks and whites, all one way or the other. Nonetheless, he recognized the need for practicality. When he electrified America with *Common Sense*, he displayed consummate skill as a political pamphleteer by not only stressing principles and abstract reasoning but also appealing to the self-interest of Americans. Much of his radicalism stems from his uncompromising individualism, his belief that no one human being has the right to tell another what to do. Consistent with this principle, he refused to accept the notion, generally held then as now, that generations were continuous; instead, he saw them as replacing one another and, as a result, argued that all laws and all constitutions should be remade anew with each generation; one had no right to bind another. Issues should be settled on the basis of what is right, as determined by reason, not on the basis of tradition or precedent.

Although Thomas Paine was one of the most potent forces in bringing about the American Revolution, he did not represent the dominant views. He refused to accept the notion of sovereignty in the government. Only the people are sovereign and government is their servant, a servant that is made necessary by their wickedness, not by an ordinance of God. He favored a redistribution of income, not to eliminate the rich but to provide that no one is to remain poor while others are not. Partly because of these attitudes that showed less sensitivity to property rights than to human rights, Paine was virtually ignored after the Revolution, and worse, was shunned by his adopted countrymen when he was in need in later years. Also contributing to his difficulties was his essay "The Age of Reason," in which he forthrightly laid out his views on religion and attacked churches and other institutionalized restrictions, as he saw them, upon the minds of humanity. Paine was a Deist, a rational religionist with a strong ethical sense, but he was considered to be an atheist. Even if true, this would have been irrelevant, but it nonetheless served to shatter those vestiges of respect that had survived the disdain directed against his radicalism.

Common Sense is, of course, the greatest example of Paine's polemical style, but the bulk of his political philosophy is to be found in *The Rights of Man*; also interesting is the series of papers called *The Crisis*. *Agrarian Justice* is the work that sets forth most of his social proposals, such as those designed to eliminate poverty and provide for those in need.[12]

Americans were, and remain, uneasy with the spirit of Thomas Paine. A President such as Gerald Ford can quote his patriotic calls to revolution, but things stop there. Paine was saddened by the ill-treatment from the country that he loved and helped to create; he would be sadder still were he to discover that many of the social ills that he devoted his life to alleviating still exist and some have worsened. No doubt he would take small comfort from the fact that his strident calls, if they were to be heard, would make many Americans as nervous as when he first uttered them.

Principles of the Declaration of Independence

Encouraged by dedicated pamphleteers such as Thomas Paine and activists such as Samuel Adams, a Lockean American through and through, America revolted and broke its political ties with England. American revolutionary thought is beautifully presented in one of the world's classic radical political documents, the Declaration of Independence. In writing the Declaration, adopted by the Second Continental Congress on July 4, 1776, Thomas Jefferson not only relied upon the prevailing influences from John Locke but captured the spirit of specifically American radical individualism as it existed during the revolutionary fervor.

The Declaration begins by saying that a "decent respect for the opinions of mankind" requires that the reasons for separation from England should be made clear. There is thus a note of prudence as well as the assumption that humankind is reasonable and will react favorably to a reasoned argument, and that opinions are to be valued. The second paragraph enumerates "self-evident truths," reflecting the traditional American assumption that natural law could be disclosed upon reasoned analysis:

> We hold these truths to be self-evident, that all men are created equal, that they are endowed by their Creator with certain unalienable Rights, that among these are Life, Liberty and the pursuit of Happiness. That to secure these rights, Governments are instituted among Men, deriving their just powers from the consent of the governed. That whenever any Form of Government becomes destructive of these ends, it is the Right of the People to alter or to abolish it, and to institute new Government, laying its foundation on such principles and organizing its powers in such form, as to them shall seem most likely to effect their Safety and Happiness.

There could be no clearer statement of the right of revolution or of the principle that government is the servant, not the master, of the people and that it serves at their pleasure. Fully as clear is the emphasis upon the individual human being as the basic unit of society and government, and the assumption that the foremost consideration is the basic right of each human being to live in freedom. This is not to say that Jefferson intended to assert that these principles may be proven in the scientific sense or that everyone agrees with them. They are rather moral propositions that are based upon natural law and stipulate the correct and ethical paths for citizens and governments to take. He intended them to be statements of truth, absolute and unchangeable.[13]

The Declaration is a splendid example of much of the best in American political thought. In these modern secular times, we are frequently uncomfortable with the abstract, unless it can be quantified, and with statements of absolutes. Historically, one can point to the continuing abuse of Indians, the subordinate status of women, and even the existence of human slavery at the same time that Americans were praising the principles of the Declaration, principles that asserted that all were equal and that the only legitimate rule was with the consent of the ruled. However much this may fault practice, it does not detract from the majesty of the document, nor does our discomfort with absolutes render the principles of the Declaration any less than still the soundest justification for human freedom in the American political tradition. The Declaration proclaims the only justification that deems freedom to be an end in itself, not subordinate to the good of society or some other consideration.

When practice differs from theory, it often is possible to compartmentalize the two so that each continues relatively unaffected by the other until some factor precipitates a change. The persistence of such contradictions may be seen in the existence of slavery for nearly a century after the Declaration, with discrimination against blacks and mistreatment of Indians still with us. For evidence that women should be considered in this discussion, one may turn to an exchange of correspondence between Abigail Adams and her husband John. On March 31, 1776, Abigail wrote:

> I long to hear that you have declared an independency—and by the way in the new Code of Laws which I suppose it will be necessary for you to make I desire you would remember the Ladies, and be more generous and favourable to them than your ancestors. Do not put such unlimited power into the hands of the Husbands. Remember all Men would be tyrants if they could. If perticuliar care and attention is not paid to the Laidies we are determined to foment a Rebelion, and will not hold ourselves bound by any Laws in which we have no voice, or Representation.
>
> That your sex are Naturally Tyrannical is a Truth so thoroughly established as to admit of no dispute, but such of you as wish to be happy willingly give up the harsh title of Master for the more tender and endearing one of Friend. Why then, not put it out of the power of the vicious and the Lawless to use us with cruelty and indignity with impunity. Men of Sense in all Ages abhor those customs which treat us

only as the vassals of your Sex. Regard us then as Beings placed by providence under your protection and in immitation of the Supreem Being make use of that power only for our happiness.[14]

In the course of John's reply, he wrote on April 14:

As to your extraordinary Code of Laws, I cannot but laugh. We have been told that our Struggle has loosened the bands of Government every where. That Children and Apprentices were disobedient—that schools and Colleges were grown turbulent—that Indians slighted their Guardians and Negroes grew insolent to their Masters. But your letter was the first Intimation that another Tribe more numerous and power-full than all the rest were grown discontented.—This is rather too coarse a Compliment but you are so saucy, I wont blot it out.[15]

Abigail's response on May 7 was as follows:

I can not say that I think you very generous to the Ladies, for whilst you are proclaiming peace and good will to Men, Emancipating all Nations, you insist upon retaining an absolute power over Wives. But you must remember that Arbitrary power is like most other things which are very hard, very liable to be broken.[16]

The first cautious movements toward revolution came because the colonists considered themselves entitled to the traditional rights of Englishmen and could therefore satisfy themselves that they were upholding the English constitution by defying the English government when in their opinion it denied them their rights. Both the more radical rights of man arguments and this essentially conservative approach continued to be currents within the revolutionary movement. As conservatives, the one camp tended to look to retention of their traditional liberties; as liberals, the other tended to anticipate the future and hope for new ones. It is unfortunate, it is tragic, that despite the quality of thought that the Revolution produced there was so little recognition even among the advocates of the rights of man that their principles were all-embracing but their habits and practices restrictive.

NOTES

1. With regard to the racist attitudes of the Puritans, see the excellent study by G. E. Thomas, "Puritans, Indians, and the Concept of Race," *New England Quarterly* 48 (March 1975).

2. Quoted in Alan P. Grimes, *American Political Thought* (New York: Holt, Rinehart and Winston, 1960), p. 75.

3. *The Works of Benjamin Franklin*, vol. 3, John Bigelow, ed. (New York: G. P.

Putnam's Sons, 1904); see also Franklin's *Autobiography* (New York: Signet, 1961), pp. 140–142.

4. "The Rights of the British Colonies Asserted and Proved" (Boston: Edes and Gill, 1764), passim.

5. Quoted in Josiah Quincy, Jr., *Reports of Cases Argued and Adjudged in the Superior Court of Judicature of the Province of Massachusetts Bay Between 1761 and 1772* (Boston: Little, Brown, 1865), p. 474; parts of the opinion are reprinted in A. T. Mason and Richard Leach, *In Quest of Freedom*, 2nd ed. (Englewood Cliffs, N.J.: Prentice-Hall, 1973), p. 142. A writ of assistance is a general search warrant, not limiting the places to be searched or the subject of the search—now outlawed in the United States by the Constitution.

6. See V. L. Parrington, *Main Currents in American Thought*, vol. 1 (New York: Harcourt Brace Jovanovich, 1954), pp. 224–237.

7. See "Considerations on the Nature and Extent of the Legislative Authority of the British Parliament" (1774), in *The Works of James Wilson*, vol. 2, James DeWitt Andrews, ed. (Chicago: Callaghan, 1896).

8. See *The Works of John Adams*, vol. 4, Charles Francis Adams, ed. (Boston: Little, Brown, 1851).

9. See John Adams and Daniel Leonard, *Novanglus and Massachusettensis* (Boston: Hews & Gass, 1819).

10. Thornton Anderson, *Jacobson's Development of American Political Thought*, 2nd ed. (New York: Appleton-Century-Crofts, 1961), p. 137.

11. For example, although Germany began a comprehensive system of social insurance, or social security programs, in the 1880s, the United States waited almost fifty years, until 1935, to adopt the Social Security Act. Even then, the taxation supporting the social programs in this country was strikingly regressive, and the act made no provision for health care benefits, which came only with the passage of "Medicare" legislation in 1965.

12. See *The Complete Writings of Thomas Paine*, 2 vols., Philip S. Foner, ed. (New York: Citadel Press, 1945); for a comprehensive analysis of his attitudes toward politics, see Mary Donna McGaughey, "Thomas Paine's Theory of Participatory Democracy" (M.A. thesis, California State University, Long Beach, 1972).

13. For a perceptive analysis of Jefferson's theory of revolution, see Harris Mirkin, "Rebellion, Revolution, and the Constitution: Thomas Jefferson's Theory of Civil Disobedience," *American Studies* 13, no. 2 (Fall 1972), 61–74; on Jefferson's general ideas on politics, see Adrienne Koch, *The Philosophy of Thomas Jefferson* (New York: Columbia University Press, 1943), esp. part 3.

14. Quoted in Alice S. Rossi, ed., *The Feminist Papers* (New York: Columbia University Press, 1973), pp. 10–11.

15. Ibid., p. 11.

16. Ibid., p. 13.

ADDITIONAL READINGS

Appleby, Joyce. "The New Republican Synthesis & the Changing Political Ideas of John Adams." *American Quarterly* XXV (December 1973).

Bailyn, Bernard. *Pamphlets of the American Revolution, 1750–1776.* Cambridge, Mass.: Harvard University Press, 1965.

———. "Political Experience and Enlightenment Ideas in Eighteenth Century America." *American Historical Review* LXVII (January 1962).

———. *The Ideological Origins of the American Revolution*. Cambridge, Mass.: The Belknap Press of Harvard University Press, 1967.

Baldwin, Alice M. *The New England Clergy and the American Revolution*. Durham, N.C.: Duke University Press, 1928.

Becker, Carl L. *The Declaration of Independence: A Study in the History of Political Ideas*. New York: Vintage, 1958 [1922].

Dana, William R. "The Declaration of Independence as Justification for Revolution." *Harvard Law Review* XIII (January 1900).

The Essential Thomas Paine. New York: Mentor Books, 1969 (selections from Paine's political writings).

Hartz, Louis. "American Political Thought and the American Revolution." *American Political Science Review* XLVI (June 1952).

Jensen, Merrill. "Democracy and the American Revolution." *Huntington Library Quarterly* XXII (August 1957).

Malone, Dumas. *Jefferson the Virginian*. Jefferson and His Time, vol. 1. Boston: Little, Brown, 1948.

Rossiter, Clinton. "The Political Theory of Benjamin Franklin." *Pennsylvania Magazine of History and Biography* LXXVI (July 1952).

———. "The Political Theory of the American Revolution." *Review of Politics* XV (January 1953).

———. *The Political Thought of the American Revolution*. Seedtime of the Republic, part III. New York: Harcourt, Brace and World, 1963.

Stourzh, Gerald. "Reason and Power in Benjamin Franklin's Political Thought." *American Political Science Review* XLVII (December 1953).

Wishy, Bernard. "John Locke and the Spirit of '76." *Political Science Quarterly* LXIII (September 1958).

Wright, B. F. *American Interpretations of Natural Law*. Cambridge, Mass.: Harvard University Press, 1931.

4

The Constitution and Its Critics

The most important function of a constitution is limiting the exercise of power. Although the fundamental principles that accomplish this task may be largely unwritten, as in the case of the British constitution, the predominant practice among constitutional systems today is to establish governments upon written constitutions. It was the success of the American experiment that popularized written constitutions throughout much of the world, and it was the Anglo-American tradition that gave the greatest boost to constitutionalism in modern states.

Constitutionalism, essential adherence to a body of principles that limits the exercise of power, is based upon the belief that there are certain things that it is improper for governments to do, even majority governments. This notion is obviously related to the conception of a higher law that resulted from the assumption that there is a power beyond that of government. In the American tradition the Constitution is the result of an attempt to codify the dictates of higher law so that they will serve as the precise legal ground for the existence and the functioning of the entire political process.[1] Just as a written constitution was a significant American innovation in world political practice, so too was its logical consequence, judicial review. If the written constitution is to be the fundamental law to which all other laws must conform, it was a natural development for the interpreters of the law, the courts, to refuse to enforce any governmental act that they deemed inconsistent with the Constitution.

Although judicial review has not been so widely copied elsewhere as has the practice of a written constitution, it remains a significant contribution and one that is crucial to the operation of governments in the American system.

Precedents for a Written Constitution

In fashioning a scheme based upon written constitutions, Americans were not operating in a vacuum. They were the inheritors of centuries of British traditions of constitutionalism that included such written documents as Magna Carta, and they had had considerable experience with constitutionalism and with written documents that served as partial constitutions before the 1787 convention in Philadelphia. In the postrevolutionary years the states had all drawn up constitutions of their own, except for Rhode Island and Connecticut, whose very liberal colonial charters remained adequate for the time being. Earlier, the colonies had written charters that served as their constitutions, some of which, such as the Mayflower Compact and the Fundamental Orders of Connecticut, they had created themselves. The Fundamental Orders established a majority vote of the freemen for the annual selection of officers. More notably democratic was the Plantation Agreement at Providence that Roger Williams and his fellow Rhode Islanders drew up in 1640. It provided for a town meeting to establish general policy, with five "disposers," whose terms were only three months, to govern between meetings. Even with this short term, there were mechanisms to call the meeting together at any time to remove a disposer in the event he was deemed to have abused his authority. The system also provided for settlement of disputes by arbitration, and the Agreement specifically guarded, as it put it, the "liberty of conscience." As in the other colonies, however, those permitted to participate in politics were limited to those "who held stock in the town." Rhode Island's General Court declared in 1641 that the colony was built upon "a Democracy, or Popular Government," and the parliamentary patent (authorizing document) granted in 1643 and the royal charter in 1663 safeguarded the colony's institutions.[2]

After the Revolution, however, state leaders combined English traditions modified by the unique American environment with the notion of compact, or the contract theory of government, to produce something more than the limited statements of the past. The American constitutions thus produced, based as they were upon a contract theory that embodied a conception of the higher law, became the first truly comprehensive documents of politics, the first writings serving as the foundations of entire states and their political subdivisions. In fact the new states, after having British authority removed, had the opportunity of putting theory into practice by creating documents that would be the basis for political order. Politically speaking, they were almost literally in a state of nature as envisioned by John Locke, and they reacted according to the Lockean formula.

All of the new state constitutions took a suspicious view of governmental power, with the greatest distrust reserved for the executive. Virginia led the way, followed by most of the others, in adopting a bill of rights that identified certain liberties of the citizen that were to remain free from government interference. In addition, the states, adopting the principle that power should check power, provided for checks and balances and separation of powers. Each state separated the executive from the legislature and established independent courts; all except Pennsylvania, Vermont, and Georgia set up bicameral legislatures so that there would even be checks within the legislative branch itself. In practice, though, the executive branch lacked the veto or power to appoint and was so weak as to result in a system of legislative supremacy. No doubt this came about because of the hostility that Americans as colonists had developed toward royal governors during long periods of struggle between the legislatures, which the colonists saw as protecting their interests, and the governors, whom the colonists viewed as speaking for special privilege.

The state constitutions also tended to be vastly more democratic than would have seemed possible elsewhere. They typically reduced the requirements for voting so that in most states the majority of white adult males had the franchise, and they gave voters heavy influence upon officeholders by setting up annual elections. As wide as the franchise was by world standards, there was hardly any thought given to expanding it to all adults. Despite the occasional humane view expressed during colonial times by such figures as Samuel Seabury and Roger Williams, or by the Quaker John Woolman in his criticisms of slavery, there were no serious proposals to give the vote to blacks, Indians, or women. Many critics of the Declaration of Independence, including the royal governor of Massachusetts, the hated loyalist Thomas Hutchinson, had condemned what they concluded was American hypocrisy. Hutchinson argued that Americans spoke of rights and equality and yet deprived "more than an hundred thousand Africans of their rights to liberty and *the pursuit of happiness*, and in some degree to their lives."[3] Not even this cogent argument had any effect, however, and the argument itself ignored women.

The state constitutions were permeated by a fear of power. They generally resulted from actions by the legislatures or from special conventions and were not submitted to the people for their approval, a practice severely criticized by some. Nevertheless, they did originate in bodies that represented the people, and it is clear that they were intended to bind all parts of government including the legislatures. The checks and balances reflected a view of the corrupting influences of power and a belief that institutions were necessary to prevent the holders of power from abusing their authority. The constitutions accepted the need for power in government, but only for tightly controlled power, and in the early stages tended to reflect the belief that the legislature most clearly represented the people. This belief would be modified in a few years to the view that all of the branches were merely differing modes of representation.

In 1780 Massachusetts devised a new procedure for the formulation and installation of a constitution, and it generally has been followed at the state level ever since. It involves the creation of a popularly elected convention to devise a written constitution, and a popular referendum, or vote, upon the document. The tendency to identify government by consent with government by majority approval is apparent.

The early state constitutions were not immune from criticism, as is illustrated by Jefferson's trenchant analysis of the Virginia document in his *Notes on the State of Virginia*.[4] He explained the "very capital defects" as resulting from lack of experience in the science of government and used democratic arguments to explain wherein these defects lay. His criticism centered upon unequal representation, lack of real separation of powers (regardless of formal arrangements), legislative supremacy, and a bicameralism in the legislature that failed to provide for the representation of different interests in each chamber. He noted that the Virginia Senate was chosen at the same time and by the same electors as the House of Delegates and compared the situation—which, he reasoned, would produce "men of the same description"—unfavorably with that in some other states in which the interests of property found representation in one house and those of the people in the other. It is clear from this that Jefferson not only had no objection to representing property but asserted that it, or some factor other than popular interest, should be represented in a separate chamber. The purpose for this proposal, however, was to isolate the nonpopular influence, so that it would not permeate both chambers and thereby completely dominate the legislature.[5] His piercing comment, "an *elective despotism* was not the government we fought for,"[6] summarizes many of the objections not only to the state constitutions but later to the United States Constitution as well.

The preferences of the figures influencing the postrevolutionary state constitutions varied considerably from the radical democracy of the Revolution to the more sober tastes of the conservatives. Despite the differences there were certain agreements as well. Benjamin Franklin, for example, and John Adams—to some extent representing, respectively, the radical notions and those that might be called "classical republicanism"—agreed in their rather pessimistic assessment of human nature and the degree to which self-interest would prevail in any government. Their differences, however, were reflected in the institutional arrangements that they supported: Franklin argued for unicameralism and the greatest influence for the people, as embodied in the Pennsylvania Constitution of 1776, whereas Adams, one of the drafters of the Massachusetts Constitution of 1780, stressed the follies of popular passions and the need for balance and a mixed government that could preserve the interests of varied groups but be captured by none. That the assumptions underlying the constitutions were similar from state to state, however, is indicated by the similarity of the documents.

The Articles of Confederation

It was the Continental Congress, an emergency body that had initially sprung up in 1774 to provide some mechanism for uniting the colonies during the Revolution, that had requested the states to draw up constitutions. The Continental Congress had no actual legitimacy, but in the short period of its existence it helped to fill the vacuum left by the withdrawal of British power. The original Congress had delegates from only twelve of the states, but in 1775 all thirteen sent delegates, and it was this body that on July 4, 1776, adopted the Declaration of Independence. Because of the need for a form of central government with powers adequate to carry on the war and the desires of some for a national organization to continue beyond the war's duration, the Congress quickly began work on the first step toward an American national constitution and brought forth the Articles of Confederation in 1777. The scheme required the approval of all the states before it could take effect, and by 1779 all had ratified the document except for Maryland. Maryland finally approved in 1781, and the Articles became effective after some other states had agreed to cede certain western lands to the nation.

National government under the Articles consisted solely of a unicameral Congress in which each state delegation cast one vote. Important actions required the assent of nine states and amendment of the Articles required the approval of all thirteen. Although the Congress was given some restricted judicial authority over interstate disputes and marine affairs, there was no provision for an executive or a judiciary. At first the Congress appointed ad hoc committees whenever necessary for performance of its limited executive functions, but soon it created permanent departments under its direction. There was no chief executive; the "president" was merely the presiding officer of the Congress. The tendency to fear power and to restrict its exercise was evident in every provision. Because Americans were even more fearful of a national government than of their state governments, the Articles declared that "each state retains its sovereignty, freedom, and independence." Moreover, the document says that the states had entered into merely a "league of friendship with each other."[7] They had clearly opted for continuation as virtually independent nations and created an institution that served more as a consultative council reflecting state views than as a national government. Thus the Articles did not create a national state in the modern sense but established instead essentially a league, or confederation, of independent units. So weak was the central power that there was no meaningful provision for financing. The Congress could in theory obtain operating funds from the states through levies upon them, but it could not enforce payment. There were attempts to enact a tariff to create national revenue, but such an action required the consent of all of the states and at least one was always in opposition. Almost as great a weakness was the lack of power over individual citizens, who were subject only to their respective state governments.

Despite the weaknesses of the central authority under the Articles, there were considerable accomplishments. Such agencies as the departments of Foreign Affairs, Finances, and War, all of which Congress created in 1781, if permitted to develop might well have evolved into a cabinet with a resulting parliamentary form of government; this could have been more efficient in many ways than the government that the founders created and at the same time have been at least as responsive to the people.

By far the most significant action under the Articles was the passage of the Northwest Ordinance of 1787 governing the Northwest Territory, the national lands north of the Ohio River. The Ordinance included a bill of rights for residents of the territory that dealt with such things as the right of habeas corpus, trial by jury, freedom of religion, prohibition of cruel and unusual punishment, and the guaranteeing of contracts. It adopted an innovative procedure for admitting to the confederation, on a basis of full equality with the original states, new states that might be created from the area; it thereby set a precedent for the creation of new states from other American national lands and influenced procedures for dealing with the evolution of colonial units into autonomous nations in various parts of the world. One of the Ordinance's most notable features was its prohibition of slavery in the Northwest Territory; it set the tone for much of the subsequent development of the American West and might have averted the Civil War had the Congress gone further and adopted Jefferson's suggestion that slavery be prohibited in all western lands, to the south as well as to the north.

Unfortunately for the advocates of decentralization, the very weak central authority was hardly able to function at all in many instances because of its inability to exert sanctions to enforce even the few powers that it was supposed to have. Such inadequacies were seized upon by those favoring strong central power and a greater national identity. In fact, as the constitutional scholar A. T. Mason has concluded, "Perhaps the greatest service rendered by the Articles of Confederation was the impetus its shortcomings gave the nationalists, particularly James Wilson, John Jay, Alexander Hamilton, James Madison, Thomas Jefferson, and John Adams."[8]

Much of the agitation for a stronger central government came from persons fearing the lack of a sound uniform monetary system and viewing with alarm the populist tendencies within many of the states that impaired the right of contracts and favored debtor classes over creditors. A major precipitating factor was Shays's Rebellion in Massachusetts in 1786. Captain Daniel Shays, who had fought in the Revolution, led an armed revolt of farmers who marched upon Boston in protest against the depression in which the country found itself. The group shut down the courts and intimidated the legislature in order to prevent the collection of debts. Such tactics brought fear to the propertied interests, and they financed the militia, which broke the revolt. Elsewhere there were actions seen as direct attacks upon the right of property in response to popular pressure to favor debtors. The situation was most notable in Rhode Island, where debtor and agrarian interests controlled the legislature and directed governmental policy. All such developments merely strengthened the cause of the nationalists, or Federalists, who charged that a stronger central government was essential to protect property and sustain order. The concern was not limited to those favoring centralization. As Mason notes:

> It would be a mistake to conclude that all . . . precursors of antifederalism were impervious to the defects inherent in the Articles. . . . The great majority did not oppose all effort to revise the Articles. All agreed

that some revision was necessary. Shays's Rebellion did not impress Federalists alone. Included among those who favored stronger government before 1787 were George Mason, Patrick Henry, Elbridge Gerry, George Clinton, James Monroe, William Grayson, John Francis Mercer, and James Warren. All were destined to become staunch Antifederalists.[9]

On the other hand, there were those who saw Shays's Rebellion as a healthy reaction, not something to be feared. In writing to James Madison concerning the features that he liked and did not like about the proposed Constitution, Thomas Jefferson said:

> I own I am not a friend to a very energetic government. It is always oppressive. The late rebellion in Massachusetts has given more alarm than I think it should have done. Calculate that one rebellion in thirteen states in the course of eleven years, is but one for each state in a century and a half. No country should be so long without one. Nor will any degree of power in the hands of government prevent insurrections. France with all its despotism, and two or three hundred thousand men always in arms has had three insurrections in the three years I have been here in every one of which greater numbers were engaged than in Massachusetts and a great deal more blood was spilt. In Turkey, which Montesquieu supposes more despotic, insurrections are the events of every day. In England, where the hand of power is lighter than here [i.e., France], but heavier than with us, they happen every half dozen years.[10]

On balance, though, the sound and sober members of the community deplored and feared the rebellion and the factors leading to it, and it sounded the death knell of the confederation.

Characteristically the question of the states versus an external power would dominate the discussion of a constitution as it had the discussions that led to the Revolution and to the Articles of Confederation. Both as colonists and as citizens under the Articles, Americans had become accustomed to two levels of authority. It was natural that they would think in terms of some sort of dual system when they met to devise a new government.

The Constitutional Convention and Ensuing Debate

It is unnecessary here to go into great detail regarding the devising of the Constitution because it is a familiar story. At the suggestion of the Congress of the confederation, a convention met in Philadelphia in 1787; the sole purpose of the convention, however, was to amend the Articles to provide for a more workable central government.

Despite the strict limitations upon the power of the convention, the delegates, who represented all the states except Rhode Island, which had refused to participate, quickly concluded that the structure under the Articles was not viable and that it was necessary to disregard the authority by which the convention had been established and to propose a completely new governmental structure. Just as the new nation had come into being with a violent reaction against authority that led to a revolution, so the first stable and enduring government grew from disobedience to authority.

Although the convention in theory represented the states and the people of America, the population at the time was divided into two categories consisting essentially of those of wealth on the one hand and those who were small farmers and workers—that is, debtors who agitated for inflationary policies—on the other. Almost completely, the convention represented lawyers and business-oriented interests; in other words, it largely reflected the values of one faction and ignored the other. However narrow the interests of the delegates may have been, it is to their credit that they tended to follow the example of the Declaration of Independence in thinking in universal terms and couching their language in words that were not limited to class interests. Although their principles may have been, and certainly were to some extent, shaped by their biases, and although practice in many instances fell short of the principles, the fact remains that the delegates acted upon principle as they saw it.

Largely because of the fear of central power and the suspicion that the delegates represented elite interests, there was considerable controversy over ratification in several of the states. Ultimately, all thirteen ratified the document, but only after the proponents promised that the first Congress under the new government would propose a "bill of rights" for the states to ratify. The Bill of Rights, in the form of the first ten amendments, therefore became a part of the new Constitution. The Federalists thus won the day, although not without compromise. It is interesting to note that the name "Federalist" was wisely chosen, but not really accurate; the Federalists tended essentially to be nationalists whose talk of federalism was a pragmatic recognition that the existence of the states was not to be treated lightly, whatever the preferences of those favoring strong central power.

The period beginning with the debates over the Articles and continuing until after ratification of the Constitution was marked by dissension, emotion, and factional interest, but, more important, it was also characterized by political speculation and theorizing of a high order. It was a period of ferment that produced many profound political writings and placed into practice many of the results of what once had been abstract theorizing. Among the ideas contending for acceptance were those that would enshrine an aristocracy into permanent positions of power, as advocated by Alexander Hamilton; those advanced by William Paterson of New Jersey that the Articles of Confederation should merely be revised (the original purpose of the convention); and the middle ground, which the convention adopted at the urging of James Madison and the Virginia delegation, that set up federalism as it exists today combining a strong central government with states that retained powers over citizens.[11]

Despite the famous compromises of the convention, there was almost complete agreement upon the provisions that were to become the basic principles of the Constitution; these occasioned little debate at the time, and many of the momentous questions that plagued the delegates, such as large state interests versus those of the small states, seem hardly to have arisen at all after the convention. The major principles of the Constitution were highly consistent with the Lockean foundations of much of American political thought, especially the thought of the predominant interests that controlled the convention. There was no question that the consent principle was valid and that power should be considered as flowing from the people. There was also no suggestion, at least in the convention, that the people should run the government without checks; democracy was accepted only as one principle among several that were equally valid. All were agreed upon some form of federalism, and all accepted the principle that powers should be separated. Because the convention accepted power as necessary, but dangerous, the people were assured that whatever government was proposed would be limited. Also, the founders had great faith in institutions. They believed that their version of the good society could be achieved if the proper institutions were created. The correct balance of institutions could permit the necessary exercise of power yet at the same time prevent its abuse by power holders.

Such agreement on fundamentals reflected not only a shared background and acceptance of the mainstream tenets of American political thought, but also the narrow range of interests represented in the convention. In the country at large there were tensions between the wealthy and the workers, between tidewater and backcountry, between small agriculture and large, between manufacturing and agriculture, between debtors and creditors, between slaveholding interests and the rest of the nation, between nationalists and those whose allegiance remained wholly with their states, between advocates of various religions or none, and a myriad of other groupings. Such tensions contributed greatly to the controversy regarding ratification, and they also influenced the production of some of the world's greatest political literature.

With respect to the arguments surrounding the Constitution's ratification, the critics won their point regarding the danger of having no bill of rights, and the lack was speedily remedied. The question of national versus state power eventually brought about a civil war and has not totally been laid to rest today. Those Anti-Federalists fearful of too great power in the national executive, such as George Mason and Patrick Henry of Virginia, issued scathing criticisms that have largely been ignored in the development of American politics, but with the recent concern engendered by the belated recognition of the inflated powers of the presidency, it appears as if their arguments should not have been dismissed so lightly. The immediate task facing the advocates of the Constitution, however, was to overcome the Anti-Federalist fears sufficiently to achieve ratification. To this end a series of eighty-five essays appeared in New York newspapers under the name of "Publius," and they have justly been recognized as not merely polemics but classics of political statement; as *The Federalist*, they embody the soundest description and justification of the basis of the American political system.

The authors, Alexander Hamilton, James Madison, and John Jay, argued that the Articles were inadequate as the foundation of a government and that they left liberty and property unprotected. The Constitution, they assured the reader, would remedy the defects of the Articles and provide ample protection for liberty and property while guaranteeing the security of the nation. Much of the analysis was devoted to the proposed federal system that would establish a powerful, but limited, national government while preserving the states and their rights, and to a study of the separation of powers that would be fundamental to the new national government. Hamilton forcefully argued, in *The Federalist*, No. 15, that there was considerably more danger from weakness at the national level than from strength and that the centrifugal forces would need constantly to be checked, and Madison, in No. 45, supported his contentions. One of the most well known of the essays is Madison's No. 10, in which he condemns "faction" and reflects his concern for the public good as opposed to special interests. The Constitution does not mention parties, and modern democracies have found it impossible to work without them, but Madison's comments indicate both a hope that government could operate upon a principle of the good of the whole rather than a pandering to groupings and an assumption that government under the Constitution would work in that manner. He not only failed to anticipate the development of modern party systems but deplored any tendency in their direction.

Throughout *The Federalist* there is consistent emphasis upon the principle of consent. The people are to rule through the republican principle of elected representatives, and they are the foundation of political power. All power, however, must be limited, and the limitations accepted most approvingly by Publius resulted from checks and balances, as in the admiring references to Montesquieu in *The Federalist*, No. 47. The goal is a mixed form of government combining both democratic and aristocratic elements. In providing balance, in fact, Hamilton even anticipated judicial review and in No. 78 outlined the practice that the Supreme Court under the leadership of Chief Justice John Marshall adopted a decade and a half later. It is the concern for balance that Nos. 48 and 70 use as a foundation for arguing in favor of a strong, or "energetic," executive to guard against legislative tyranny.

Is the Constitution Reactionary?

In recent decades revisionist scholars have frequently questioned the accomplishments of the founders and their motives. The earliest and most prominent of these critics was Charles A. Beard, who in 1913 created considerable controversy with his study *An Economic Interpretation of the Constitution of the United States*.[12] Beard contended that those who designed the new government desired primarily to limit the extent of democracy in order to safeguard financial security for themselves and the wealthy classes and to preserve their elite status. The discussion has come to center upon the nature of the Declaration and the Constitution, with critics of the Constitution comparing its relative conservatism unfavorably with the Declaration's radicalism.

Unquestionably there are vast differences in the tone of the two documents. Some assert that the Constitution is merely the result of a practical translation into functioning governmental institutions of the radical rights of man arguments that the American revolutionaries hurled at Europe through the Declaration. Those arguing in this fashion say that the Declaration and the Constitution are simply two sides of the same coin and that the need for sober consideration of practicalities demanded more caution in the Constitution, whereas there was no need for restraint in drawing up a statement of revolution, which by its very nature depended upon extreme statements for its effect. In other words, it is easier to proclaim abstract principles than to place them into practice in the real world.

The question will never be settled. There is no doubt that the Constitution is a more conservative document than the Declaration and is as concerned with practicalities as with principles of eternal truth. Whether that makes it a conservative repudiation of the principles of the Declaration, though, is not so obvious. The Constitution is pervaded throughout with checks upon the power of the people. The amending requirements, for example, specify more than majority desire and do not even permit popular participation in the process. The powerful Supreme Court consists of appointive justices with life tenure. All legislation must receive approval of a Senate that originally was not subject to popular election and still represents areas rather than population. The electoral college and many other features of the original Constitution and the Constitution as it exists today are far from the Declaration's spirit of radical individualism. It is an oversimplification, however, to conclude without further examination that all antidemocratic features are reactionary. Appointive selection of judges and lifetime tenure, for example, may work in some situations to defend liberty when popular passions as expressed through a legislative body might restrain them. Even if the founders had been devoted to the democratic principle, which for a variety of reasons they were not, a concern for liberty might have dictated limitations upon democracy without becoming reactionary. The most consistent emphasis in the Constitution is a reflection of the fear that most early Americans, regardless of class and economic interest, had of concentrations of governmental power. The Constitution was designed fundamentally to limit the power of the national government; although in many instances the mechanisms were not and are not democratic, the intent in the historical sense was profoundly liberal.

This is not to ignore the role of economics and self-interest on the part of the founders, but it is difficult to separate naked self-interest from a true commitment that may be clouded by time, place, and background. One can easily rationalize support for policies that would bring personal benefit as support for that which is right, but not all such support can be written off as mere rationalization. Objective considerations may upon occasion dictate actions that aid oneself for reasons that are unselfish; more frequently, however, a person may truly believe that he or she is acting upon unselfish principle when the view expressed may be clouded by circumstances, such as economic grouping or fundamental assumptions of the culture.

Professor Beard, therefore, may have overstated his case. Certainly the authors of the Constitution were influenced by personal considerations and by economic factors, but it is far from clear that economic issues were the sole criterion by which they shaped the new government. Although the principles may have reflected a cultural bias, a concern for principle was at least a part of the work of the convention. Beard's notable accomplishment was in calling attention to the role and importance of economics, which can no longer be disregarded.

The Constitution should be viewed in this light. It was the product of a small elite group in a certain time and place. They were acting in their own interest but in most cases appear to have been convinced that they also were acting in the interest of the entire society, and in fact of the world. Their product was far from perfect; its greatest defect was in preserving an institution, human slavery, that was not only illiberal but malevolent. The writers were not ideologues, as some of the revolutionaries had been. On balance, their preferences were for human liberty, but they were willing to compromise to achieve what they considered to be the good society. Their achievements were solid, although flawed in some respects. For instance, they failed to recognize the dangers in concentrations of private power. To criticize this failure, though, would be to criticize their inability to foretell the future. It would have been impossible in the late eighteenth century to anticipate the development and effects of corporate industrialism that created the possibility of huge accumulations of private power.

The subsequent development of American politics indicates that the Constitution was a splendid reflection of the basic assumptions of mainstream American political thought. In terms of the presuppositions of the American people, it is probably true that the Constitution was the best possible codification of the principles and rhetoric of the Declaration that could survive in this society. It would have been difficult, therefore, and probably impossible, for the founders or any other group to have produced anything superior to it; the United States Constitution appears most fully to represent the political spirit that has motivated this special branch of Western civilization, America.

NOTES

1. See, for example, Edward S. Corwin, *The "Higher Law" Background of American Constitutional Law* (Ithaca, N.Y.: Cornell University Press, 1967).

2. See Francis N. Thorpe, *The Federal and State Constitutions, Colonial Charters, and Other Organic Laws of the States, Territories, and Colonies,* vol. 6 (Washington, D.C.: U.S. Government Printing Office, 1909), pp. 3205–3211.

3. Quoted in Bernard Bailyn, *The Ideological Origins of the American Revolution* (Cambridge, Mass.: The Belknap Press of Harvard University Press, 1967), p. 246.

4. (New York: Harper Torchbooks, 1964).

5. For a discussion of this point, see ibid., pp. 111–124.

6. Ibid., p. 113.

7. See Articles II and III.

8. *Free Government in the Making*, 3rd ed. (New York: Oxford University Press, 1965), pp. 135–136.

9. Ibid., p. 142.

10. Letter of December 20, 1787, in *The Papers of Thomas Jefferson*, vol. 12, Julian R. Boyd, ed. (Princeton, N.J.: Princeton University Press, 1950–1971), p. 441; see also Harris Mirkin, "Rebellion, Revolution, and the Constitution: Thomas Jefferson's Theory of Civil Disobedience," *American Studies* 13, no. 2 (Fall 1972), 62–68.

11. On the convention, see Max Farrand, ed., *The Records of the Federal Convention of 1787*, 3 vols. (New Haven, Conn.: Yale University Press, 1911).

12. (New York: Macmillan, 1913).

ADDITIONAL READINGS

Bennett, Walter H. *American Theories of Federalism*. University, Ala.: University of Alabama Press, 1964.

Corwin, E. S. *The "Higher Law" Background of American Constitutional Law*. Ithaca, N.Y.: Cornell University Press, 1967 [1928].

Crosskey, William W. *Politics and the Constitution in the History of the United States*. Chicago: University of Chicago Press, 1953.

Eidelberg, Paul. *The Philosophy of the American Constitution: A Re-interpretation of the Intentions of the Founding Fathers*. New York: Free Press, 1968.

Farrand, Max, ed. *The Records of the Federal Convention of 1787*. New Haven, Conn.: Yale University Press, 1937.

Friedrich, Carl J., and Robert G. McCloskey. *From the Declaration of Independence to the Constitution: The Roots of American Constitutionalism*. Indianapolis: Bobbs-Merrill, 1954.

Hofstadter, Richard. *The American Political Tradition*. New York: Vintage, 1958, chap. 1.

———. "Beard and the Constitution: The History of an Idea." *American Quarterly* II (Fall 1950).

Koch, Adrienne, ed. *Notes of Debates in the Federal Convention of 1787 Reported by James Madison*. Athens, Ohio: Ohio University Press, 1966.

Latham, Earl, ed. *The Declaration of Independence and the Constitution*. 3rd ed. Lexington, Mass.: D.C. Heath, 1976 (a broad selection of readings).

Lewis, John D., ed. *Anti-Federalists versus Federalists: Selected Documents*. Scranton, Pa: Chandler, 1967.

McIlwain, C. H. *Constitutionalism, Ancient and Modern*. Rev. ed. Ithaca, N.Y.: Cornell University Press, 1947.

Patterson, C. P. "The Evolution of Constitutionalism." *Minnesota Law Review* XXXII (April 1948).

Peek, George A., ed. *The Political Writings of John Adams: Representative Selections.* Indianapolis: Bobbs-Merrill, 1954.

Roche, John P. "The Founding Fathers: A Reform Caucus in Action." *American Political Science Review* LV (December 1961).

Smith, David G. *The Convention and the Constitution: The Political Ideas of the Founding Fathers.* New York: St. Martin's Press, 1969.

Solberg, Winton U., ed. *The Federal Convention and the Formation of the Union of the American States.* Indianapolis: Bobbs-Merrill, 1958.

Wormuth, Francis D. *The Origins of Modern Constitutionalism.* New York: Harper, 1949.

5

The Early Republic

The Constitution of the United States was based upon a pessimistic view of human nature but an optimistic assessment of the potential of institutions to control the human tendency toward corruption. The Founding Fathers were individualists and firmly believed, however skeptical they were of democracy and the capabilities of the masses, that the only true justification for political authority was the consent of the governed and that the only purpose of government was to operate in the interests of the people. This much is clear, and to this extent the early Americans in the republic were united and distinguished from most of the rest of the world.

The beliefs of those favoring the Constitution and those opposing it, the beliefs of those advocating centralization and those favoring strengthening the states and institutions of localism, and the beliefs of those groupings that coalesced into the Federalists and their antagonists, the Anti-Federalists, or Democratic-Republicans, were therefore all reflections of a pervasive liberal atmosphere in America. Historically, conservatism stresses tradition, hierarchy, religion, duty as opposed to rights, and the organic nature of the state, that is, the rejection of the individual as the unit of politics and the assumption that the state is more than the sum of the citizens that comprise it. By these standards, postrevolutionary America, with its individualism, fear of power, and emphasis upon rationality as opposed to tradition, was profoundly liberal. There is little politically that suggests any significant tendency toward classical conservatism.[1] There was nevertheless a definite split into two factions. A strict definition would class both factions as liberals in the historical sense, but for purposes of simplicity it is convenient to speak of the two camps as "liberal" and "conservative," recognizing that such a description makes sense only within an American setting and does not attempt to place the "conservative" actually within the historical tradition of conservatism. Both the liberal group, who favored more reliance upon the people, and the conservative group, who feared the people, tended to accept the principle that the individual is the unit of government. Moreover each recognized the need for limitations upon the exercise of power, with the liberals fearing most the power to be exercised by government and the conservatives tending to fear most the power of the people. There were those who generally are regarded as among the conservative camp whose greatest concern was the concentration of power regardless of which group was to exercise it. Both James Madison and John Adams, for example, were fearful of power as such, having no faith in the ability of any single group to wield unchecked power with either wisdom or virtue. In a popular government, of course, the power of the people and the power of the government should be directly related.

As they worked out the details of the new government, the Founding Fathers endeavored to pit power against power. Madison said in *The Federalist*, No. 51, that "ambition must be made to counteract ambition." He proceeded to admit that such an approach did not reflect well upon human nature but argued that the very existence of government itself was "the greatest of all reflections upon human nature." He wrote that "if men were angels, no government would be necessary," and maintained that the greatest difficulty facing the designer of a government was to enable the government to control the governed yet insure that it would control itself. The difficulty leads directly to the search for a mixed government with divided powers that check one another. What institutions can accomplish the goal of establishing a government that is adequately powerful yet adequately restrained? Among the Founding Fathers there was no search for a Platonic philosopher king whose virtue and ability would provide restraint, no search for qualities within humanity that would provide the necessary safeguards, and no questioning of the assumption that proper institutions would provide the proper answer.

In the early years of the republic considerable tension arose between two of the fundamental elements of the new government, democracy and constitutionalism. The founders had established a government that combined democratic aspects with clear limitations upon democracy. Their attempt was to provide simultaneously an effective government and a protected liberty. They did not view democracy as the primary protection for freedom; rather they assumed that liberty could be protected only by checks upon democracy, or upon "popular passions," and that it was property instead of democracy that contributed most to its preservation.

The liberty that they most cherished was freedom from irregularities in the economy. Richard Hofstadter has pointed out that the delegates to the constitutional convention had no interest whatsoever in extending liberty to those Americans who needed it the most, black slaves and white indentured servants. The Constitution itself accepted slavery, and there was not even any discussion of indenture. Hofstadter correctly noted that the delegates did not regard civil liberties any too tenderly, and that "it was the opponents of the Constitution who were most active in demanding such vital liberties as freedom of religion, freedom of speech and press, jury trial, due process, and protection from 'unreasonable searches and seizures.' These guarantees had to be incorporated in the first ten amendments because the Convention neglected to put them in the original document."[2]

The greatest fear of the delegates tended to be of the "propertyless masses" that would probably develop along with urban areas. The founders placed their faith in the widespread ownership of land, and the states, which set the requirements for voting, reflected this faith. Just as the early colonies limited the principle of consent to freemen or stockholders in the towns, so did the early republic limit political participation to those who had at least a minimum of property. The founders had done just what they had intended. They viewed themselves as moderates who rejected political extremes, and the government that they created reflected not only their class interests but also their sense of moderation and their adherence to republican principles, as republicanism and moderation were understood in the eighteenth century. Although their work was not perfect, and although it did involve compromises that sacrificed some of the principles that still appeal forcefully from the Declaration of Independence, they did produce a masterwork of practical politics.[3]

They also enshrined some practices that were exaggerated by the rise of corporate industrialism to such an extent that private threats to liberties became in the late nineteenth century at least the equal of governmental threats. The founders in general were much closer to Locke's thought than to that of Hobbes. Nevertheless, in adopting along with Hobbes the philosophical position that recognized self-interest as the greatest of human forces, they set up an economic situation based upon fierce competition, not recognizing that subsequent economic and technological developments would provide the major contenders with a vast amount of power—enough, in fact, to run roughshod over the rest of society. The eighteenth-century principles of moderation became in the nineteenth century practices that showed great bias in favor of property rights as opposed to human rights. Many of the biases have now been eliminated, but many persist.

One reason for the bias toward property rights in the initial Constitution and the early republic was that the split into relative liberal and conservative factions did not represent a split between propertied and nonpropertied interests, but between interests that tended to coalesce around two kinds of property. The more liberal Republican faction that resisted the tendencies toward centralization, that spoke of human rights and opposed the development of industrialization and urbanization, consisted largely of the holders of landed property. The Federalists, on the other hand, were more likely to be men of commerce and manufacturing. Those who were debtors and those who lacked property, insofar as they were politically active, tended to align themselves with the landed group, whose agrarian principles would have benefited them more than the policies of the Federalists.

So distinct were the two factions during the early years that they became thoroughly identified with their respective leaders, Alexander Hamilton, the conservative Secretary of the Treasury, and Thomas Jefferson, the Secretary of State, who led the liberal opponents of Hamiltonian centralization. The two men were so forceful, and their doctrines so characteristic of two of the major thrusts in American thought, that they have given their names to the conflicting tendencies, "Jeffersonianism" and "Hamiltonianism," that still influence much American political dialogue. Such scholars as the late V. L. Parrington, in fact, at the risk of great oversimplification, have tended to interpret virtually the whole of American politics as a struggle between these two forces. Before turning to the details of the political struggle between Jefferson and Hamilton, it is instructive to examine the foremost principles of their political thought.

The Political Philosophy of Thomas Jefferson

Thomas Jefferson was fully within the liberal tradition. His emphasis was upon human rights and limitations upon the power of government. He stressed the value of education, and he worked to establish free public education for all. He was hostile to the growth of urban areas and considered cities to be "sores upon the body politic." He favored the development of an American republic based upon states' rights and small, independent farmers, whose virtue would be insured by remaining close to the soil and far from the places of corruption. He argued that each generation should decide its own policies and not rely upon tradition or be bound by decisions made by its forefathers. He favored strict construction of the Constitution to limit the national government by preventing it from assuming powers not explicitly stated in that document, and he placed his greatest faith in local institutions as being those closer to the people and less susceptible to corruption. He was relatively optimistic with regard to human nature and the ability of human beings to govern themselves without external coercion. He feared the corrupting influences of power, however, and prescribed rigid limitations upon power holders. Above all, he placed his faith in human reason.

By the time of the Enlightenment, that new wave of speculation about politics in the eighteenth century that stressed both science and skepticism toward authority, natural law had come to imply natural rights. Jefferson's emphasis upon natural law and natural rights in the Declaration of Independence (see pp. 46–47) could not have been clearer. Similarly clear is his concern with the right of the people to determine their own government, regardless of restricting institutions. Although his thought reflects close acquaintance with the existing literature of natural law and political philosophy, Jefferson was more than a follower of Locke or of currents in French thought. In short, he was American. In the words of Adrienne Koch:

> Jefferson's interpretation is exceptional . . . in two respects. First, his elaboration of the full moral implications of republican theory went further than that of the continental or English writers. Second, his patience and inventiveness with the political devices necessary to the operation of republicanism were greater and, incidentally, more native to him and thus to America than derivative from the English or the French.[4]

In his later years, Jefferson proposed a system of political wards that has been unjustifiably ignored. He would have divided the entire nation into a hierarchy of units with its base in autonomous wards that would be self-governing and free to handle all questions that were local in nature. Hannah Arendt was one of the very few to have taken note of Jefferson's suggestions, and her analyses are extraordinarily perceptive. As she pointed out:

> Had Jefferson's plan of "elementary republics" [wards] been carried out, it would have exceeded by far the feeble germs of a new form of government which we are able to detect in the sections of the Parisian Commune and the popular societies during the French Revolution. However, if Jefferson's political imagination surpassed them in insight and in scope, his thoughts were still traveling in the same direction. Both Jefferson's plan and the French *sociétés révolutionnaires* anticipated with an

almost weird precision those councils, *soviets* and *Räte* which were to make their appearance in every genuine revolution throughout the nineteenth and twentieth centuries. Each time they appeared, they sprang up as the spontaneous organs of the people, not only outside of all revolutionary parties but entirely unexpected by them and their leaders. Like Jefferson's proposals, they were utterly neglected by statesmen, historians, political theorists, and, most importantly, by the revolutionary tradition itself.[5]

She qualified the statement by mentioning some exceptions, but the point remains that neither Jefferson's plan nor actual developments in subsequent revolutions made any difference with regard to political theory or practice.

Jefferson's concern was participation. He considered the people to have acted during the Revolution and to have participated in the events that concerned them. During more settled times, however, public actions came to be relegated solely to the government.[6] Even county government was too large to permit actual experience in self-government as opposed to representative government for its citizens, and the possibilities were progressively worse at the state and national levels. Viewing this development, Jefferson decided that the fundamental basis of republican government demanded, as Arendt noted, "the subdivision of the counties into wards," the creation of "small republics," within which "every man in the State" would be "an acting member of the Common government, transacting in person a great portion of its rights and duties, subordinate indeed, yet important, and entirely within his competence. . . . These little republics . . . would be the strength of the great one."[7]

The purpose of the "small republic" would not be to strengthen the majority, but to enhance the power of each citizen. This was similarly the goal of the advocates of participatory democracy in the 1960s and early 1970s. Two hundred years later, we still have virtually no mechanism for permitting the citizen to participate in making policies that directly concern him or her and in influencing decisions that affect the quality of life, except the mildest of actions, the occasional casting of a vote. Voting, unfortunately, brings no evidence to the citizen that participation has any direct influence upon the course of politics.

Jefferson was vague regarding the specific functions of the wards. Arendt contended that the vagueness was intentional and that it is evidence that he was suggesting a new form of constitutional order that would be the only nonviolent alternative to frequent revolutions if liberty were to survive. If this is correct, if Jefferson intended to suggest a new form of government rather than a reform of the old one, he must be regarded as vastly more radical than has been recognized. Arendt has broadened our understanding of Jefferson considerably by identifying the direction of his thought. Freedom was the aim of the Revolution, and Jefferson thought true freedom would exist only when a person could share in the public power as an individual, and not merely as a member of a majority, or of the mass.[8]

Jefferson's views of humanity did not imply that he believed that the average person was capable of great intellectual feats or that high governmental office did not require special competence. He trusted the people, however, to elect to office those who possessed the wisdom and the virtue that would be needed. He agreed with John Adams, with whom he conducted a regular correspondence in the last years of their lives, that there was an aristocracy of the intellect. It was this aristocracy of ability that Jefferson trusted the people to choose as their leaders.

If it is true that despite the honor paid to Jefferson much of the greatness of his thought has not widely been recognized, it is also true that he was often inconsistent. His actions as a strong President were at variance with many of his doctrines; practicalities led him to retreat to some extent from emphasizing decentralization and the limiting of governmental power. Moreover, in spite of his opinions regarding the rights of man, there were instances in which he violated his own principles of civil liberties.[9]

Nowhere are the inconsistencies of his thought clearer than in his writings on Indians, women and blacks. In *Notes on the State of Virginia*, responding to allegations that the American continent produced animal life that was inferior to that of the Old World, he produced facts and figures to the contrary and stressed his beliefs that Indians were the equal of whites and that any significant differences between the two groups were cultural.[10] In discussing Indians, he expressed attitudes of sexual equality as well; commenting that he had observed Indian males to dominate females, he noted that he believed this to be "the case with every barbarous people. With such, force is law. The stronger sex imposes on the weaker. It is civilization alone which replaces women in the enjoyment of their natural equality."[11] With regard to blacks, however, his views were strikingly different. He admitted the great injustices to which they had been subjected and argued that such injustices added to the dangers to white society, should slavery be abolished as he advocated. But he never freed all of his own slaves, even at his death, and he favored colonization of blacks elsewhere, citing alleged physical and mental differences that would make it unlikely for whites and blacks to live together peaceably on a basis of equality even if the blacks had not bitterly resented their treatment. Although he phrases his conclusion with some caution, he wrote, "I advance it, therefore, as a suspicion only, that the blacks . . . are inferior to the whites in the endowments both of body and mind."[12] Such conclusions come easily with reference to persons over whom one has total control. Jefferson had some hesitation about his own feeling that blacks were naturally inferior because it obviously contradicted the views that he had incorporated into the Declaration of Independence. If differences between blacks and whites were owing solely to culture and education, on the other hand, then clearly blacks and whites could mingle ultimately on an equal basis. His own discussion indicates that he objected to this possibility on purely racist grounds, upon grounds that were more aesthetic than rational.[13] Jefferson accepted the idea of black inferiority, but wavered on the cause; finding no position that satisfied him, he came increasingly to evade the question as time passed.

An example of Jefferson's reluctance to deal with the issue directly may be seen in his response to a communication from Benjamin Banneker, a free black man and a gifted mathematician. Banneker was largely unschooled but had educated himself and prepared an astronomical almanac, although he spent his life as a farmer. In reaction to the comments on black capabilities in *Notes on the State of Virginia*, he wrote to Jefferson, then Secretary of State, and enclosed a copy of the almanac. His letter was a tightly reasoned social and political argument equating American slavery with the conditions that Americans had fought against in ending their status as "slaves" to Great Britain and calling attention to the contradiction in the fact that Americans could argue forcefully against their own slavery, yet simultaneously hold others in bondage. Quoting Jefferson's own language from the Declaration of Independence, he noted that it was self-evidently true that all men are created equal and that they are endowed with inalienable rights, including the rights to life, liberty, and happiness. He ended by relating his own accomplishments and using them as evidence that black mental abilities are no different from those of whites, and that the apparent inferiority of blacks resulted from their deprived condition.

In response, Jefferson thanked him for the almanac in a brief letter and wrote:

> No body wishes more than I do, to see such proofs as you exhibit, that nature has given to our black brethren talents equal to those of the other colors of men; and that the appearance of the want of them is owing merely to the degraded condition of their existence. . . . I can add with truth, that no body wishes more ardently to see a good system commenced, for raising the condition, both of their body and mind, to what it ought to be, as far as . . . circumstances . . . will admit.[14]

Jefferson's reply was evasive, though he nominated Banneker to be a member of the commission that was to survey the new national district. He also praised Banneker in a letter to the French politician Condorcet, saying that he was a "very worthy and respectable member of society" and that the "want of talents" observed in blacks may be the "effect of their degraded condition."[15]

The Political Philosophy of Alexander Hamilton

As much as any other American statesman of the period, despite some of his youthful comments to the contrary, Alexander Hamilton leaned toward the doctrines of Hobbes. Like his contemporaries, he favored republicanism. He accepted the notion that governmental authority is to be founded upon consent, yet he desired to strengthen the power of the government in order to provide the most firmly established state possible. He agreed that government must be limited, but his notions of limitations were far from those of Jefferson. As much as anything else, he looked to the virtue of rulers as a source of limitation. Hamilton believed that the rich and the wellborn possessed the ability and wisdom to govern and that legislation should be directed toward establishing their rule. He greatly feared the mob and took direct issue with Jefferson's notion of the people's capacity for self-government. Essentially he was a nationalist, desiring to build the strongest possible nation and believing this possible only with a strong central government and an economy built upon manufacturing, not the agrarian society that Jefferson favored; he viewed Jefferson's preference for an empire of small, independent farmers as romantic nonsense. Rather than sharing Jefferson's fear of cities and their potential for mobs and corruption, he welcomed the coming of urbanism as making possible the growth of industrialism by providing a pool of labor. Aid to industry, currency manipulation, and a national debt he accepted as beneficial mechanisms for strengthening the economy.

Many of Hamilton's views would be seen today as grossly antihumanitarian. Woodrow Wilson allegedly once remarked that Hamilton was a great man, but not a great American. It is true that America in general has adopted Jeffersonian rhetoric and has in theory responded most readily to it, but when examining American practice, it would be difficult to demonstrate that Hamilton's policies were unrepresentative of American actions. In this sense Wilson was mistaken. Although Hamilton did not talk the way most Americans talk, he acted as Americans often act; he was different in being candid about it. The basic distinction between Hamilton and Jefferson turned upon the question of power. Hamilton's major concern was the adequacy of power, whereas Jefferson's was the adequacy of the limitations upon power. This sheds light upon Hamilton's emphasis on a strong national government and upon Jefferson's preference for decentralization.

In terms of personality another distinction is that whereas Jefferson frequently dealt with the moral aspects of governmental actions, Hamilton tended to concern himself solely with the practical consequences as they related to national power. Despite Jefferson's more romantic temper and his faith in the people, he was realistic in recognizing the need to control all power strictly. In one ironic respect, the realist Hamilton was more guilty of romanticism than Jefferson in that he placed his faith in the ability of the wellborn to rule with wisdom and virtue with minimal restraints.

Federalists Versus Republicans: Political Developments

The new administration under President Washington came quickly to be dominated by Hamilton's conservative policies. The conservative majority in the Congress was hesitant to adopt changes in the Constitution, despite the agreements in many states that ratification was contingent upon the adoption of a bill of rights, but James Madison reviewed the amendments that the state ratifying conventions had suggested and selected those he believed would protect liberty without damaging the fabric of the infant government. Only twelve of those that he presented survived congressional action, and ten of the twelve were ratified by the states, becoming the Bill of Rights.

Even the Bill of Rights was far from the ringing defense of natural rights that Jefferson had built into the Declaration. It was a noteworthy advance in world political practice, but it was not protected from change that might come from future amendment. The Eleventh Amendment, in fact, although not directed at a guarantee within the Bill of Rights, did eliminate the right of citizens, or any persons, to bring suit in federal court against a state other than their own. Moreover, the Congress specifically excluded from its proposed amendments one that would have made the Bill of Rights binding upon the states as well as upon the national government. As it was adopted, the Bill of Rights protected Americans only against the central government, not against an action by a state. The fact that many states continued established churches for a time illustrates its limitations. The intention may have been to safeguard rights not mentioned by adopting the Ninth Amendment, which declared that failure to list a right did not prove that it was not to be protected, but the Ninth Amendment was completely ignored. Only recently have some begun to look anew at that amendment as a possible protection, for example, of privacy or the environment.

Under Hamilton's leadership, centralization proceeded rapidly. Congress moved to enact a tariff to protect manufacturers, and it laid excise taxes and used force to collect them. These policies were a part of Hamilton's program to strengthen the central government, if need be at the expense of the noncommercial groups. He specifically brought about an excise tax upon whiskey as a means of showing the power of the new government to regulate the individual citizen. The farmers of western Pennsylvania, who were among the more hostile to the newly established order, generally converted their grains into whiskey for ease of transportation. Because the tax financed national actions of which they disapproved and which benefited them not at all, and because it threatened their very livelihood, they refused to pay and took to arms. Hamilton welcomed the confrontation, and troops crushed the revolt, known as the Whiskey Rebellion.

In response to Hamilton's leadership, Congress enacted the Funding Act of 1790 to redeem the outstanding state debts as well as those of the confederation and those accumulated under the Continental Congress, a move that enriched speculators. In 1791 it passed legislation for the creation of a Bank of the United States, which not only went contrary to the laissez-faire ideas of Adam Smith that had become popular in this country, but also raised serious constitutional questions. James Madison, considered the foremost expert on the Constitution, led the opposition in Congress. Arguing that the Constitution clearly limited the national government and that this was the express intention of the constitutional convention, Madison nevertheless lost to a strong Federalist majority that rejected his pleas.

Despite Congress's action, Madison's reasoning troubled President Washington, who turned to his cabinet for opinions on the constitutionality of the National Bank. Jefferson wrote that the Tenth Amendment reserved to the states or to the people all powers not delegated to the national government, and that "to take a single step beyond the boundaries thus specially drawn around the powers of Congress, is to take possession of a boundless field of power, no longer susceptible of any definition."[16] This statement is a clear assertion of the doctrine of strict construction of the Constitution.

Hamilton, for his part, produced a masterful argument in favor of loose construction. It has been remarked that "next to *The Federalist*, his argument on the constitutionality of the bank is perhaps the most important single contribution to American political thought in the first years of the Union. In it Hamilton made the first substantial statement of the doctrine of implied powers, which he had earlier suggested."[17] Hamilton argued that inherent in the very definition of government is the principle that every power vested in a government is sovereign and presupposes the power also to exercise any means necessary to carry out a permitted action, so long as the methods are consistent with the goal and are not otherwise prohibited. As to the charge that his reasoning would lead to uncontrolled power, he wrote:

> But the doctrine which is contended for is not chargeable with the consequences imputed to it. It does not affirm that the National Government is sovereign in all respects, but that it is sovereign to a certain extent;—that is, to the extent of the objects of its specified powers.
>
> It leaves, therefore, a criterion of what is constitutional and of what is not so. This criterion is the *end*, to which the measure relates as a *means*. If the *end* be clearly comprehended within any of the specified powers, and if the measure have an obvious relation to the *end*, and is not forbidden by any particular provision of the Constitution, it may safely be deemed to come within the compass of the national authority. There is also this criterion, which may materially assist the decision: Does the proposed measure abridge a pre-existing right of any State or of any individual? If it does not, there is a strong presumption in favor of its constitutionality.[18]

Edmund Randolph, the Attorney General, agreed with Jefferson that the bank was unconstitutional, but when Henry Knox, the Secretary of War, supported Hamilton's position Washington signed into law the bill creating the bank.

Hamilton quickly added to his program with two more great reports, *Report on the Establishment of a Mint* and *Report on the Subject of Manufacturing*. Reasoning that manufacturing, not agriculture, was the key to building the strength of a state, he advocated all-out government aid to industry and based his authority for such a program upon the same reasoning that he advanced in favoring the bank. Efficiency was his watchword; a side benefit of an industrial state was that it would permit the use of labor that might otherwise be wasted, such as that of women and children, many of whom, he asserted, might be of a "tender age."

Jefferson was convinced that the Hamiltonian program was directed toward the aggrandizement of the government to the extent that it might be deliberately paving the way to the establishment of a monarchy. Eventually, he resigned from Washington's cabinet in protest. In 1796 he placed second to John Adams in the presidential race and thereby became Vice President, as was provided by the original Constitution before the passage of the Twelfth Amendment.

In 1798, under pressure from his own Federalist party resulting from the increasingly bitter dispute with the Jeffersonians, Adams signed into law the infamous Alien and Sedition Acts, which made it a crime to criticize the government. In view of Jefferson's attitude favoring strict construction of the Constitution, it was almost inevitable that he would forcefully challenge the acts as beyond the scope of the national government; they exceeded not only the limitations of the Constitution as outlined in the First Amendment, but grossly violated the spirit of a government based upon notions of liberty. The Kentucky and Virginia Resolutions, the former essentially a product of Jefferson and the latter introduced by John Taylor and urged upon the legislature by Madison, were responses by the Jeffersonians, who would have found it difficult to have criticized the acts directly without facing jail. The Kentucky and Virginia legislatures circulated their resolutions among the other states, receiving hostile replies from those dominated by Federalists, but publicizing widely the authoritarian nature of the Federalist legislation. The following year, in 1799, Kentucky adopted an even stronger resolution.

In substance, the resolutions stressed the contractual nature of the Union. They asserted that it was created by the action of sovereign states and that the resulting national government was strictly limited in its powers. If national powers were limited, some other agency had to be the judge of those limitations because a limit that would be interpreted by the government that was itself the agency to be limited would be no limit at all. The states, therefore, as the original contractors to the formation of the Union, should determine when the national government was within its stated powers or was exceeding them. The second Kentucky Resolution went so far as to imply the possibility of state nullification of federal acts. It contended "that the several states . . . have the unquestionable right to judge of the infraction; and, *That a Nullification of those sovereigns, of all unauthorized acts done under color of that instrument is the rightful remedy.*" Nevertheless, it drew back from an open advocacy of independent state action by assuring "that although this commonwealth, as a party to the federal compact, will bow to the laws of the Union, yet it does, at the same time, declare, that it will not now, or ever hereafter, cease to oppose, in a constitutional manner, every attempt at what quarter soever offered, to violate that compact."[19] In Virginia the Federalist responses drew an answer from Madison, who again emphasized that the states, which originally had contracted to form the Constitution, were the proper parties to interpret it. Although Madison later denied that his position supported South Carolina's attempts at nullification, he used the term "inter position," and in years to come elements in the South quoted him in defense of their moves toward interposition, that is, interposing state power to shield its citizens from action by the national government, and nullification.[20]

The Kentucky and Virginia Resolutions preceded the case of *Marbury* v. *Madison* in 1803, when the Supreme Court asserted the right of judicial review. They were attempts within the new nation to determine which agency must be charged with the power to interpret the Constitution, a question upon which the specific language of the Constitution is silent. Although many at the constitutional convention had assumed that the courts would exercise this function, the Jeffersonians were highly displeased with what they considered the judiciary's usurpation of power, because the courts were totally Federalist as a result of the "midnight appointments" by which John Adams had packed them with his supporters in the last days of his Federalist administration.

The specific controversy surrounding the Alien and Sedition Acts died a natural death after Jefferson was elected President in 1800. His administration allowed them to lapse in 1801, their expiration date. Partly because of changing national sentiments, and partly because of internal splits within the Federalists between the extreme advocates of Hamiltonian policies and the more moderate factions who adhered to Adams, the Jeffersonian victory spelled the end of the old Federalist party, except as it persevered for some years in the judiciary. However much one may allow for exaggeration, those who interpret the election of Jefferson as the "Revolution of 1800" have some logic on their side. It is nevertheless ironic that Jefferson in power became a strong President and at times went considerably beyond the boundaries of strict constitutional construction.

Other Exponents of Jeffersonian Philosophy

Although Jefferson is so closely identified with a prominent current of American political thought that it carries his name, he did not systematically expound upon his principles in a comprehensive philosophical treatise. For much that is to be found in the tradition of "Jeffersonianism," one must turn to other writers to supplement Jefferson's own diverse writings. The two other persons most closely associated with the tradition are James Madison and John Taylor of Caroline County, Virginia.

Madison is known as the "Father of the Constitution" as well as the author of much of *The Federalist*. Like Jefferson, he owed a great debt to Locke, and he based his political philosophy upon the notion of contract. He followed Montesquieu in favoring separation of powers, and he favored a middle approach between the localism of Jefferson and the ardent nationalism of Hamilton. Probably as a result of Jefferson's influence, he came to recognize the provisions of the Bill of Rights as useful, although he feared that the greatest danger to liberty would probably result from majority tyranny, against which constitutional prohibitions would be of little effect. Like Jefferson, he viewed legitimate government as based upon consent, and he accepted the foundation of government as majority rule contingent upon the preservation of natural rights. He differed from Jefferson in that he placed a greater emphasis upon the rights of property, though both favored a representation of property interest within one branch of the legislature. Madison also took a more legalistic view than Jefferson of constitutionalism. Jefferson believed in a "revolution" every twenty years; legislation should last only for a specified period so that each generation would enact its own rather than be enslaved by the past. Madison feared that such continual shifts would introduce an unacceptable instability in government. He was more of a traditionalist than Jefferson and also emphasized governmental structure to a greater degree. Essentially the major difference in their tempers is that Madison was more closely oriented toward the practical. As a practical theoretician, one of his foremost accomplishments was to assist in the establishment of a system that would provide both liberty and authority in a large republic, a subject that was his lifelong concern.[21]

John Taylor exemplified Jeffersonian principles with no hint of Jefferson's broad humanitarianism or his understanding of the practicalities of statecraft. He is known primarily for his attacks upon Federalist programs, finally including even attacks upon Jefferson and Madison for having compromised with some Federalist principles, and for his ardent defense of states' rights, which came ultimately to undergird the arguments of the secessionists. Taylor's first significant work, and his most important, was *An Inquiry into the Principles and Policy of the Government of the United States*, written in 1814. He is known also for three later works: *Construction Construed and Constitutions Vindicated*, in 1820; *Tyranny Unmasked*, in 1822; and *New Views of the Constitution*, his last work, written in 1823.

As a militant agrarian, Taylor naturally favored decentralization and opposed the fiscal policies of the rising commercial interests, interests that were well represented by the Federalists. More so than has been common among Americans, Taylor attempted to present a systematic political philosophy, one that explicitly rejected the assumptions underlying the theories of John Adams and the nation-building programs of Alexander Hamilton. Prior to the adoption of the Constitution, Adams had written a three-volume work entitled *A Defence of the Constitution of Government of the United States of America*, published in 1787 and 1788. In it he laid the groundwork for his theories of mixed government, contending that power was naturally divided into three branches and that each deserved representation. In every form of government he identified a "first magistrate, a head, a chief," a "senate or little council," and the people. The council reflected the power of the aristocracy, which was a naturally occurring phenomenon and inevitable. It was this theory of aristocracy as the product of nature that Taylor condemned in his *Inquiry* more than twenty-five years later.

Aristocracy, Taylor argued, was artificial, not natural, and resulted from economics. Government arose from moral principles, not natural or physical causes, and thus did not take the same form in all circumstances and did not "naturally" divide citizens into classes. Adams was therefore mistaken to assume that one form of government was the best. Taylor also denied that human nature was unchanging, thereby maintaining consistency in his views that governmental forms would and probably should differ in response to different conditions. It follows that the form of government is irrelevant; it is its functioning that is important. The proper evaluation of a government involves not outward form but rather moral principles. Evaluators should seek answers to the questions: What are the principles upon which the government acts, what policies does it adopt, and what is its general character?

Taylor condemned both Adams and the authors of *The Federalist* for concentrating upon form and institutions. In his view, they were unduly influenced by the British model and by Montesquieu's writings. The strength of Taylor's thought is his recognition that substance is more important than form and that any meaningful analysis must probe beneath the surface. His weaknesses are his dogmatism and his tendency to oversimplify drastically; he perceived the world in blacks and whites. He divided the American economy into agrarian interests and the world of commerce, representing the forces of good and those of evil, respectively, with politics as essentially a Manichean struggle between them. His opposition to the National Bank, to tariffs, and to the nationalizing tendencies of John Marshall's

Supreme Court thus transcended mere politics and became a moral crusade.

Also in the Jeffersonian tradition and beginning with the republic itself, spontaneous political groups, Democratic-Republican clubs, formed throughout America. The clubs were joined together through federations with the aim ultimately of expanding into international associations leading to democratic societies throughout the world. They tended to go beyond Jefferson to Thomas Paine, and even to Jean Jacques Rousseau, for their philosophical underpinnings.[22] The clubs represented the radical spirit of individualism reflected in the Declaration of Independence, and their spirit of equalitarian optimism and faith in human potential anticipated the development of many utopian groups and societies in nineteenth-century America.

Some have contended that "nationalism, elitism, and power characterized the theory of the Federalists, whereas limited government, democracy, and human rights characterized the theory of the Jeffersonians."[23] It is true that Jeffersonianism and Hamiltonianism became stark contrasts that in varying forms have continued to affect American politics and political thought. It would be a mistake, however, to fail to recognize the diversities that existed within each stream of thought. John Adams did not initiate the Alien and Sedition Acts passed during his administration, although he enforced them vigorously. Despite this, he generally reflected a moderate temper that was sharply different from that expressed by the more extreme faction of the Federalists who followed Hamilton. Adams and Jefferson, despite all their differences, had much more in common than either of them recognized until the friendship of their later years.

Similarly, it is at least as unwise to consider Jeffersonianism as a simple and consistent movement. During Jefferson's administration there was action by many states to stifle criticism of the Jeffersonians that rivaled the Federalist policies under the Alien and Sedition Acts. Among those classified as Jeffersonians, emphases ranged from the institutional concerns of Madison to Taylor's disregard of institutions and his consideration solely of function; Jefferson himself was somewhere in between. Generally the Jeffersonians did stress natural rights, agrarianism, and the great potential for popular education. With the possible exception of such dogmatic figures as Taylor, the prominent Jeffersonians clearly considered their vital principles to be human liberty, equality, and dignity. It is this core of Jeffersonianism that speaks to us today. It is this core moreover that rises above the contradictions in theory and in practice that are so easy to identify.

There is one factor that united both factions, however much they disagreed regarding its attainment: the assumption that there is a public good, that it can be ascertained by reasonable persons, and that it is the function of government to work toward it. The assumption betrays an optimism that would be disputed by many moderns.

NOTES

1. See, however, Allen Guttmann's *The Conservative Tradition in America* (New York: Oxford University Press, 1967) for a discussion of how conservatism in America has expressed itself in other than political ways.

2. *The American Political Tradition* (New York: Vintage, 1948), pp. 10–11.

3. Ibid., pp. 12–17.

4. *The Philosophy of Thomas Jefferson* (New York: Columbia University Press, 1943), p. 149.

5. *On Revolution* (New York: Viking, 1965), p. 252; Koch, ibid., pp. 162–165, also notes the idea of wards, however briefly, and refers to them as one of Jefferson's "most significant and original ideas for implementing representative democracy."

6. According to Arendt, Jefferson apparently came to his conception of the ward system late in life. He did not mention the Constitution's failure to include wards when he issued his criticisms of the document based upon its lack of a bill of rights. The absence of such a criticism from his analysis of the Constitution, coupled with the fact that among his writings only some letters that he wrote in 1816 outline the system, indicates that his ideas had developed considerably after his service in government had ended. See Arendt, ibid., p. 253.

7. Ibid., p. 257.

8. Ibid., pp. 258–259.

9. See Leonard W. Levy, *Jefferson and Civil Liberties: The Darker Side* (Cambridge, Mass.: The Belknap Press of Harvard University Press, 1963).

10. *Notes on the State of Virginia* (New York: Harper Torchbooks, 1964), pp. 55–59.

11. Ibid., p. 57.

12. Ibid., p. 133.

13. See ibid.

14. Reprinted in George Ducas, ed., *Great Documents in Black American History* (New York: Praeger, 1970), pp. 22–27.

15. Quoted in Koch, *Philosophy*, pp. 118–119.

16. See his "Opinion on the Constitutionality of the Bank," *The Papers of Thomas Jefferson*, vol. 19, Julian P. Boyd, ed. (Princeton, N.J.: Princeton University Press, 1950), pp. 275–282.

17. A. T. Mason and Richard Leach, *In Quest of Freedom*, 2nd ed. (Englewood Cliffs, N.J.: Prentice-Hall, 1973), p. 126; see also *The Federalist*, No. 23.

18. "Opinion on the Constitutionality of the Bank of the United States," *The Works of Alexander Hamilton*, vol. 3, Henry C. Lodge, ed. (New York: G. P. Putnam's Sons, 1885), p. 180.

19. Jonathan Elliot, *The Debates in the Several State Conventions on the Adoption of the Federal Constitution*, vol. 4 (New York: Burt Franklin, 1888), p. 545; the Virginia Resolution is included in this volume, pp. 528–529, as are the two Kentucky Resolutions, pp. 540–545.

20. See Diane Tipton's excellent monograph, *Nullification and Interposition in American Political Thought*, publication No. 78 of the Division of Government Research, The Institute for Social Research and Development (Albuquerque: University of New Mexico, January 1969), chap. 2.

21. See Adrienne Koch, *Jefferson and Madison: The Great Collaboration* (New York: Alfred A. Knopf, 1950).

22. See A. J. Beitzinger, *A History of American Political Thought* (New York: Dodd & Mead, 1972), pp. 304–307.

23. Alan P. Grimes, *American Political Thought* (New York: Holt, Rinehart and Winston, 1960), p. 173.

ADDITIONAL READINGS

Adams, Henry, ed. *Documents Relating to New England Federalism, 1800–1815.* Boston: Little, Brown, 1877.

Beloff, Max. *Thomas Jefferson and American Democracy.* New York: Collier Books, 1962.

Boorstin, Daniel J. *The Lost World of Thomas Jefferson.* Boston: Beacon Press, 1964.

Bowers, Claude G. *Jefferson and Hamilton: The Struggle for Democracy in America.* Boston: Houghton-Mifflin, 1953.

Brant, Irving. "James Madison and His Times." *American Historical Review* LVII (July 1952).

Caldwell, Lynton K. *The Administrative Theories of Hamilton and Jefferson: Their Contribution to Thought on Public Administration.* Chicago: University of Chicago Press, 1944.

Corwin, E. S. *The Doctrine of Judicial Review: Its Legal and Historical Basis.* Princeton, N.J.: Princeton University Press, 1914.

———. *John Marshall and the Constitution.* New Haven, Conn.: Yale University Press, 1919.

Dauer, Manning J. *The Adams Federalists.* Baltimore: Johns Hopkins University Press, 1953.

———, and Hans Hammond. "John Taylor: Democrat or Aristocrat?" *Journal of Politics* VI (November 1944).

Dorfman, Joseph. "The Economic Philosophy of Thomas Jefferson." *Political Science Quarterly* LV (March 1940).

Fischer, David Hackett. *The Revolution of American Conservatism: The Federalist Party in an Era of Jeffersonian Democracy.* New York: Harper Torchbooks, 1965.

Foner, Philip S., ed. *Thomas Jefferson.* New York: International Publishers, 1943.

Griswold, A. Whitney. "The Agrarian Democracy of Thomas Jefferson." *American Political Science Review* XL (August 1946).

Haraszti, Zoltan. *John Adams and the Prophets of Progress.* Cambridge, Mass.: Harvard University Press, 1952.

Hofstadter, Richard. "Thomas Jefferson: The Aristocrat as Democrat." In *The American Political Tradition.* New York: Vintage, 1958, chap. 2.

Koch, Adrienne, and Harry Ammon. "The Virginia and Kentucky Resolutions: An Episode in Jefferson's and Madison's Defense of Civil Liberties." *William and Mary Quarterly,* 3rd Series, V (April 1948).

Mason, Alpheus T. "The Nature of Our Federal Union Reconsidered." *Political Science Quarterly* LXV (December 1950).

Miller, John Chester. *The Federalist Era, 1789-1801.* New York: Harper, 1960.

Morris, Richard B., ed. *Alexander Hamilton and the Founding of the Nation.* New York: Dial, 1957.

Padover, Saul K., ed. *The Complete Madison.* New York: Harper, 1953.

Parrington, V. L. *Main Currents in American Thought.* New York: Harcourt, Brace, 1954, vol. 2, pp. 1-26.

Patterson, C. Perry. "James Madison and Judicial Review." *California Law Review* XXVIII (November 1939).

Peterson, Merrill D. *The Jefferson Image and the American Mind.* New York: Oxford University Press, 1960.

———, ed. *The Portable Thomas Jefferson.* New York: Viking, 1975.

Rutland, Robert A. *The Birth of the Bill of Rights, 1776-1791.* Chapel Hill: University of North Carolina, 1955.

Smith, James Morton. *Freedom's Fetters: The Alien and Sedition Laws and American Civil Liberties.* Ithaca, N.Y.: Cornell University Press, 1956.

Stourzh, Gerald. *Alexander Hamilton and the Idea of Republican Government.* Stanford: Stanford University Press, 1970.

"A Symposium on Jefferson." *Ethics* LIII (July 1943).

Wiltse, Charles M. *The Jefferson Tradition in American Democracy.* Chapel Hill: University of North Carolina, 1935.

Wright, Benjamin F. "The Philosopher of Jeffersonian Democracy." *American Political Science Review* XXII (November 1928); on John Taylor.

6

Jacksonian America

Even after the Federalist party had died as a significant and identifiable force, much of its program remained. Hamilton had placed the economy upon a strong foundation, and Americans have always found it difficult to argue with material success. The Democratic-Republicans adopted tariffs, and Madison himself as President in 1816 approved a second Bank of the United States (the first had been chartered in 1791 for twenty years and had been permitted to expire in 1811). The Supreme Court, headed by Chief Justice John Marshall, asserted the right of judicial review and in such landmark decisions as *McCulloch* v. *Maryland*, which denied a state the power to tax an agency of the national government, not only continued but accelerated the thrust toward national centralization. It is with good reason that a well-known text has a section titled "Hamilton's Constitution Reinforced: John Marshall."[1]

Jacksonianism: Extension of Suffrage and Rising Black Consciousness

As national centralization proceeded apace, the older Federalist emphasis upon privilege was submerged by a rising popular sentiment for democracy and by resulting changes within the states. Historians have given the name "Jacksonianism" to these democratizing tendencies of the period, which peaked with the political campaigns and presidency of Andrew Jackson. In the two decades beginning around 1820, a revolution of sorts occurred within the states that was at least as significant as the better-known "Revolution of 1800" in which the Jeffersonians came to power nationally.

So great was the sentiment for increasing popular participation that there came a rush within the states, beginning with Massachusetts, New York, and Virginia, to revise their constitutions in order to extend the franchise and permit greater popular power. Adding to the thrust of the reform movement was the fact that new states with minimal if any property qualifications for suffrage were being admitted to the Union; also, the workingmen's parties that formed during the late 1820s agitated for an increasing degree of democracy. The changes did not come easily, and the debates within the amending conventions were frequently rancorous.

Some of the most prominent of American statesmen participated actively. Former President John Adams, Supreme Court Justice Joseph Story, and Senator Daniel Webster all represented the conservative side in Massachusetts, as did Chancellor James Kent in New York. In Virginia the active participants included two former Presidents, James Madison and James Monroe, Chief Justice John Marshall, and the vitriolic John Randolph of Roanoke, a powerful member of the U.S. House of Representatives. Most of the debates centered upon such things as the removal of property requirements for voting or the provisions in some states' constitutions that made the state senates, as A. T. Mason notes "the guardian of property," or "the rich man's citadel."[2]

The liberals sought to relax or remove such restraints on popular participation by invoking the familiar doctrine of the American Revolution, the rights of man arguments. The conservatives resisted, fearing that any easing of the restrictions would result in attacks upon the rights of property. The liberals responded that America was different from Europe, that it was not characterized by sharp divisions into economic classes, and that essentially all groups in society had an interest in preserving the rights of property, since even the poor hoped to become property holders and persons of substance some day. Typically, Madison called for moderation and compromise; equally in character were John Randolph, who, caustic and bitter to the end, argued that no government could divorce property from power, and John Marshall, who pleaded for the supremacy of the judiciary, saying that a judge should be answerable only to himself and to God. Mason remarks that one cannot read the discussions without a sense of paradox that in a free government the "moral ideals of political freedom and equality" are "coupled with impassioned insistence that inevitable economic inequality must be maintained by constitutional safeguards."[3]

Ironically, the conservatives in these debates tended to analyze American society in a manner that anticipated Karl Marx's *Communist*

Manifesto of the middle of the century. They viewed America as rife with tension between economic classes and intense struggle between the rich minority and the poor majority, with the rich erecting constitutional barriers to preserve their prerogatives against the people. After the liberals won their reforms, however, the conservatives recognized that their own rhetoric of class conflict was a danger to themselves and modified their attitudes quickly to agree with the liberal position that America was not a class society, and that all, as potential property holders, had an equal interest in maintaining protection for property. There could hardly be a better indication of the essentially liberal nature of American society than the fact that both factions in a bitter dispute would come to accept the same materialistic basis for economics and politics, and equally, that they would both reject radical rhetoric.

The movements to liberalize the state constitutions finally laid to rest one of the old tenets of conservatism, the stake-in-society theory. According to this theory the more material goods a person has, the more he stands to lose; therefore, justice demands that a person have political power in direct proportion to his wealth, with the wealthy, who have the most to lose, dominating all decisions of government. One's stake in society thus is proportionate to one's holdings. This argument fails to recognize that all have the same ultimate stake in society in that all need to protect their lives and liberties. The purely economic interpretation that a person's stake in society is based upon wealth ignores many facets of human existence and should have been settled almost two centuries before in the debates between the officers and men of Cromwell's army (see p. 10).

Contradicting the tendency toward greater political equality was the acceptance by most whites of the continued existence of black slavery. Prior to the adoption of the Constitution, most respectable political oratory that had dealt with the question criticized slavery. The Constitution, however, had accepted it as a fundamental institution in the new nation. Moreover, with the end of the Revolution and the turning of attention to the practical matters of everyday politics, there was little more to be heard of the rights of man, arguments that however little they may have been directed toward blacks at least contained within themselves some hope for them. There were still arguments against slavery, but they tended to stress colonization elsewhere, not an acceptance of free blacks within American society.

For a variety of reasons, there are few records remaining that give much indication of black thought in the early republic. It seems, however, that although some favored colonization, most politically aware blacks feared it and recognized that much of the sentiment for deportation pertained to the free black population and did not include the ending of slavery. There were black leaders who sought to intensify group consciousness and pride, some of whom, such as David Walker, called for armed rebellion to eliminate their chains. More common were black conventions that began in the 1830s with the aim of building black confidence and identifying blacks as oppressed Americans.[4]

The status of American blacks had not improved during the early years under the Constitution, but despite their deprived condition they did develop group awareness and produce some significant commentaries on politics. As early as 1788, for example, a free black from Maryland, writing under the pseudonym "Othello," produced an "Essay on Negro Slavery" that dealt with the moral implications of the institution and also the detrimental effects that it had upon the nation.[5] He argued that it encouraged sloth and "voluptuousness" and damaged the image of the American nation in the world because so long as slavery existed America's claims to represent liberty could not be wholly accepted. He noted that Rhode Island was condemned by the other states for not yet having agreed to the Constitution but that it deserved the highest praise for having halted the slave traffic within its borders. Similarly he praised Pennsylvania for its policies leading to abolition but held South Carolina guilty of detestable conduct because of its having made it a crime to teach slaves to read, thereby attempting to enslave the minds as well as the bodies of those in bondage.

Worker Agitation:
Thomas Skidmore and Frances Wright

Along with the stirrings of black Americans there were those from other groups who felt oppressed by economic institutions and social conventions. Economic pressure led to the beginnings of a movement that ultimately failed in this country, underscoring the distinctiveness of American conditions because such movements found success in many European nations and in the mother country itself. This movement was an attempt to establish political parties based upon laboring groups. The immediate question that initiated the efforts was the ten-hour day. In Philadelphia workers were agitating for a reduction to ten hours, whereas in New York the ten-hour day already prevailed but employers appeared to be threatening to lengthen it. The Workingmen's party in New York was formed in 1829, two years after the one in Philadelphia. The New York group is of more interest to students of political thought because of the ideas of some of its noteworthy figures. Both parties were short-lived; only traces remained in New York by 1831.[6]

During its brief existence in New York, the Workingmen's party spread to many portions of the state. Despite the economic basis of their grievances, the workers tended most to protest political conditions that provided greater representation for the rich than for others. They complained of a lack of true democracy in political affairs, the dominance of parties and bosses, and legislation that was to the interest of the "aristocratical" as opposed to the "producing" classes. According to John R. Commons, "All these commonplace difficulties in the way of practical democracy were regarded with angry, hurt surprise by men to whom the doctrines of the Declaration of Independence were unquestionable, fundamental truth."[7] The first general meeting produced resolutions that simultaneously reflected a radicalism far from the mainstream of American thought and a Lockean temper that was remarkable for its sharing of fundamental assumptions with much of the mainstream. In asserting their refusal to work beyond the ten-hour day, the mechanics of New York resolved:

> that all men hold their property by the consent of the great mass of the community, and by no other title; that a great portion of the latter hold no property at all; that in society they have given up what in a state of nature they would have equal right to with others; and that in lieu thereof, they have the right to an equal participation with others, through the means of their labour, of the enjoyments of a comfortable subsistence.[8]

The resolution clearly bore the mark of the early leader of the Workingmen's party, Thomas Skidmore. Skidmore's thought was strongly influenced by Thomas Paine, but had some originality as well. His proposals came to be called "agrarianism," probably because of the similarity that much of them had to Paine's suggestions in *Agrarian Justice*. Skidmore, a mechanic, ran as a Workingmen's candidate for the New York legislature and lost by a mere handful of votes. His party originally was committed to the agrarian program, but it is doubtful whether many truly understood the radical nature of his ideas.[9] His effectiveness was probably severely damaged when he produced his book, *The Rights of Man to Property! Being a Proposition to Make It Equal among the Adults of the Present Generation: and to Provide for Its Equal Transmission to Every Individual of Each Succeeding Generation, on Arriving at the Age of Maturity.*[10]

Skidmore contended that everyone in the state of nature had an equal right to property and that resources were so abundant that

there were no significant disputes. As population increased, however, abundance diminished and inequality began when human
beings ceased to be nomadic and first accumulated property individu-
ally. He argued that the process was sufficiently slow that at first
there were no disagreements regarding accumulation, since there
was still an abundance. By the time that there came to be too little for
everyone to accumulate without limit, however, the practice of
holding title had come to be accepted without really being examined;
the only question raised was whose title, not whether there should
be a title at all. He likened the contemporary system to one that
permitted the first person to a table to eat his fill and then to
determine among those who came later who should eat what and
under what conditions. Title to property, he asserted, is fraudulently
based upon the good fortune of the property holder in having
received it from someone who established it generations earlier
merely by having arrived first. He argued, furthermore, that it is this
artificial inequality that leads to the injustices found in society. He
believed that without inequality in property there would be equal
justice, and even that it is inequality that leads to wars and conquests.
Without inequality, he wrote, no one would agree to fight in a war,
the only reason to risk one's life being the economic gain possible to
someone who might otherwise go hungry.

Skidmore proposed that the people immediately choose a convention that would order a general division of property. Because this
would cause turmoil and property holders might hide their assets,
the convention would order the suspension of all business. Recognizing that this would effectively eliminate all government as it was
constituted, he provided for a committee of safety that would
conduct society's affairs until a new convention could set up a new
government "on principles corresponding with *all* the rights of man."
Such a government would eliminate the situation that requires a
laborer to work for an employer, a relationship that he contended
was the same as slavery since the worker effectively had no choice
but to follow orders from someone else or to starve. Basically,
however, his concern was the division between the rich and the poor,
and he anticipated the development of class consciousness that has
marked most of socialism since Marx.[11]

Skidmore's radicalism not only caused him to lose power within
the Workingmen's party but also gave the party's opponents additional arguments against it. After Skidmore the party's attention
turned to advocacy of a "state guardianship" educational system that
would have provided equal education for all in the way that he would
have provided equal property. State guardianship would have estab-

lished state boarding schools for all children so that class distinctions would not matter. This was similar educationally to Skidmore's thought in economics, originating not with him, but with the new leaders of the soon-to-disintegrate party, Robert Dale Owen and Frances Wright.

Because of the agitation from the workers there were some political reforms, but laboring parties never succeeded in obtaining a foothold in the United States. In the 1830s New York State passed a mechanics' lien law, abolished imprisonment for debt, and greatly increased appropriations for education. Another result was that many in the rising trade union movement argued against direct political involvement, based upon the fate of the Workingmen's party.[12]

Skidmore died in 1832. Despite his abrasive personality and his radicalism, he had gained much respect. Even his enemies praised his "open candour, his independence of spirit," and "his fearless contention for his own rights and the rights of the poor man."[13] He is hardly remembered today, however, and he had little if any effect upon the American mainstream. Except for his book, he wrote nothing besides his daily paper, *Friend of Equal Rights*. Nevertheless, he is significant in having been one of the few to carry on the tradition of Thomas Paine and in his efforts to provide a voice for his fellow workers and to demonstrate to them that they need not turn to others for leadership. Whatever the merits of his proposals, and however unpolished his presentation, he represents a healthy example of a politically active American who was both a worker and an abstract thinker.

When the Workingmen's party came under the influence of Frances Wright, it was inevitable that its future would be as controversial as its past; not only was Fanny Wright an irreverent and outspoken radical, she was a woman who gave public lectures and questioned all conventions that she deemed to be senseless, whether economic, political, social, or sexual. It must be remembered that there was no higher education for women at the time and that it was considered unseemly for a woman to assert herself in the slightest. For example, when Emma Willard founded a school for girls in New York and added to the subjects of geography, history, and mathematics a bit of physiology, "mothers visiting a class at the Seminary in the early thirties were so shocked at the sight of a pupil drawing a heart, arteries and veins on a blackboard . . . that they left the room in shame and dismay."[14] If a sober study of physiology appeared to be indelicate, how much more so was Fanny Wright's bold questioning of many of society's most fundamental assumptions?

Wright was the daughter of a Scottish tradesman who had excited the animosity of his neighbors by underwriting a cheap edition of Thomas Paine's *The Rights of Man*. She was born at the end of the eighteenth century when revolutionary notions were current, and she early championed any causes that aroused her sympathy. She had developed a feeling for the United States in her childhood after hearing a Tory aunt discourse upon the wickedness of the colonials who had rebelled against their king. Because of the revolutionary doctrines upon which America was founded, she sailed to the New World upon becoming of age, explaining that she preferred to go to a country inhabited by free men rather than one filled with ruins and populated by slaves.[15] Returning to England in 1820, she published a book describing the democratic institutions in the United States in so complimentary a fashion that she attracted the praise of European liberals and the disapproval of many aristocrats.

In the next few years Wright traveled widely and made important acquaintances, including the French General Lafayette, who became her close companion to the embarrassment of his family.[16] She accompanied the general to America when he toured the country in 1824, and she turned her attention to the evils of slavery. During her previous tour, she had visited Jefferson at Monticello and had discussed the institution with him after having earlier observed the deplorable conditions on board a slave ship leaving Virginia for the Savannah slave markets. By early 1825 Lafayette had embarked upon a tour of the southern states, and she left his company to establish an experimental community in the West that would educate slaves to prepare them for freedom. She sent copies of her plan to numerous persons and had carefully searched statutes to determine that there was no legal impediment. She had Lafayette send Jefferson her plan and asked for his support, but the former President responded that at the age of eighty-two he would embark upon no new enterprise, not even the great one that she proposed, and added that her powers of mind might do much to excite others.[17]

Wright visited utopian communities in Pennsylvania and Ohio to observe them in action and purchased 640 acres near Memphis to found her own community, Nashoba. In February 1826 the community got under way with Fanny and her sister Camilla, George Flower with his wife and three children, and eight slaves, five male and three female. She intended not only to educate the slaves for freedom but to provide a society with no restraints upon intellectual development and to encourage free association with congenial companions. She sought to eliminate both chattel slavery and also what she considered to be the slavery of marriage. Each person was to be free to live with whomever he or she wished and to change partners whenever desired, regardless of color. Her shocked critics called it "Fanny Wright's Free Love Colony" and were delighted in 1829 when the community failed and she joined Robert Dale Owen in his experimental socialist community in New Harmony, Indiana.[18] Thereafter, she published widely and became an unusually effective public lecturer, concentrating her energies upon women's rights, and social, racial, and economic justice.

As if her other activities were not enough to excite their fury, religious conservatives were outraged at her attacks upon the clergy and her free thought. She founded a newspaper, the *Free Enquirer*, purchased an old Methodist church that she converted into a hall of science, and provided programs of medical care and social services for the poor. It was at this time that she became active in the Workingmen's party.[19] Her publishing and editing activities were quite varied, but the substance of her thought is captured by her *Course of Popular Lectures*.

Consistently, Wright stressed political equality and economic betterment for deprived groups. She attacked the American practice of judging a person's worth by his income and argued that society, although founded upon the principles of freedom, had retained the evils of British and European aristocratic attitudes, and the English common law, which she denounced in scathing terms as unsuited to a nation of liberty. She charged that the clergy oppressed the minds of the people, and for these and other efforts, she was described by them as the "Priestess of Beelzebub." Her keen mind and extraordinary oratorical skills aroused the fear of all her enemies. They heckled her at lectures and frequently sabotaged the lights or operated smoke-producing machines. She was "a woman impervious to the voice of virtue and case-hardened against shame," and a "female monster whom all decent people ought to avoid." She answered in newspapers of her own and continued her efforts throughout the 1830s; in the latter part of the decade she continued to write, but otherwise retired from the public arena.[20]

According to one commentator, Robert Whittenmore, "What Frances Wright stood for, few men even today care or dare to preach. Yet, if she offended, she offended gloriously. The role of women, the life of the Negro, the rights of the workingman, the freedom of the press—all were bettered for her efforts."[21] It is always difficult to preach ideas that are out of tune with one's time; it is all the more difficult for a woman in times when she is subject to abuse simply for being a woman, to dare to think and speak.

Andrew Jackson's Thought

There were many currents that are notable during the 1820s and 1830s, most of them considerably less radical and more in tune with the ideas of the majority of Americans than the attitudes of such nonconformists as Skidmore and Wright. A wave of change swept through American culture that effectively closed the eighteenth century and firmly established the nineteenth, thereby ending the period of a struggling new state and settling in as a nation. Although this wave has been summed up in the term "Jacksonianism," Andrew Jackson can hardly be judged to have been its cause. He did, however, have the talent and the personality to ride the wave that many historians, in a somewhat exaggerated fashion, have interpreted as ushering in an era of "the common man." Jackson was not a common man and did not consider himself to be. By the frontier standards of his day, he was an aristocrat who was reasonably well educated. He was a lawyer and a military man, but hardly a foot soldier; he was a general. Nevertheless, he excited the popular imagination as few Americans have, and he clearly adopted the rhetoric of the common man.

Jackson was a rugged man of action, not a philosopher or a writer. His own ideas are important only insofar as they represent Jacksonianism as a new mode of thought in America, and essentially they are available only in his addresses and official messages. Jackson spoke largely as a Jeffersonian and adopted much of the rhetoric associated with the Jeffersonian movement. One distinguishing feature, however, was Jefferson's strong emphasis upon education and Jackson's disdain for it. Jacksonianism represented more the rising small business and commercial orientation of the United States than it did, as folklore would have it, "the workers." In fact, Jackson appears to have been the first American President to have used federal troops against workers in a labor dispute.[22] The Jeffersonians had represented largely the landed aristocrats; although they had the general support of the backcountry and the low-income groups, the main reason was that there was nowhere else for such groups to turn. When they did turn elsewhere, after having become sufficiently active in the political system to have a true effect, the result was Jacksonianism. Gone was the aristocratic orientation and the emphasis upon a static agrarianism. The new mood called for growth and expansion, for new forms of economic opportunity. Rather than the Jeffersonian yeoman farmer, the Jacksonian looked to the rising tradesman as the foundation of American society.

The Jeffersonian background was basically the tidewater South with its many rivers and its geographic inducements to self-sufficiency. The newer thrust came from workers in the cities and from the growing backcountry areas that tended to turn to Washington for help in transporting goods to market. With the diminution of the older aristocracy, there was a great deal more truly democratic sympathy than formerly, as was reflected in the modifications of the older state constitutions and the relatively liberal constitutions of the newer states. As suffrage restrictions fell, there came some slight beginnings of sentiment for granting the vote to women and free blacks. In any case, popular participation in politics increased greatly for a variety of reasons, and the Jacksonian movement began the Democratic party. There were indirect effects as well, as presidential electors began to be chosen by popular vote rather than by state legislatures, and as the parties turned to the nominating convention to choose their candidates instead of selecting them by congressional caucus. It may be difficult for some to recognize today that the adoption of the convention, first used at the presidential level by the Anti-Masonic party in the election of 1832, was actually a more democratic device than had previously existed. The Jacksonian movement also brought, consistent with its disdain for education, an emphasis upon rotation in office, with little regard for qualifications and an open acceptance of the spoils system by which the victorious party could place its adherents in public positions. But as important as any change was the shift toward a much more powerful executive. Jackson infused the veto with more power by using it with more vigor and less restraint than his predecessors. Even at the state level the tendency was away from the old eighteenth-century fear of the executive toward a view that the executive as well as the legislature represented the people. If one incident among the complex factors can be assigned more importance than others, it probably was Jackson's fight against the Bank of the United States.

Jackson vetoed the act rechartering the National Bank and used language sharply distinguishing the interests of the privileged from those of the mass of citizens. He contended that it was his responsibility as much as the Supreme Court's to judge the constitutionality of an act and that he opposed the bank also on constitutional grounds. His veto has been widely interpreted, therefore, as an attack upon privilege in favor of the workers, but many of his supporters had opposed the bank for quite different reasons; not only did it work to the advantage of some of the wealthy classes, but it tended also to restrain the enthusiasm of wildcat banks in the West and dampen the growing capitalist interests. Given Jackson's irascible personality, it probably is true that his hostility toward Nicholas

Biddle, the bank's director, was an important factor in his decision. Daniel Webster spoke for Jackson's opponents when he disputed Jackson on constitutional grounds, saying that Jackson was in error in denying to the judiciary the power of constitutional interpretation and in claiming to share with Congress the power of originating statutes. He also charged the President with seeking "to inflame the poor against the rich."[23] Nevertheless, Jackson prevailed.

At the core of Jacksonianism seems to be the beginning of much of modern American political thought with its twin emphases upon the rights of the people and those of the community. It recognized the capabilities of the average citizen considerably more than the Federalists, and also more than most of the Jeffersonians, had done. As a rule American movements have been strongly optimistic regarding the future of the nation, none more so than Jacksonianism. Contrary to their Jeffersonian predecessors, the Jacksonians also had no fear of using the national government to achieve their goals for the nation.

Interpreters of Jacksonian America

Two of the most perceptive treatments of Jacksonian America came from unlikely sources, one a Frenchman and the other a man of letters. Alexis de Tocqueville, a young French aristocrat, visited the United States in the 1830s to study its prison system. Upon returning to France, he produced a monumental work, *Democracy in America*,[24] that explained the workings of American democracy in minute detail to a curious Europe. On the whole his treatment is quite favorable, although Tocqueville was no democrat. It is difficult to summarize his extensive treatment, but he discussed the workings of democracy in the United States and its potential in a world undergoing radical changes. He did not anticipate Frederick Jackson Turner's frontier thesis, which attributed the American character to the existence of the frontier, nor did he assign environmental factors key importance in the development of American democracy. He assumed that it was the temper and moral spirit of Americans that led them to experiment and to succeed. He emphasized the tendency of Americans to associate together in groups and warned of the danger of majority tyranny. He praised democracy for raising the level of the average person but noted that it emphasized equality more than liberty, presenting a potential for danger.

Tocqueville was astonishingly astute, and his work is as comprehensive and thorough as any ever written about American society and politics. He outlined the workings of democracy, including what he considered to be its strengths and weaknesses, with considerable fairness. He also demonstrated great foresight, and many of his predictions were borne out. Although written in 1835, his work even today is indispensible for students of American culture.

The other analysis came from an American, James Fenimore Cooper, known for his Leatherstocking tales. His book *The American Democrat* is one of the few examples of formal political philosophy that has been produced in the United States, and, as such, it is strange that it is not better known. Cooper had returned from an extensive stay in Europe and wrote a frank study of the workings of democracy as he saw them. He was manifestly critical, but, as he was careful to stress, his criticism did not result from hostility to democracy. He was, he contended, "as good a democrat as there is in America. But his democracy is not of the impracticable school. He prefers a democracy to any other system, on account of its comparative advantages, and not on account of its perfection. He knows it has evils; great and increasing evils, and evils peculiar to itself; but he believes that monarchy and aristocracy have more."[25]

Such a disclaimer was of no benefit; Cooper was strongly assailed for his criticisms and suspected of favoring aristocracy. In truth, Cooper had an aristocratic temperament. He was a wealthy man with strong feelings of class consciousness. Nevertheless, he was a Jacksonian Democrat. One explanation of the apparent paradox is that Cooper was one of the few remaining landed gentry, and his interests were threatened more by rising finance and industrial capitalism than by popular participation in government. He praised many American institutions and the intelligence of the people. He favored a broadened suffrage, which he saw as bringing about popular control of the government and a greater diffusion of political power. He had no great faith in the infallibility of the public, but, as was consistent with his view of democracy itself, he did not believe that popular control would lead to decisions that were less wise than control by a few; in fact, he thought government under popular control would be considerably less likely to become tyrannical. He, like Tocqueville, recognized the dangers of the tyranny of the majority, but he also recognized that any form of government carries with it the potential of tyranny and feared that the lack of government would be even worse.

Cooper's work in some ways is reminiscent of Tocqueville's. It is much more concise but also goes to the heart of the workings of American democracy, its philosophical underpinnings, and its consequences. Cooper was stuffy and could be tiresome, but he was not hostile to the America of his times, as he was charged with being. He strongly believed in liberty, and popular rule with all its faults seemed to him to be the best way to achieve it. Some of his judgments were wrong, others questionable. He too, however, speaks to us today, which makes it even worse that he has been almost totally ignored.

Other comments upon Jacksonianism came from the historian George Bancroft. Probably no person more exemplified the optimism prevalent regarding the new democracy or the future of the American dream. He welcomed the era of the common man and implied that God had ordained for America a special mission in the world, a notion that, when translated as "Manifest Destiny," was to have disastrous results in years to come (see pp. 128–129). Nevertheless, his was a voice raised in support of human dignity and the equality of all. He had faith in popular judgment and in the worth of all persons. He is best known for his lifetime's work, *History of the United States*, which depicted the rising democracy in glowingly optimistic terms from which he never retreated. In associating natural rights with popular rule he expressed a confidence that others might judge naive in that he allowed for no possibility of conflict between them. His infectious buoyancy is captured in his talk "The Office of the People in Art, Government and Religion."[26] In it he remarked that spirit in mankind leads the people to truth, and this spirit, implanted by God, is conscience. Moreover, rather than being limited to an elite few or to a nation, it is universal.

However simplistic Bancroft may have been in his treatment of democracy, he was consistent in his belief in liberty and popular rule. Moreover, he was far in advance of his time in his rejection of racism and assumptions of cultural superiority. He saw all human beings as children of God, and as such all were entitled to the same human dignity. Regardless of his limitations, America could have done much worse, and indeed has done much worse, in its choice of spokesmen.

One spokesman of the period who differed somewhat from the customary views was the German immigrant Francis Lieber, who had obtained a Ph.D. from Jena and then fled from Germany because of political difficulties with the police. Lieber popularized the academic study of physical education and also originated the *Encyclopedia Americana*, upon which he worked from 1829 to 1833.[27] As a political theoretician he was a follower of the German philosopher Immanuel Kant, and he brought out two formal treatises, *A Manual of Political Ethics*, in 1838, and *On Liberty and Self-Government*, in 1853. He denied the existence of natural rights and rejected contract and state-of-nature theories. He did, however, speak of "primordial rights," such as freedom of thought, communication, and physical integrity, but his major emphasis was upon the right of acquisition, that is, property.

Lieber emphasized the organic nature of the state and anticipated much of modern social science by his insistence upon an empirical approach. He wished to protect liberty against the one, the few, or the many and therefore rejected the infallibility of public opinion and majority rule. He also adopted a racist view of culture, stressing the "superiority" of the "Teutonic race," specifically the Anglo-Saxons. Although his views won some acceptance in the South, he felt uncomfortable in his position at South Carolina College and joined the faculty of Columbia University. Subsequently, he became Lincoln's expert on international law.[28] Although little known today, Lieber had considerable influence upon generations of American students.

The Jacksonian period embraced many varying themes and has been interpreted in a variety of ways, but there is one point upon which there is widespread agreement: Jacksonianism brought pervasive changes to American thought and practice. However differently scholars may evaluate the meaning or effect of Jacksonianism, it is clear that it brought an era to completion and began another.

NOTES

1. A. T. Mason and Richard Leach, *In Quest of Freedom*, 2nd ed. (Englewood Cliffs, N.J.: Prentice Hall, 1973), p. 136.

2. *Free Government in the Making*, 3rd ed. (New York: Oxford University Press, 1965), pp. 405–406.

3. Ibid., p. 407.

4. See John H. Bracey, Jr., August Meyer, and Elliot Rudwick, eds., *Black Nationalism in America* (New York: Bobbs-Merrill, 1970), pp. xxx–xxxiii.

5. Reprinted in George Ducas, ed., *Great Documents in Black History* (New York: Praeger, 1970), pp. 28–38.

6. See Frank T. Carlton, "The Workingmen's Party of New York City: 1829–1831," *Political Science Quarterly*, 22 (1907), 401–415; and John R. Commons, et al., *History of Labor in the United States*, vol. 1 (New York: Macmillan, 1918), part 3, chap. 3.

7. Commons, ibid., p. 232.

8. Quoted in ibid., p. 235.

9. See ibid., pp. 242–243; see also Carlton, "The Workingmen's Party," 413–414.

10. (New York: A. Ming, Jr., 1829); see Commons, ibid., p. 245, fn. 38. In the event Skidmore's book is unavailable, selections can be found in anthologies. For example, chapter 8, which captures his major arguments, is reprinted in Merle Curti et al., eds., *American Issues*, 4th ed., vol. 1 (New York: Lippincott, 1971), pp. 233–241, and an abridgment of chapter 2 is included in Joseph Blau, ed., *Social Theories of Jacksonian Democracy* (New York: Liberal Arts Press, 1954), pp. 355–364.

11. See Commons, ibid., p. 237.

12. See Carlton, "The Workingmen's Party," 415. A mechanics' lien law provides a workman with the power to retain or sell property upon which he has performed labor if the customer refuses to pay for the work.

13. Commons, *History of Labor*, p. 237.

14. Barbara Deckard, *The Women's Movement* (New York: Harper & Row, 1975), p. 246.

15. Alice Felt Tyler, *Freedom's Ferment* (New York: Harper Torchbooks, 1962), p. 206.

16. Ibid., p. 207.

17. Alice S. Rossi, ed., *The Feminist Papers* (New York: Columbia University Press, 1973), pp. 91–92.

18. Robert C. Whittemore, *Makers of the American Mind* (New York: Morrow, 1964), pp. 109–111.

19. Rossi, *The Feminist Papers*, pp. 93–99.

20. See Tyler, *Freedom's Ferment*, pp. 208–211 (quotations are on pp. 210, 211).

21. *Makers of the American Mind*, p. 110.

22. See Harvey Wish, *Society and Thought in Early America* (New York: Longmans, Green, 1950), p. 404.

23. *The Works of Daniel Webster*, 12th ed., vol. 3 (Boston: Little, Brown, 1860), pp. 418–447.

24. 2 vols. (New York: Vintage, 1957).

25. James Fenimore Cooper, *The American Democrat*, 3rd ed. (New York: Vintage, 1956), p. 4.

26. In Blau, *Social Theories of Jacksonian Democracy*, pp. 263–273.

27. Wish, *Society and Thought*, pp. 292–293.

28. Ibid., pp. 524–525.

ADDITIONAL READINGS

Curti, Merle. "The Age of Reason and Morality, 1750–1860." *Political Science Quarterly* 68 (September 1953).

Ekirch, Arthur A. *The Idea of Progress in America, 1815–1860.* New York: Peter Smith, 1951.

Grossman, James. "James Fenimore Cooper: An Uneasy American," *Yale Review* 40 (Summer 1951).

Hofstadter, Richard. "Andrew Jackson and the Rise of Liberal Capitalism." In *The American Political Tradition.* New York: Vintage, 1958, chap. 3.

Hugins, Walter. *Jacksonian Democracy and the Working Class: A Study of the New York Workingman's Movement 1829–1837.* Stanford: Stanford University Press, 1967.

James, Marquis. *The Life of Andrew Jackson.* Indianapolis: Bobbs-Merrill, 1937.

Meyers, Marvin. *The Jacksonian Persuasion, Politics and Belief.* Stanford: Stanford University Press, 1966.

Nye, Russell B. *George Bancroft: Brahmin Rebel.* New York: Knopf, 1944.

Ostrander, Gilman. *The Rights of Man in America, 1606–1861.* Columbia: University of Missouri Press, 1960.

Parrington, V. L. *Main Currents in American Thought.* New York: Harcourt, Brace, 1954, vol. 2, pp. 131–145.

Peterson, Merrill D., ed. *Democracy, Liberty and Property: The State Constitutional Conventions of the Early 1820's.* Indianapolis: Library Arts Press, 1965.

Schlesinger, Arthur M., Jr. *The Age of Jackson.* Boston: Little, Brown, 1945.

Sellers, Charles, Jr. "Andrew Jackson Versus the Historians." *Mississippi Valley Historical Review* XLIV (March 1958).

Somit, Albert. "Andrew Jackson as a Political Theorist." *Tennessee Historical Quarterly* VIII (June 1949).

Spiller, R. E. *Fenimore Cooper, Critic of His Times.* New York: Russell and Russell, 1963.

Ward, John William. *Andrew Jackson: Symbol for an Age.* New York: Oxford University Press, 1955.

Williamson, Chilton. *American Suffrage from Property to Democracy, 1760–1860.* Princeton, N.J.: Princeton University Press, 1960.

7

Romantic Response

With the rise of Jacksonianism, the coming of industrialism, and the increase in population, as early as the 1820s there were some who voiced concern for the future of the person in society. Within a few years such concern had become sufficiently prominent as to constitute a movement of its own. In addition to Frances Wright there were those such as Dorothea Dix, who campaigned for humane treatment for those in mental institutions; women were beginning to speak out. The most notable fact, however, is the character of the movement that sought to better the lot of those who had virtually no influence upon the forces that affected them. The character of the movement was such that it may well be termed America's romantic experience, and the most interesting part of it all—too diffuse to constitute a movement and therefore more of a mood, related to the broader movement and yet apart from it—was Transcendentalism.

By the time the nineteenth century had settled in and the harshness of New England Calvinism had been modified considerably, there had arisen a new, liberal religious movement, Unitarianism. Unitarianism was a rational religion, humanistically oriented in reaction to the other-worldliness of Calvinism. Unitarianism shared with Calvinism a strong intellectual tradition and an emphasis upon scholarship, but whereas the Calvinists had accepted the Bible literally, Unitarians examined it critically, using newly developed scholarly standards and rejecting the older biblical literalism.[1] Unitarianism, in turn, gave birth to Transcendentalism. Transcendentalism was a spirit that flourished briefly in New England, glorifying individualism and the human consciousness, and recognizing the need for the coldness of intellectualism to be softened by intuition and emotion, but certainly not rejected. Apart from their American backgrounds and their native experiences, the Transcendentalist writers were most influenced by German idealism, as represented especially in the writings of Immanuel Kant and J. W. von Goethe, and the wave of English literary romanticism expressed by Thomas Carlyle, Samuel Taylor Coleridge, William Wordsworth, and others. There was also influence from such sources as the mystic Emanuel Swedenborg as well as from the Orient and France.[2]

Transcendentalism began in Boston in 1836 when a group of writers, many of whom were Unitarian clergymen, started to meet regularly for discussion in the home of George Ripley. The membership of the group fluctuated constantly, and there was never more than a loose association for purposes of intellectual stimulation. Nonetheless, there appeared to their detractors to be something sinister and conspiratorial in their doctrines, and they began referring to the group as the "Transcendental Club." The name apparently was intended to be one of derision, but it prevailed. The group actually was too loosely formed to be a "club," and probably no two Transcendentalists ever would have agreed completely on philosophical underpinnings. As Emerson put it, they only agreed in having fallen upon Coleridge and Wordsworth, and Goethe, then on Carlyle, with pleasure and sympathy.[3] Nevertheless, there were core beliefs that most of the Transcendentalists would have accepted.

The only work by a Transcendentalist that approaches being a comprehensive treatment of their thought appeared anonymously in 1842 as a pamphlet entitled "An Essay on Transcendentalism." Its author seems to have been Charles Mayo Ellis, who became a lawyer and worked for antislavery causes.[4] Ellis maintained that the Transcendentalist belief was founded upon a conception of human nature as being composed of three elements: appetites, or love for food and pleasure; rationality, or love for truth; and religious aspirations, or spirituality. A human being is something more than a physical object, more than an animal, and more than an animal with reason. Ellis applied the term "transcendental" to those considerations of humankind that deal with the spiritual. The Transcendentalists contended that ideas could be innate; by this they meant that human beings possessed ideas and understandings that came neither through the senses nor through reasoning, but derived instead from divine inspiration or from God's presence in the world. Ellis countered the famous remark of French philosopher René Descartes, "I think, therefore I am," with the simpler statement "I exist," and argued that no further proof of one's existence is necessary or possible.

The goal of the Transcendentalist was no less than the perfection of the world. Ellis wrote that human beings do not create goodness anymore than the sun creates the sense of seeing, but that just as one must open one's eyes to see the light, so one must turn open eyes toward right and beauty in order to perceive them. This notion is related to the idea of natural law as available to all by the exercise of right reason, but it was not the same because the Transcendentalist did not rely solely upon reason; rather the emphasis was upon a consciousness of the absolute, more the result of intuition than of reason. With regard to politics Ellis demonstrated a practical spirit. Even if it could be shown that every aspect of the government were wrong, he believed reform still should be slow and cautious. It must proceed, however, and enlightened persons must work to bring about improvement.

Transcendentalism was clearly concerned intimately with religion as well as with literature, and religious emphases within the group outweighed those of aesthetics. The Transcendentalists' religious concerns, however, were not doctrinal but ethical. As such, they were led directly to considerations that bore upon the established order and upon the social and political system of the United States. As much as anything else, Transcendentalism was a reaction to an emerging industrialism that appeared to subordinate human and ethical values to those of a business order. It was also essentially a youthful movement against the constricting opinions of older generations.

Ralph Waldo Emerson, one of Transcendentalism's most prominent adherents, summed up its origin and character best in his essay "Historic Notes of Life and Letters in New England."[5] He wrote that there are always two parties—that of the past, the Establishment, and that of the future, the Movement (his own terms, interestingly enough). The development of Transcendentalism came when the party of the future brought into the open a conflict between the intellect and the emotion and created also new divisions in politics. The mind had become conscious of itself, and with the recognition of the importance of the self came the modern notion that the nation existed for the individual.

At the invitation of Mr. and Mrs. George Ripley, Emerson, Margaret Fuller, Theodore Parker, Orestes Brownson, William Henry Channing, and others met for the first time in the group that later came to be called Transcendentalist. Emerson wrote that nothing came of their meetings except the journal called *The Dial*, which began under Margaret Fuller's editorship and remained obscure for four years. If ideas have any force, this judgment is incorrect because some of the most forceful ideas in American history came from the Transcendentalists, ideas that are as impor-

tant today as then, and perhaps even more so. The Transcendentalists had influence far beyond their small numbers, and they included
such important figures, besides Emerson and Fuller, as Henry David
Thoreau and Walt Whitman. One would have a greatly flawed
interpretation of American political thought if these persons and
their transcendental orientation were ignored, and it would also be
unfortunate to fail to examine their one group effort at political and
social reform, the Brook Farm communitarian experiment. Noteworthy, too, is the acceptance of tremendous diversity within the fold,
ranging from those who adhered to the socialist theories of the
Frenchman Charles Fourier to the arch-individualist Thoreau.
Rather than attempting to summarize a group that defies attempts to
summarize, it is better to investigate the Brook Farm experiment and
the major ideas of some of the most prominent Transcendentalists.

The Brook Farm Community

Brook Farm had its beginning in 1840 and initially was called Ripley's
Farm. The community was located some distance from Boston and
included a fascinating variety of persons, some of whom went on to
become great figures in American literature. Besides the Ripleys,
there were Margaret Fuller, Charles Dana, Nathaniel Hawthorne,
and others. The group urged Emerson to join them, but, although he
expressed sympathy with the experiment, he considered all societies,
including that at Brook Farm, to be prisons, and he did not desire to
exchange one prison for another. Emerson's individualism kept him
from Brook Farm, although the effort, paradoxically, was designed to
achieve the height of individualism through the mechanism of a
community wherein each person was free to develop intellectually
and to combine manual and intellectual labor. Emerson could not be
convinced. He wrote that he wished to be, but that to go to Brook
Farm would be to violate his longstanding theory that one person "is
a counterpoise to a city—that a man is stronger than a city, that his
solitude is more prevalent and beneficient than the concert of
crowds."[6]

  Ripley spoke for the group in describing its goals to Emerson.
Brook Farm was an attempt to provide each person with a responsibility to engage in manual labor appropriate for his or her personality. Each would receive the benefits of his or her own labor and the
community would benefit simultaneously. The ultimate goals were
to guarantee that labor would be adapted to the tastes and talents of
all and to establish "a more natural union between intellectual and
manual labor" than existed.[7] Under such circumstances personal

relations would be more wholesome because the competition of the world would be eliminated. An anonymous article describing the community, written by a friend who was not a member, made clear the importance of the experiment as viewed by the participants. Rather than immersing themselves in something of purely local significance or of interest only to themselves, they intended to settle "two of the most important problems of human life": the reconciliation of labor with "elegance of mind and manners" and the "independence of the Faculty of education." Without elaborating, the author proceeded so far as to say that it might "be proved the new church."[8]

Elizabeth Peabody, in an article for *The Dial* entitled "Plan of the West Roxbury Community,"[9] captured the humane spirit of the Brook Farm participants and their basic principles. She wrote that the whole soul of humanity was contained within each man and woman and that the community existed for those who felt oppressed by society. "Whoever is satisfied with society, as it is; whose sense of justice is not wounded by its common action, institutions, spirit of commerce, has no business with this community." With regard to education the intent of the group was to concentrate upon the inward needs of each pupil, both male and female, old and young. From our vantage point of a century and a half later, such rhetoric suggests hackneyed clichés, but at the time of Brook Farm it not only was innovative, it was sincere. Because of their ability and their sincere desire to contribute to intellectual growth, the school that they established was the most successful of their enterprises. Yet those at Brook Farm did not divorce intellectual development from their principles. As Peabody wrote, "Transcendentalism belongs to no sect of religion, and no social party. It is the common ground to which all sects may rise, and be purified of their narrowness; for it consists in seeking the spiritual ground of all manifestations."

Such a visionary grouping may have been doomed to failure, at least so "practical" persons are likely to conclude, and fail it did. There came to be personal conflicts and some disillusionment regarding basic goals. Hawthorne, for example, who had never been a Transcendentalist but had been attracted to the experiment, was so exhausted by physical labor that he found it impossible to write. For him, there could apparently be no union between intellectual and natural labor; as he wrote to his wife, "A man's soul may be buried and perish under a dungheap or in a furrow of the field, just as well as under a pile of money."[10]

For whatever reason, the original intensely individualistic orientation of the community weakened. Under the influence of Albert Brisbane it was converted into a "phalanx," following the teachings of Charles Fourier, who promoted a system of socialism based upon an extreme division of labor and upon attempts to achieve community by applying science and the "laws" of human behavior. Fourier divided human beings into twelve categories with various subtypes and contended that a group of 800 would include all of the necessary variety for the success of any community. He did provide, though, for more than a doubling of the number to allow for error. In any case, the phalanx was no more successful than the earlier experiment had been.

The group had been founded in hope. Soon it came under the influence of Fourier's principles of association, which, however noble their purposes may have been, were starkly different from the initial impulses. Convers Francis wrote to Theodore Parker with a tone that conveyed the change:

> I always feel a distrust of all plans like Fourier's, which would seem to say, "go to now, by means of mechanical arrangements and progressive series we will construct a perfect form of society." It seems too much like applying mathematics and mechanism to a free soul, too much like attempting so to arrange mankind, that the square of the oblique diagonal of conduct shall be equal to the two squares of the base of nature, and the perpendicular of education.[11]

Nothing could have been more in contrast to the Transcendentalist spirit with its distrust of institutions and its faith in the perfection, not of the mass, but of the human individual. Brook Farm officially became a phalanx in 1844 and was already in many ways effectively destroyed before a disastrous fire in 1846 destroyed the physical properties as well. After the fire, Brook Farm remained only in memory.

Ralph Waldo Emerson and Margaret Fuller

Insofar as a group of intense individualists can have one, the high priest of the Transcendentalist mood was Emerson. Virtually everything that he wrote, beginning with his 1836 essay "Nature" and continuing on through a prolific lifetime, is pertinent. His most significant writings include "Nature," "The American Scholar," "The Divinity School Adress," "Self-Reliance," "The Over-Soul," and "Politics." Emerson was Lockean in basing his thought upon the individual, but quite foreign to Locke's thought in rejecting his emphasis upon institutions, which Emerson considered at best to be necessary evils. He accepted the notion of the contract origin of the state, in a sense, and yet he thought of the contract as solely between individuals. The state he considered to be generally ludicrous, and at best to be nonexistent, since it was nothing more than the people and had no organic existence of its own.

Emerson's primary interest was ethical and his orientation was toward a glorification of the individual human consciousness. Nevertheless, he was drawn to political concerns. He could accept as the foundation of a just society neither the emphasis of the Democrats upon the mass nor the concern of the Whigs, the successors to the Federalists, for property interests. The only basis for a social and political order that made good government possible was the morality and good will of the individual. In his essay "Politics" he wrote that the state existed to educate the wise man and that with the wise man's appearance the state would become unnecessary and cease to exist. He had, he wrote, benign feelings toward the state, so long as it did not trouble him. He would pay his taxes. The state was a poor dumb cow to whom he would give its clover without begrudging it, and with whom he would not pick a quarrel. If, however, the poor cow tried to hook him, he would cut its throat.[12]

This was not mere bravado. The Transcendentalist believed that an unjust state depended upon the existence of a slavish people and that each person had not only the right to resist an unjust state, but the duty. When righteous persons resisted, the state could not stand. This did not imply resistance in all cases, but only when the state "tried to hook" them. Emerson, like all the Transcendentalists, was concerned with authority and recognized only the authority of the individual conscience that could grasp the truth through an intuition that transcended reason. Whether in intellectual matters or in politics, the American should throw off all authority except that which he or she recognized as consistent with the principle of individualism. Why should one person obey another if not because that person was right? And if that person were right, the reason to obey would not be because of official position or an intellectual position of commanding authority, but because the individual himself recognized the rightness of the order. V. L. Parrington and others have contended that Emerson was in the Jeffersonian tradition, and in some ways he was, but in a mystic and romantic sense that Jefferson could never have recognized.

Emerson was drawn to politics, but only reluctantly. He spoke against slavery and worked against the annexation of Texas as a plot to extend it, but he was never at home in politics. He never became the activist that many of his friends and some of the other Transcendentalists became. His greatest importance was as an inspiration to others who contributed more to politics than he but who might not have done so without his example.

One of the most interesting figures among the Transcendental-ists, and a tragic figure as well, was *The Dial's* first editor, Margaret Fuller, who was the only woman among the Transcendentalists to approach Emerson in prominence. Possessed of one of the keenest intellects in the nation, and indeed in American history, she was educated as a man in a world that oppressed women. Along with many of the Transcendentalists, she wrote prolifically, often turning her hand to poetry. Her failure to produce lasting contributions to literature was probably more the result of other factors than of lack of talent. In one respect, however, her contributions tower above those of almost all other Transcendentalists and had both social and political implications. She produced the first soundly reasoned and carefully justified treatise in America advocating the elimination of restraints upon women. She was not shrill, but she spoke freely regarding society, politics, and even sexual relations. As was to be expected, she suffered for it. Her great book is *Woman in the Nineteenth Century*, and its greatness lies in its having been not only the first of the feminist works and still one of the best, but also a work that did not limit itself narrowly to considerations of women's rights. She, as a true Transcendentalist, was concerned with the liberation of all people. As Perry Miller remarked, women's rights were only a "subordinate part of the most comprehensive program of nineteenth-century liberation. She was a great radical, and so we should remember her."[13]

Margaret Fuller avoided separating women's interests from those of men. She believed that all persons had to be happy and virtuous if anyone is to achieve perfect happiness or virtue. Human-ity had a dual character, masculine and feminine; if they were in perfect harmony, they would fulfill one another. Unhappily, "there is no perfect harmony in human nature." When men, because of superior physical power, began to dominate women, they educated women as servants and thereby found themselves kings with no queens, not recognizing that woman was half of man. This did not leave women powerless, but it forced them into the exercise of power that was degrading both to them and to men. They had to resort to the servile arts of cunning and unreasonable emotion.

There would be objections to equality, Fuller recognized, as supporters of the Equal Rights Amendment discovered as late as the third quarter of the twentieth century, but she contended that women, just as men, should do as they wished and be what they wished. "Let them be sea-captains, if you will," she wrote; "*all* need not be constrained to employments for which *some* are unfit." She urged the independence of both sexes, but not because she did not think that the sexes needed one another. Rather, because they do need one another, women had come to "an excessive devotion, which has cooled love, degraded marriage, and prevented either sex from being what it should be to itself or the other."[14] These and other observations had, and have, profound implications for the social and political order beyond those that relate merely to feminism, as important as those are.

Walt Whitman and Orestes Brownson

One of the best-known Transcendentalists was also one who differed most from many of the others. Walt Whitman, the poet of America, with his Quaker heritage, New York upbringing, and working-class background came to sing the praises of the nation. He, too, was an individualist, but his faith was also in the common people as a group. His most familiar works are his poetic masterpiece, *Leaves of Grass*, and his extended essay praising America in prose, *Democratic Vistas*. Alone among the Transcendentalists he preached an abiding democratic religion and a triumphant American nationalism that was not a petty exercise in racism or imperialism but was to extend the reign of the common people throughout the world.

In a sense Whitman was the bridge between the Transcendentalists and Jacksonian democracy as the people understood it. He condemned in prose and poetry all forms of discrimination against human beings, including slaves, paupers, homosexuals, prostitutes, and other outcasts of society, thereby extending the range of democratic thought considerably. He was in the Jeffersonian tradition, as well as the Jacksonian, but he brought to those traditions the humanitarianism of the Transcendentalists. He also added a rejection of relentless conformity to which either tradition could lead. Not often in America have exuberant nationalism and genuine humanitarianism been combined. Nationalistic or not, it is perhaps significant that Whitman was fired from his post as a clerk in the Department of the Interior because of allegations that *Leaves of Grass* was immoral. It was not enough to support; one had also to conform.

Whitman was unique among the Transcendentalists because of his nationalism, but it is Orestes Brownson who fits into a discussion of Transcendentalism only with some difficulty because he was one of the group only for a relatively brief time and then rejected it completely. At one time, Brownson was among the most radical of Americans. He had been reared as a strict Calvinist, becoming first a Congregationalist and then a Presbyterian, but later moved, always seeking, through Universalism, Unitarianism, and Transcendental-ism. He came to reject Emersonian individualism politically as well as religiously, causing most of the Transcendentalists to shun him as a turncoat.

Brownson typifies many who search for absolutes and fail to find them. At one time an ardent Democrat and a socialist, for a while he assisted Fanny Wright and Robert Owen in their efforts on behalf of the New York Workingmen's party. His views were influential because of the forums that he commanded. He edited the *Boston Quarterly Review* and *Brownson's Quarterly Review*, and contributed widely to other periodicals. In his socialist period he strongly championed democracy and equality, contending that bad legislation resulted not from too much democracy, but from not enough. As with many reformers who fail, he became disillusioned and came ultimately to advocate strong authority. He rejected not just the extremes of democracy in politics but individualism in religion as well, coming full circle to conversion to the Roman Catholic Church. He remained a militant Catholic to the end of his life. The harsh critic of capitalism had come to the position that the only true freedom could be found under the constraints of authority. Having lost his faith in the people, Brownson concluded that the Roman Catholic religion was necessary to sustain liberty because only a religion free from popular control, a religion that stood above the people and could command them, could restrain attacks upon liberty and remain free from corruption.[15]

Since the people are fallible and subject to corruption, he con-tended, democratic theory itself was inadequate because it was predicated upon the essential goodness of human nature; a govern-ment responsive to people committing error would be a government in error. His solution was to retain democratic government but to control the people through the medium of religion, insuring that their government would be one of virtue and intelligence. The church would supply the virtue and intelligence, and the people would maintain their government consistent with its teachings. Thus to control the government wisely, the people must serve a master. Brownson accepted the importance of a fundamental moral law and considered other tenets beside it to be of small importance. Although he was not a follower of Thomas Hobbes, Brownson demonstrated that a Hobbesian spirit had some influence in America when he wrote that "we have heard enough of liberty and the rights of man. . . . It is high time to hear something of the duties of men and the rights of authority."[16]

The turning point had come with the defeat of the Democrats in

1840. Brownson had worked hard for the party and continued for a time to attempt to reenergize Jacksonian democracy. In 1843 he merged his *Quarterly* with John Louis O'Sullivan's *Democratic Review* in an effort to revive the voice of Jacksonianism. Even by this time, however, his opinions had changed and he had come to downgrade the ability of people collectively and to stress the need for power over them.

He also came to deal with the people politically as an organic whole, rather than as merely an aggregate of individuals, and he denied the existence of a state of nature. In some ways the tone of his writings is more medieval than modern. No one has produced a more interesting criticism of the predominant strain of Lockean assumptions in American political thought. It is all the more interesting that he retained an emphasis upon a qualified democracy with a limited majority rule. His articles progressively alienated O'Sullivan's readers to the extent that O'Sullivan dissolved the relationship at the end of the year. The following year, 1844, Brownson announced his conversion.[17] One might note the parallel with some of the liberal voices of the 1950s and early 1960s who, disillusioned with the direction of American politics, by the 1970s had come consistently to argue from a position that stressed duties and power rather than rights and liberties, and the collective rather than the individual, thus adopting a stance that gives every appearance of a new conservatism.

Henry David Thoreau

Among the many significant contributions to American political thought that grew out of the Transcendentalist ferment, the most significant came from Henry David Thoreau, one of the most prominent political theorists America has produced. Although, like other Transcendentalists, his intent was not to produce political philosophy, Thoreau moved almost inevitably in the direction of politics because of his social and ethical concerns. He was relatively little known during his lifetime but later came to have considerable influence. In the United States his influence was both direct and indirect by way of Asia. Mohandas Gandhi, the architect of Indian independence, had read Thoreau and made use of many of his ideas. Martin Luther King, Jr., in turn, read Gandhi and through him was attracted to Thoreau. Although the route was a roundabout one, Thoreau's writings assisted in formulating the theory that shaped the civil rights movement of the 1960s.

Thoreau found early that a consistent adherence to principle is likely to bring difficulty. He graduated from Harvard in 1837 and returned to his home, Concord, where he began to teach school. His job lasted less than a month because he was unwilling to beat the children of the school, as demanded by the town fathers. He later faced squarely the character of society and found it to be degrading to each person's humanity. He questioned the desirability of devoting the major part of one's life to earning money, and he recognized the evil inherent in the system of slavery and the danger that it presented to the integrity of every person. He called upon all citizens to examine the nature of political authority and to obey only when the actions demanded were reasonable and could be accepted with no violation of conscience. Clearly, Thoreau was the kind of person whom administrators and officials, desiring speedy obedience and the efficient functioning of all institutions, find highly irritating.

Thoreau's thought was fundamentally consistent with and reflective of Emerson's. The striking difference was Thoreau's activism: Emerson spoke and wrote, and Thoreau spoke, wrote, and acted. In order to become closer to nature and to know himself better—in order, as he put it, to live deliberately—Thoreau withdrew from society and for more than two years lived near Walden Pond. He created his own shelter and provided for his own food and clothing. He did not retreat to Walden because of antisocial feelings but because he had concluded that he could come truly to understand himself and his place in nature only by seeking a solitude that would for a time eliminate the discordant and distracting pressures. From this experience he produced his masterpiece, *Walden*.

Thoreau thought that human beings were corrupted by institutions, and also by work. He recognized the necessity of work but condemned the Puritan ethic that had infected Americans with the notion that work itself is noble. He believed that the function of a person in the world was to live, not to work, except as work was required. The duty of each person was to be true to himself and to his own conscience, not to work for its own sake, follow governmental dictates, or pressure others to conform to one's own ideas. Thoreau went beyond Emerson and carried the Transcendentalist arguments to their logical extremes. He is the most prominent American exponent of philosophical anarchism. Some writers contend that Thoreau was not truly an anarchist because he stressed the desirability of cooperation and did not call for the abolition of all government, and because he wrote "unlike those who call themselves no-government men, I ask for not at once no government, but at once a better government."[18] This depends, of course, upon the definition of anarchism. For years political scientists considered anarchism to be a wholly negative philosophy, an antipolitical philosophy, and therefore refused to dignify it by study. If this negative definition is accepted, certainly Thoreau was not truly an anarchist. In recent years, however, some theorists have suggested that anarchism presents considerably more potential than one of total negation of government. Surely a system that is designed upon cooperation rather than coercion deserves to be called political, and yet such a system in theory might dispense with the customary mechanisms of state power. If anarchism is defined in this more complex and perhaps more perceptive way, if anarchism presents some theoretical possibilities for becoming the foundation of a political system, however remote the probabilities, then Thoreau should certainly be ranked with those who might thus be called "political anarchists."

Rather than advocating the complete elimination of government, Thoreau argued the primacy of the individual conscience. When government is wrong, it not only is the right but the duty of the person of conscience to resist it, if only by withdrawing and refusing to cooperate. He believed that the willingness of citizens to resist and to refuse to carry out immoral dictates of government would be the necessary corrective and would bring a government to its knees. To this end he refused to pay his poll tax, a tax then levied upon all ablebodied men in Massachusetts. He refused because of his conviction that the Mexican War, to which Massachusetts was sending troops, was an effort to extend the system of slavery. Emerson paid his fine, and after one night he was released. His experience brought him to write his classic essay "Resistance to Civil Government," shortly to be renamed by others "Civil Disobedience."[19]

Thoreau argued that neither state nor society has an organic existence but that they are only the sum of individual citizens. He wrote that he accepted the motto "that government is best which governs least," but finally came to the conclusion that that government is best which governs not at all. Since government is an expedient only, he refused to recognize as his government any political organization that was also the slave's government. He carried the theory of consent to its logical conclusion, contending that it applied to each person, not merely the people as a whole:

> It is not a man's duty, as a matter of course, to devote himself to the eradication of any, even the most enormous wrong; he may still properly have other concerns to engage him; but it is his duty, at least, to wash his hands of it, and, if he gives it no thought longer, not to give it practically his support. . . . If the law is such a nature that it requires you to be an agent of injustice to another, then, I say, break the law. Let your life be a counter friction to stop the machine.

Thoreau maintained that all machines had their friction and that therefore no government could be perfect—and it should not be expected to be. When, however, the friction came to have its machine, it was time to smash it. Aristotle over 2,000 years before had discussed the question of the good citizen under a bad regime; Thoreau similarly proclaimed that prison is the proper place for a just man under a government that imprisons any unjustly. He pointed out that a minority is powerless when it conforms to a majority, but that it can become irresistible when it clogs by its whole weight:

> If the alternative is to keep all just men in prison, or give up war and slavery, the State will not hesitate which to choose. If a thousand men were not to pay their tax-bills this year, that would not be a violent and bloody measure, as it would be to pay them, and enable the State to commit violence and shed innocent blood.

"Civil Disobedience" has been reprinted countless times and is widely read. That it is not merely impractical romanticism is indicated by the experience of the American judicial system during the later years of the Vietnam War, especially the experience of the U.S. District Courts on the West Coast. This has not been widely publicized, and for obvious reasons the government did not wish it to become common knowledge, but so many young men had refused to register for the draft or had refused to report for induction that it became impossible to prosecute them all. Apparently thousands "clogged the system" as Thoreau recommended and rendered it almost ineffective. What would have been the result had the same resistance occurred nationwide?

In general, Thoreau advocated nonviolent resistance only. He opposed bloodshed. Nevertheless, the example of John Brown's strike at slavery with a raid on Harper's Ferry caught Thoreau's imagination as few things had. Here was a man striking out against injustice and breaking his contract with a government that had refused to honor its end of the bargain.[20]

Thoreau had met and had high regard for Walt Whitman, who sang the praises of America. Thoreau, too, would sing the praises of an America that permitted people to be themselves. His writings may serve as a counterfriction in these days of rampant technology, intrusive government, and the invasion of privacy. Some would question whether government would be possible at all in a society that took Thoreau too seriously; others might ask whether it would have been better if Thoreau had not merely been read, but acted upon before the coercive state had become, in Lewis Mumford's words, a mega-machine. Surely it is revealing that Thoreau, and indeed all the Transcendentalists, can be dismissed by some out of hand because of their contention that the foundation of government must be the moral individual.

The age of the Transcendentalists was an age of ferment. Many sought a form of community that was not being satisfied by American society as they knew it. Several groups withdrew to form new societies apart from the larger state, some religious, some secular. Brook Farm and New Harmony were only two of almost one hundred utopian communities established in the United States between the Jacksonian period and the Civil War.[21] These communities varied widely, but they all sought a form of government and society that avoided the extremes of competition and provided their citizens something to live for other than material things. It was during this period, also, that numerous reform movements directed toward peace, abolition, the elimination of social evils such as alcoholism, and almost every imaginable cause grew like mushrooms. Related to these developments was the tendency even to form new religions, by such groups as the Millerites, the Mormons, and the Shakers as they developed in America.[22] With the coming of the Civil War, most of the energies directed toward reform were consumed by the internal conflict, and so the significance of what Alice Felt Tyler has called "Freedom's Ferment" may not have been fully recognized. Apparently something was lacking that Americans were seeking. Whether the lack has ever been remedied is doubtful.

NOTES

1. For an excellent brief discussion of Unitarianism, see Yehoshua Arieli, *Individualism and Nationalism in American Ideology* (Baltimore: Penguin, 1966), pp. 252–259.

2. The best brief treatments of Transcendentalism are to be found in Alice Felt Tyler, *Freedom's Ferment* (New York: Harper Torchbooks, 1962), pp. 47ff.; V. L. Parrington, *Main Currents in American Thought*, vol. 2 (New York: Harcourt Brace Jovanovich, 1954), pp. 338–340 and 371ff.; Perry Miller, ed., *The Transcendentalists* (Cambridge, Mass: Harvard University Press, 1950); and Perry Miller, *The American Transcendentalists* (Garden City, N.Y.: Doubleday/Anchor Books, 1957).

3. Quoted in Tyler, ibid., p. 50.

4. Miller, *The American Transcendentalists*, pp. 20–21; selections referred to from Ellis' "Essay" are on pp. 21–35.

5. In *The Portable Emerson*, Mark van Doren, ed. (New York: Viking, 1965), pp. 513–543.

6. In Henry S. Sams, ed., *Autobiography of Brook Farm* (Englewood Cliffs, N.J.: Prentice-Hall, 1958), pp. 4–5.

7. Ripley to Emerson in ibid., pp. 5–8.

8. "The Community of West Roxbury, Mass.," in ibid., pp. 24–29; quotations are on p. 29.

9. In ibid., pp. 62–72; quotations are on pp. 65 and 71.

10. In ibid., p. 21.

11. In ibid., p. 118; both Francis and Parker were adherents of Transcendentalism, and both were Unitarian ministers, of whom Parker was among the most prominent.

12. In *Essays: Second Series*, rev. ed. (Boston: Houghton Mifflin, 1891), pp. 189–211.

13. *The American Transcendentalists*, p. 330.

14. Selections quoted are reprinted in ibid., pp. 330–338; quotations are on pp. 334–335.

15. Ralph Henry Gabriel, *The Course of American Democratic Thought*, 2nd ed. (New York: Ronald, 1956), p. 57.

16. Ibid., pp. 58–61; quotation is found on p. 60.

17. Miller, *The American Transcendentalists*, pp. 338–340.

18. See, for example, Alan P. Grimes, *American Political Thought* (New York: Holt, Rinehart and Winston, 1960), pp. 206–208, and A. T. Mason and Richard H. Leach, *In Quest of Freedom*, 2nd ed. (Englewood Cliffs, N.J.: Prentice-Hall, 1973), pp. 219–220; Thoreau is quoted from Grimes, p. 207.

19. In *The Writings of Henry D. Thoreau: Reform Papers*, Wendell Glick, ed. (Princeton, N.J.: Princeton University Press, 1973), pp. 63–90; quotations here and below are on pp. 71, 73–74, and 76.

20. See "A Plea for Captain John Brown," in ibid., pp. 111–138, and other comments pp. 139–153.

21. See Arthur Bestor, Jr., *Backwoods Utopias* (Philadelphia: University of Pennsylvania Press, 1950).

22. See Tyler, *Freedom's Ferment.*

ADDITIONAL READINGS

Arvin, Newton. *Whitman*. New York: Macmillan, 1938.

Bates, Ernest Sutherland. *American Faith, Its Religious, Political, and Economic Foundations*. New York: W. W. Norton, 1940.

Beatty, Richmond C. "Whitman's Political Thought." *Southern Atlantic Quarterly* XLVI (January 1947).

Brooks, Van Wyck. *The Flowering of New England: 1815–1865*. New York: E. P. Dutton, 1947.

———. *The Times of Melville and Whitman*. New York: E. P. Dutton, 1947.

Cameron, Kenneth W. *Emerson The Essayist: An Outline of His Philosophical Development Through 1836*. Raleigh, N.C.: Thistle Press, 1945.

Canby, Henry Seidel. *Thoreau*. Boston: Houghton Mifflin, 1939.

Frothingham, Octavius B. *Transcendentalism in New England*. Boston: American Unitarian Association, 1903.

Goddard, Harold C. *Studies in New England Transcendentalism*. New York: Columbia University Press, 1908.

Harding, Walter. *The Days of Henry Thoreau*. New York: Knopf, 1965.

Krutch, Joseph Wood. *Henry David Thoreau.* New York: W. Sloane & Associates, 1948.

Ladu, Arthur I. "Political Ideas of Orestes A. Brownson, Transcendentalist." *Philological Quarterly* XII (July 1933).

———. "The Political Ideas of Theodore Parker." *Studies in Philology* XXXVIII (January 1941).

Madison, Charles A. "Henry David Thoreau: Transcendental Individualist." *Ethics* 54 (January 1944).

Miller, Perry. "Jonathan Edwards to Emerson." *New England Quarterly* 13 (December 1940).

———. "Emersonian Genius and The American Democracy." *New England Quarterly* (March 1953).

———. *The Golden Age of American Literature.* New York: Braziller, 1959.

Parrington, V. L., Jr. *American Dreams: A Study of American Utopias.* Providence: Brown University Press, 1947.

Stoller, Leo. *After Walden: Thoreau's Changing Views on Economic Man.* Stanford: Stanford University Press, 1957.

Van Doren, Mark. *Henry David Thoreau: A Critical Study.* New York: Russell and Russell, 1961.

8

National Power and Nationalism

Nationalism can refer either to consolidation of political power—the growth of the nation as opposed to the centrifugal tendencies of the states—or it may have to do with the development of national spirit and a concern, sometimes exaggerated, with the position of the United States in world affairs. This chapter will use "nationalism" to refer to the latter phenomenon and will distinguish it from the growth of national power. The two are, of course, related. A sense of being an "American" rather than merely a citizen of a state made possible the growth of national power at the same time that it encouraged an American solidarity in facing other nations and peoples.

The Growth of National Power

The controversy over national power began even before the Constitution and formed the nucleus of the dispute over ratification. Almost as soon as the Constitution became the foundation of the new government, the dispute regarding the extent of national powers and questions of national versus state authority became the center of much of American politics. To a large extent the issue was the argument over loose as opposed to strict construction of the Constitution, as reflected in the Jeffersonian and Hamiltonian antagonism over the creation of a national bank and other related policies.

The action of the government in creating the bank did not still the debate between those favoring loose construction and their opponents, despite the fact that Thomas Jefferson, the most prominent spokesman for strict constructionism, acted upon the loose constructionist doctrine of implied powers after he became President to justify such things as the annexation of Louisiana in 1803 and the embargo of foreign trade in 1807.

If there ever had been doubt regarding the eventual outcome, the Supreme Court's crucial role made the victory of those supporting national power almost a sure thing. Almost as soon as the Union came into existence, the court began exercising the power of judicial review over the acts of the states. In 1796, for example, the court in the case of *Ware* v. *Hylton* struck down an act of the Virginia legislature which provided that debts owed by Virginians to British creditors be paid instead to the state; the basis for the decision was that the act was in violation of the 1783 peace treaty. Although the court did not overrule an act of Congress until *Marbury* v. *Madison* in 1803, it anticipated such an action as early as 1796 in *Hylton* v. *United States*, in which it reviewed a congressional act and found it consistent with the Constitution; ruling as it did that the act was constitutional clearly raised the possibility that it might have issued a contrary ruling and declared the act to be unconstitutional.

The state resentment at abuse of national power that had led to the Kentucky and Virginia Resolutions of 1798 had little if any effect in slowing the development of centralization. The Supreme Court rounded out its decisions in 1810 in *Fletcher* v. *Peck*; previously it had voided state laws that it judged in conflict with federal legislation or treaties, but now it overruled an act of the Georgia legislature that sought to cancel contracts made as a result of actions by a previous legislature. The ground was violation of the contract clause of the U.S. Constitution, marking the first case in which the court struck down state action as in conflict with the Constitution. Continuing the trend was a decision in 1816 in which the court responded to the position taken by the Virginia Court of Appeals and its Chief Justice, Spencer Roane, that the federal courts had no jurisdiction to hear appeals from the decisions of state courts. In *Martin* v. *Hunter's Lessee* the Supreme Court affirmed that its appellate power extended to any appropriate case regardless of which court rendered the original decision, including state courts.

Probably the one decision that more than any other intensified the consolidation of national power was *McCulloch* v. *Maryland* in 1819. John Marshall, the great Federalist Chief Justice, wrote the opinion that enshrined in American constitutional practice the principle that no state could tax an instrumentality of the United States government. The issue was Maryland's attempt to tax the Baltimore branch of the National Bank out of existence. Marshall reasoned along Hamiltonian lines in holding the bank itself constitutional. He concluded, moreover, that the power to tax is the power to destroy and that agencies of the national government are therefore free from taxation by the states. Even more important was the basis for the decision. Speaking for the court, the Chief Justice concluded that although the government is one of strictly limited powers, if the goal is constitutional, then any methods of attaining the goal, if they are consistent with the goal and are not forbidden by the Constitution, are also constitutional. This decision has become a firm fixture in American constitutional law.

Although both Thomas Jefferson and Andrew Jackson maintained that each branch of government was empowered to interpret the Constitution, and although they and others since them have attacked the practices of the courts upon occasion, the Supreme Court has come to be almost completely accepted as the final constitutional arbiter and has so functioned throughout its existence. It was the early Supreme Court decisions, more than the designs of the founders or the thoughts of political philosophers, that paved the way for the development of a powerful national state. In the early years, the only political philosophy that explicitly advocated centralization at the expense of the states was the Hamiltonian brand of Federalism. The Federalists as a party died with the coming of the nineteenth century, but in placing John Marshall at the head of the Supreme Court, they succeeded in dominating the early practices that were to shape the growth of the nation. Nowhere is there stronger evidence that much of the character of the United States and its institutions was an outgrowth of political practice rather than consensus or concurrence with popular sentiment. Of course, political philosophy is important here also, but it is ironic that the ideas of a group that had been essentially discredited so far as American politics was concerned had at least as strong an impact upon the evolution of the American nation as had the ideas of their opponents, which appear to have been considerably more in keeping with the wishes of the people.

Court decisions, however, were not the only factors encouraging the growth of national power. The actions of Presidents must also be considered. Even Jefferson, whose sentiments in favor of states' rights have echoes in many legislative halls in the twentieth century, brought energy into the executive and aided the growth of the major consolidating influence, the presidency. Similarly, Jackson's use of the veto brought further power to the institution. With Abraham Lincoln, the United States actually became a "nation," as opposed to a "union," and a series of twentieth-century Presidents brought into being the full-fledged "imperial presidency" that became too obvious to ignore under Lyndon Johnson and culminated in the open disdain for the other branches of government manifested by Richard Nixon.

Along with the Supreme Court and various Presidents, Congress has played an active role in devaloping national power. It was in Congress that the rhetoric emerged that was ultimately to justify the growth of national, as opposed to state, power; court decisions laid the foundation, but political debate captured the minds of the people in a manner that Marshall's legal language could never duplicate. Originally there had been a controversy between those who contended that the Union was a contract between sovereign states and those who argued that it was instead established by the American people collectively. The dispute reached a peak in 1830 with the famous Webster-Hayne debates in the United States Senate. In debating a measure introduced by Senator Samuel Foot of Connecticut to halt the future sales of public lands, the Senate turned to discussion of the nature of the Constitution. South Carolina, the only state that had at that time forcefully advocated what later came to be the "southern" position, found its stance set forth clearly by one of its Senators, Robert Hayne. Hayne argued that states were sovereign and that they constitutionally could nullify congressional acts when they deemed such acts to be unconstitutional. Daniel Webster answered in terms that came to represent the emerging theory of the Constitution as a nationalizing document, not a mere compact among states.[1]

Webster incorporated into his constitutional theory a justification of national power that would have pleased Alexander Hamilton. Although he granted the right of revolution, he contended that there was no way under the Constitution for a state to interfere with the enforcement of national laws. If the people were to exercise their right to resist an unjust government, this would be outside the framework of the Constitution; resistance was a natural right, but it was extraconstitutional and was not sanctioned by the Constitution. If a state were to undertake nullification or interposition, it would be revolution. To Hayne's contention that he argued not for revolution but for the right of a state to resist the national government within the constitutional system, Webster responded that the question was whose prerogative it was to decide upon the constitutionality of the laws.

The federal government, Webster argued, was not merely the

agent of the states because it could not serve separate masters simultaneously; not only had the thirteen original states created the national government, but that government in turn had created the remainder of the states. He asserted that it was the power of the people, not the states, that had created "the people's Constitution" and that both the national government and the governments of the states were the creations of the people. The people had determined that the Constitution was to be supreme within the Union and that the appropriate arbiter of constitutional questions was the United States Supreme Court. The Constitution proclaimed itself the supreme law and extended to the judicial power all cases arising under it. Webster noted that nowhere in the Constitution was there a provision for state action to interpret the Constitution. To the allegation that a state might in extreme cases take upon itself the power to be the judge, he answered that in such cases the people themselves would take action without need for the state in the form of a revolution.

Webster transformed his speech into a hymn of praise for the Union. Attacking those who might contrast the growth of national power with the preservation of personal freedom, he justified the Union with a powerful central government as the greatest protector of liberty. Liberty and Union, he declared with a grand rhetorical flourish, were one and inseparable. Such rhetoric laid the groundwork for the theories of nationhood that came ultimately to be accepted.

Despite Webster's efforts, it was almost inevitable that there would continue to be disagreements regarding the locus of power given the nature of a federal structure. Americans have always been aware of the difficulties associated with two levels of authority. Their invention of federalism in its modern form raised questions that have not yet been entirely settled and that required a civil war to provide the basic pattern of the answers. Many of the basic issues in American political thought were reexamined in the years leading to the war, and such concerns as the nature of political contracts, majoritarianism, minority rights, and consent of the governed again formed the basis for intense speculation as they had in the period leading to the Revolution. In many respects the discussion on the nature of national power was different from the slavery controversy, although slavery brought the issue to the point of crisis and was the fundamental reason for most of the intense debate. Because the issues surrounding slavery have implications different from those surrounding the structure and nature of the Union, they will form a separate discussion in the next chapter.

It was the course of the Civil War that laid to rest the question of sovereignty that had dominated so much of the discussion over structure which had pervaded American politics since the adoption of the Constitution. Although there may still be disagreement concerning states rights, the advocates of national sovereignty were triumphant. No longer could it be seriously contended that the Union was a compact between states and the national government that could be abrogated by action of the parties to the contract. Even less could it be argued that the southern position of state sovereignty was viable, although Alexander H. Stephens, who had been Vice President of the Confederacy, defended the more moderate aspects of the southern argument quite ably in his *Constitutional View of the Late War Between the States*, published after the Civil War. The basic question, however, that of loyalty to state superseding loyalty to nation, was no more than a historical curiosity. The arguments of Webster carried the day along with those of diverse figures who argued for national supremacy and for the whole people, not the states, as the foundation of the Constitution. Abraham Lincoln captured the spirit of the future when he asserted that the nation was indissoluble and that it predated the Constitution.[2] It is significant that he incorporated these sentiments into his First Inaugural Address and that the Supreme Court upheld his thesis in 1869 when it ruled, in *Texas* v. *White*, that the nation was organic and indivisible and that the Confederate states, therefore, had never in fact left the Union.

With the rejection of both the extreme southern position, advocated by such spokesmen as Hayne and John C. Calhoun, and the more moderate assertions of Stephens, attention turned to varieties of nationalism. The thought of statesmen such as Webster and Lincoln for the first time joined with that of academic political philosophers. Francis Lieber (see p. 100), whose American roots were in the Jacksonian period, rejected the states' rights theories of such thinkers as Stephens and sought to provide a framework within which an organic nation could be made compatible with individual liberty. As V. L. Parrington writes:

> He gave a new turn to speculation on the origin and nature of the political state, the immediate consequence of which was the repudiation of the compact theory and natural-rights philosophy by our academic political scientists. The organic conception of the political state fell in with the centralizing movement that followed the Civil War. . . . On the whole the influence of Lieber has been rather against than for that liberty which was so dear to him, and the explanation is to be found in the tragic divorce, in his thinking, of politics and economics. His inveterate legalism and his failure to investigate the economics of politics proved in the end the undoing of his liberalism.[3]

Parrington aptly captures the contradiction that lay within Lieber's work and the extremes to which it was carried by other political scientists, such as John W. Burgess. Burgess contended that the national state must not only possess sovereignty but that it must become "the organ of interpretation in last instance of the order of life for its subjects." It was not an accident that he substituted "subjects" for "citizens," having had the way paved by Lieber's discarding of the natural rights framework of the eighteenth century that was designed to protect the person from the all-embracing power of just such a state as Burgess openly advocated. Burgess baldly wrote that no state could be conceived without sovereignty, which he defined as total power over its subjects.[4]

After the Civil War had decided the issue of secession, the Fourteenth Amendment, which followed the war, established a foundation for national, as opposed to state, citizenship. It also strengthened the federal judiciary's power to review state actions in order to force compliance with national policy. It was many years later, however, before the courts chose to interpret the amendment in such a way as to have great impact upon the states. Only in the last few decades has the Fourteenth Amendment become the vehicle for national insistence upon a program of civil rights and liberties for Americans regardless of state policy.

The greatest increases in national power have resulted not from theoretical developments but rather from crisis situations that brought forth conditions with which state governments were unable to cope. The Great Depression of the 1930s and the world war that followed quickly thereafter are the most notable. The years since World War II have seen the continuation of a wartime state because of international tensions, the demands of world leadership, and the fears of many Americans that the nation is ever in danger of becoming weak. No nation in modern times can fight a major war without devoting considerable time and energy to it on a national basis. The demands of war and of defense in a world that fears war are by far the greatest forces that strengthen tendencies toward increasing national power.

The Growth of Nationalism

Paradoxically, it is the mobility and rootlessness of Americans, a people who to some extent had broken their ties with the past and who built a new world in the Western Hemisphere, that have encouraged the development of a particular kind of nationalism.

Many currents helped form the national spirit, from the romantic good fellowship of Walt Whitman to the crudely "scientific" and racist attitudes of such writers as Francis Lieber and John W. Burgess, who reflected the German influences from G. W. F. Hegel and others who exalted the state as the embodiment of the spirit of a people. The diversity of these influences has increased the desire for Americans to explain to themselves what Americanism is and how Americans came to be Americans as opposed to transplanted Europeans.

In 1893 the historian Frederick Jackson Turner read a paper entitled "The Significance of the Frontier in American History" at a meeting of historians in Chicago during the World's Fair. Turner's frontier thesis sought to explain the development of the American character by attributing it to the existence of a frontier that continually called Americans forth from the cities to the American West. He concluded that it was the westward movement with its wilderness experience that developed much of the American spirit, including such things as the qualities of self-reliance and democracy.

Turner's thesis is inadequate in many respects, and it ignores the rich heritage that Americans brought with them from Europe; it ignores how Americans were and are connected to the rest of the world. It is important to note, however, that the Turner thesis immediately struck a responsive chord among Americans, and for a time many thought it to be a complete explanation. It told Americans that historians had concluded what they had known instinctively all along: that Americans were unique, that they were totally separate from the old and corrupt institutions of Europe, that they could make their own way in the world. Much of the earlier anti-European spirit is suggested today by the readiness of many in the United States to condemn the "effete East," the older sections of their own country.

Part of the American spirit of nationalism has been the desire for territorial conquest. Americans swept across the continent, virtually exterminating the Indians as they went. They seized, purchased, or negotiated for a vast expanse of land that had been owned by others, from Florida through the huge interior region of the Louisiana Purchase on to the Pacific Coast, taking Texas and the arid lands of the Southwest as they went. They pressed on even beyond their natural continental boundary and accumulated the distant territory of Alaska. Wherever they went, they carried with them their traditions and institutions.

The movement to acquire new land and to incorporate it into a new American empire has become known as "Manifest Destiny." Americans, from the highest leaders in the government, to the average citizen, tended to believe that it was their nation's destiny to engulf the continent, to bring enlightenment to "inferior" peoples, to spread the benefits of American civilization, and to expand the American Union. Before the end of the nineteenth century the United States had spread from the Atlantic to the Pacific, with territories far beyond.

Completion of the nation's continental boundaries ended Manifest Destiny in its classic form, but the thirst for expansion continued. The impulses that had fed it during the middle of the nineteenth century resurged at the century's end and continued past then as open imperialism. The United States was favored with immense resources, and with the thrust of nationalism it succeeded in annexing Hawaii, seizing the Philippines, wresting Cuba from Spain and reducing it for a time to a virtual American possession, joining other nations in interfering with the sovereignty and internal affairs of Cuba and China, and asserting the right to police the manners and morals of Latin America.

Many factors influenced American nationalism. Along with American wealth and power there was the heritage of success that, when combined with a political theory intended to speak for all human beings at all times and for their benefit, appeared to justify not only national development but the spread, forceful if need be, of American institutions. Americans early shared in the nationalism that has become one of the major political forces in the world. Although nationalism is a rather new phenomenon, it is now so pervasive that it is taken for granted that virtually all peoples are intensely nationalistic. So intense is the sentiment that it frequently overshadows social class, economics, politics, and other major considerations. In America as elsewhere the Marxist prediction that the interests of the working classes would lead to international unity directed against the forces of capitalism has not been borne out; workers, along with others, are so likely to be influenced primarily by nationalism that there is relatively little in the way of crossnational social and political currents, except for the huge multinational corporations. Even the insurgent movements that have brought about "wars of national liberation" have tended to be self-consciously nationalistic.

Among other factors bearing upon American nationalism are some that deserve separate treatment and are therefore considered in subsequent chapters. The nineteenth-century attitude of "realism," as opposed to the earlier American concern with absolutes, was significant, as were scientific theories that were shaking the intellectual world then. Social Darwinism was a mode of thought that interpreted social matters in a fashion that purported to be scientific and was inspired by those who sought to apply Darwin's evolutionary theories to society (see pp. 157–163). For our purposes at present, it is sufficient to say that American nationalism developed from a complex pattern of influences at work within the culture and the society and included a reaction against the European institutions from which many of the early American settlers and most of the later immigrants fled.

It is difficult to generalize about the effects of nationalism in the United States because it has taken so many different forms. On the one hand, it has led to some of the most impressive acts of international generosity in world history, including the Marshall Plan, which, however much it may also have been affected by considerations of self-interest, also helped to rebuild a continent that had been ravaged by war. On the other hand, it has upon occasion led to gross irrationalities, such as the excesses of the "red"-hunting McCarthy period in the 1950s, the World War II relocation of Americans of Japanese ancestry to concentration camps without due process of law, and the Sedition Act and the infamous Palmer raids of the period during and immediately following World War I.[5]

Similarly, American nationalism, which is an expression of American pride, has led both to some of the most noteworthy economic developments in the history of the world and to some of the most unlikely contradictions. Poverty, for example, continues to exist in the midst of affluence in this nation partly because of a reluctance to admit the existence of deplorable conditions. In purely political terms there are further contradictions. Can a nation remain true to democratic ideals at home if it subverts them elsewhere? Mark Twain asked this question early in the twentieth century when he was criticizing American imperialism in the Philippines. Such questions have been a part of American politics since the early days and are as forceful now as ever. Pride has led the nation into military excesses, which have political implications far beyond the immediate ones. It is generally true that war is simply incompatible with constitutional democracy. Democracy requires open discussion; war demands secrecy. Democracy thrives upon dissent and disagreements; war represses all opinion not consistent with the aims of the leaders. Democracy is based upon reasonable solutions; war is based upon solutions by force and violence, the greatest possible breakdown of law and order. Democracy places high value upon the individual; war subjects all to a rigid authoritarian hierarchy. The very nationlism that is based largely upon democratic theory and the American past paradoxically can bring about those situations most destructive of the institutions that brought forth the nationalistic pride.

Two of the most prominent characteristics of Americans have been a sense of mission in the world and a belief that nothing was beyond the power of the American nation to accomplish. World War I weakened both of these characteristics. Americans who had gone into the war with high ideals had been convinced that they were making the world safe for democracy. Instead, the war brought repression at home and greed and disillusionment abroad as the victors fought for national advantage at the expense of democratic principles. Both the high idealism and the subsequent disillusionment resulted in part from a naive tendency to accept views so oversimplified that they failed to account for the complexity of world happenings and failed to recognize elements of significance.

America then turned inward, and the Senate refused President Wilson's urgent pleas to permit the United States to join the League of Nations. Subsequently there came legislation incorporating into law the racist doctrines that earlier had led the nation into imperialistic ventures; it restricted immigration and based the exclusions and limitations upon national origin, not individual worth. The government, moreover, not only failed to eliminate segregation and other racist policies internally, but appeared as often as not to encourage them.

The Great Depression was a further blow to American pride and confidence, and the damage was only partially repaired by the impressive technical and industrial feats of World War II. The "cold war" that followed was prepared for not only by the currents of the twentieth century but by those extending far back into the nineteenth. The oversimplified attitude that every nation would of necessity accept the leadership of the Soviet Union or the United States overlooked the strength of nationalism in countries other than the United States and betrayed the existence of a simple-minded approach to America's place in the world that had become a part of typical American attitudes. Such inadequate interpretations brought tragic results and may be attributed at least in part to an exaggerated American nationalism that encouraged many leaders grossly to misinterpret conditions and situations in other nations. It may be that the nation has learned from its mistakes, but the cost has been enormous. A proper understanding of political philosophy could have led us in an entirely different direction.

NOTES

1. See *The Great Speeches and Orations of Daniel Webster* (Boston: Little, Brown, 1879), pp. 256–258; see also Diane Tipton, *Nullification and Interposition in American Political Thought*, publication No. 78 of the Division of Government Research, The Institute for

Social Research and Development (Albuquerque: University of New Mexico, January 1969) for a concise but detailed examination of the doctrines of nullification and interposition throughout the existence of the republic.

2. *The Collected Works of Abraham Lincoln*, vol. 4, Roy P. Basler, ed. (New Brunswick, N.J.: Rutgers University Press, 1953), pp. 252–253.

3. *Main Currents in American Thought*, vol. 2 (New York: Harcourt Brace Jovanovich, 1954), pp. 93–94.

4. Ibid., pp. 89–90.

5. Attorney General A. Mitchell Palmer directed the deportation of hundreds of aliens who had been arrested on flimsy charges and denied benefit of counsel; mere association with persons belonging to radical organizations could result in expulsion with no recourse for an alien. See Robert K. Murray, *Red Scare: A Study in National Hysteria, 1919–1920* (Minneapolis: University of Minnesota Press, 1955).

ADDITIONAL READINGS

Arieli, Yehoshua. *Individualism and Nationalism in American Ideology.* Baltimore: Penguin, 1966.

Hays, Carleton J. H. *Essays on Nationalism.* New York: Macmillan, 1926.

———. *Nationalism: A Religion.* New York: Macmillan, 1960.

Kohn, Hans. *American Nationalism: An Interpretative Essay.* New York: Macmillan, 1961.

———. *The Idea of Nationalism: A Study in Its Origins and Background.* New York: Macmillan, 1944.

Mason, Alpheus T. "The Nature of the Federal Union Reconsidered." *Political Science Quarterly* 65 (December 1950).

Merriam, Charles E. *History of the Theory of Sovereignty Since Thoreau.* New York: AMS Press, 1968 [1900].

Shafer, Boyd C. *Nationalism, Myth and Reality.* New York: Harcourt, Brace, 1955.

Snyder, Louis L. *The Meaning of Nationalism.* New Brunswick, N.J.: Rutgers University Press, 1954.

Wiltse, Charles M. "From Compact to National State in American Political Thought." In Milton R. Konvitz and Arthur E. Murphy, eds., *Essays in Political Theory.* Ithaca, N.Y.: Cornell University Press, 1948.

9

The Rights of Man Reconsidered

During the years of the Revolution Americans rallied to the rights of man. However much the radical elements inherent in such an approach may have been submerged as the republic got underway, there was general consensus upon majority rule, natural rights, the consent of the governed, and the individual as the basic unit of politics. Although the existence of slavery was an obvious contradiction to many of these principles and to the spirit of them all, that "peculiar institution" served more as an embarrassing inconsistency than as a challenge to the fundamental American liberal faith. With a few notable exceptions most political writers ignored slavery and its implications, dealing with it, if they considered it at all, only as an unfortunate inheritance that must one day be eliminated.

The change came around 1830 when some southerners began to argue that slavery, far from being a curse to the South, was a positive good. The events leading to the Civil War are well known. Less well known is the degree to which the debate over slavery included full-fledged attacks upon the American heritage and the rights of man arguments that formed the basis of the Declaration of Independence. In attacking not only the rights of man in the abstract but also the Declaration as a document, the southerners laid the groundwork for some basic changes in American political thought, changes that encouraged the modern approach based upon "realism" rather than the abstractions of the founders. The southerners lost in their attempts to retain and to expand slavery, but they nevertheless had influence in shaping future patterns of thought in America; because political language changed little, there has come to be even more divergence between action and rhetoric than before.

Background of the Debate over Slavery

Opposition to slavery had deep roots in America. Previous chapters have mentioned instances of antislavery thought and writing in colonial times. The Quakers had long condemned slavery as contrary to Christianity, and the rights of man arguments of the Revolution led many to oppose the institution as unjust and inexcusable. Abigail Adams, for example, wrote to her husband in 1774 that she considered it to be "iniquitious" to fight "for what we are daily robbing and plundering from those who have as good a right to freedom as we have."[1] In fact, the phrase "all men are born free and equal" in the Massachusetts Constitution of 1780, a phrase reminiscent of the Declaration of Independence and of classic American democratic thought, affected the movement to eliminate slavery in that state before the adoption of the U.S. Constitution. Several slaves had won suits for freedom based partly upon this section of the state's constitution, but the courts had not declared the bases for their rulings. Some writers have contended that the Quok (or Quock) Walker case destroyed slavery in Massachusetts. A. T. Mason, for example, has said that "under this provision Quock Walker, in 1781, won a suit for freedom brought against his master. This ended slavery in the Bay State."[2] The case, however, was not that clear-cut; the court ruled in Walker's favor but did not indicate upon what grounds, and part of the dispute resulted from a previous master's unfulfilled promise to free him. The more definitive case seems to have been another in which Walker was involved in 1783. In this case Walker once more sued his former master, this time on the ground of assault. Walker again was declared to be free, and the basis was the former owner's promise of manumission, or release from slavery. The judge went beyond this, though, and declared that slavery was incompatible with the new spirit "favorable to the natural rights of mankind" and with the state constitution. Although there was no formal declaration of abolition, many slaves left their masters upon the assumption that the courts would not uphold slavery, with the result that Massachusetts reported in the first census of 1790 that there were no more slaves in the state.[3]

The government under the Articles of Confederation excluded slavery from the Northwest Territory with the Northwest Ordinance of 1787, and Congress banned the importation of slaves in 1808 and in 1820 adopted the Missouri Compromise that excluded slavery from the northern part of the Louisiana Territory. Similarly, states outside the South before long adopted at least gradual abolition, leaving the American South as one of the few portions of the world that retained the practice of buying and selling human beings.[4]

Even in the South the sentiment appears to have been shifting away from favoring slavery in colonial times, except in Georgia and South Carolina. When Jefferson drafted the Declaration, he included a passage condemning the king for permitting the slave trade, but South Carolina and Georgia objected and the final draft failed to include the disputed passage. The most important factor in the southern shift toward solidarity in desiring to protect slavery was probably the invention in 1793 of the cotton gin, which permitted the growth of the cotton culture that in its early stages brought wealth to many virtually overnight, wealth that slavery enhanced immeasurably. Also significant were the efforts of John C. Calhoun and other South Carolina leaders to weld the southern states into a rigidly proslavery bloc within the Union.

Prior to the 1830s there had been many antislavery societies in the United States, most within the South. With the turn toward support of the institution, not only did the South drive antislavery societies from its midst, but it closed ranks to the extent that the South became the closest thing to a totalitarian regime that has been seen in America. Free speech was effectively eliminated, postmasters censored the mails to eliminate antislavery opinion, and nonconformists were literally in danger of their lives.

In part the southern stance was a response to the development of the abolition movement. The earlier antislavery societies had tended to be gradualist and to confine their efforts to colonization proposals and opposition to slavery's extension. The abolitionists, however, demanded an immediate end to slavery and were as harsh in their criticism of slaveholders as of the system itself. The South had become a society dominated by fear and by a sensitivity to its position as one of the last bastions of an institution almost universally condemned. Not only were their practices incompatible with the thrust of American thought, but southerners tended to believe that the rest of the Union and much of the rest of the civilized world were beleaguering them. As the development of authoritarianism in the South indicated, there was considerable fear of subversion from within as well as from without. In truth, many slaves throughout southern history had revolted, had committed sabotage, or had fled or attempted to flee. There were several uprisings, or attempted uprisings, such as the aborted plot in 1822 by Denmark Vesey, a free black, that brought terror to South Carolina. Although Vesey was betrayed and many of his followers were executed, the plot was huge and extraordinarily well organized. Not only terror but rage spread throughout the South when Nat Turner led his bloody rebellion in Virginia in 1831; by then, the South could blame the abolitionists and their agitation.

It is important to note that although most of the change in attitude had come within the South, nonsouthern Americans were hardly less racist than were southerners. Originally, there was wide agreement within both the North and the South that slavery was wrong and that there must ultimately be ways to eliminate it. In changing to the view that slavery was a positive good, however, the South came to desire that slavery spread to the territories; ultimately, it came to demand that others cease even to criticize the institution. Abraham Lincoln clearly discerned in the Supreme Court's Dred Scott decision in 1857 the implication that slavery eventually could not be prohibited even within free states. When Scott, a slave, sued for his freedom on the ground that his master had taken him into free areas, Chief Justice Roger Taney ruled for the court that blacks, free or slave, could not sue because they could never qualify as citizens. Lincoln grasped the possibilities of Taney's further reasoning that forbidding slavery in the territories would deny slaveholders the right to relocate with their "property" when other persons were free to take their property wherever they wished. Many historians, believing that slavery had reached its "natural limits," contend that much expansion could not have occurred. At best that is a strange conclusion for anyone who is familiar with the worst excesses of labor practices brought by the too rapid industrialization of the nation in the late nineteenth and early twentieth centuries. Moreover, the South had already had some success in using slave labor in nonagricultural industries, such as lumbering and manufacturing. It is difficult to believe that some of the "robber barons" when they came on the American scene would not have turned to actual slave labor had they been able.

Both the South and the North had agreed upon the Missouri Compromise, each having accepted the notion that slavery should be limited. Americans outside the South had accepted slavery where it existed and had even acquiesced in its expansion. The increasing southern demand for limitless expansion, however, finally enabled the abolitionists to persuade many in the North of the correctness of their position. At first, abolitionists were hardly more welcome outside the South than in it. They were regularly attacked, even in New England. In 1837 a mob in Alton, Illinois, murdered a Presbyterian minister, Elijah Lovejoy, and threw his printing press into the river because of his editorials against lynching. The U.S. House of Representatives in 1836 adopted its infamous "gag rule" preventing the receipt or discussion of antislavery petitions, regardless of the First Amendment, and regardless of the powerful attacks upon the resolution by one of its members, former President John Quincy Adams. When militant abolitionist William Lloyd Garrison arrived in Boston and tried to hire a church hall to deliver antislavery lectures, he was refused. As Sidney Lens noted, "Only a society of atheists would make its facilities available to this devout Baptist."[5]

Garrison founded his newspaper, *The Liberator*, on New Year's Day in 1831. Others rallied to his cause, and within a few years there were many who were writing and speaking regularly. Lens wrote that as "strange as it seems—it worked. . . . Garrison's single-mindedness, his 'impracticality,' had caused a drastic change in mood." He taunted "the conscience of a morally weak nation, and in so doing eroded its misgivings until a John Brown or an Abraham Lincoln became possible."[6] Although white Americans had no love for blacks as such, so great had the contradictions become between their professed values and the realities of slavery that at last, under prodding of militant southerners and equally militant abolitionists, they recognized the cogency of the moral issue. Probably the incidents that most directly provoked the Civil War were John Brown's raid on Harper's Ferry in 1859 and, seven years earlier, Harriet Beecher Stowe's publication of *Uncle Tom's Cabin*, the most successful piece of political propaganda, along with Tom Paine's *Common Sense*, in American history.

John P. Roche was correct in saying that slavery was crucial. It was crucial not because those outside the South considered blacks to be equal, but because they were "unwilling to allow the South to impose inequality on whites throughout the Union." He was also correct in pointing out that the suppression of civil rights, the southern veto on all legislation viewed as weakening the South's autonomy, and a proslavery foreign policy were logical and inevitable consequences of the slave system. "Indeed," Roche wrote, "the 'militant South' demanded that the whole thrust of national public policy be adjusted to the imperatives of the slave system," and, with the conclusive evidence of secession, he documented that "slavery required a rule or ruin approach to American national interest."[7]

One of the most frequent charges is that the abolitionists whipped up a crisis where none had existed, that the South ultimately would have eliminated slavery, and that the fundamental issues were economic; the South, that is, was groaning under the yoke of northern economic tyranny. Essentially accepting the thesis that slavery was a surface issue, many have contended that the Civil

War resulted from a series of blunders on each side, augmented by the conflict between the South's agrarian ideology and the industrialism of the North. Nevertheless, it is clear that slavery had advanced considerably and that nowhere in the South had it weakened; it had both expanded geographically and been intensified where it had all along existed. Rather than being a dying institution, it was vigorous and dynamic, an institution that the South was willing to fight to protect and one that the rest of the nation, admittedly belatedly, was willing to fight to keep confined. Except for the abolitionists, there was no attack upon slavery so long as it remained in the South. Even Lincoln, whose election so offended the slave states, consistently stressed that he had no intention of interfering with slavery in the states where it existed.

As for the economic argument, Allan Nevins, no friend of the abolitionists, has written that it is the flimsiest of all explanations for the war. He pointed out that Alexander Stephens, the Confederacy's Vice President, wrote during the war that the tariff, which southern rhetoric condemned as benefitting the industrial North at the expense of the agricultural South, was just what the South's own members in Congress had made it. Almost from the beginning the South had controlled the federal government, and there were few economic disadvantages that it faced that were not shared equally by the agricultural states of the Midwest—states, it may be observed, that remained loyal to the Union. There were as many unifying as divisive economic factors, and in fact the tariff on the eve of the war was the lowest since 1816.[8] With Lincoln's election, the South lost control of the presidency, but it still controlled the Congress, the Supreme Court was the same that had handed down the Dred Scott decision making slavery fundamental to the national legal system, and even the new President had assured the South that he would not and constitutionally could not move against slavery in the southern states.

Arthur Schlesinger, Jr., is one of the few contemporary writers who has recognized the moral dimensions of the slavery controversy.[9] He wrote that it was the moral issue of slavery that brought significance to the issues of the institution's expansion and of the enforcement of the fugitive slave laws. The system that the South was attempting to defend violated many of the most basic values of humanity. The evil nature of the system meant that attempts to protect it inevitably resulted in the moral and intellectual decay of the society. He pointed out that regardless of the vagueness of many moral issues, certainly human slavery is one that we can be sure is wrong, and it makes no more sense to say that there should have been no abolitionists than to say that there should have been no anti-Nazis. Schlesinger touches upon a basic truth that is too little recognized today throughout the realm of the social sciences. There is a tendency to evade moral questions in the name of a superficial objectivity. The power of southern proslavery thought was such that it contributed significantly to the climate that was to produce this tendency.

The arguments both for and against slavery fall into several clear groupings. There are the overt attacks upon the rights of man and upon abstract notions of human freedom. These form the core of the southern position, and John C. Calhoun is the most prominent advocate of that position, with George Fitzhugh probably being the most extreme. There are the more subtle attacks that are displayed by advocates, for example, of "popular sovereignty," such as Stephen A. Douglas. The antislavery positions, each compatible with the rights of man and the fundamentals of American political thought, are those of the moderates such as Lincoln on the one hand and the abolitionists on the other. It is necessary to investigate each of these positions in greater detail in order to understand not only the nature of the slavery debate but also the origin of much modern-day political thought.

The Southern Position

With the secession of the Confederate states, John C. Calhoun's argument, once confined largely to South Carolina, became the accepted position on slavery of the entire South. The form of the argument was unimportant; the defense of slavery was the goal, however argued. Such spokesmen as Albert Bledsoe and Thornton Stringfellow used biblical arguments to justify slavery; others, including Calhoun, contended that the only society that produced advances in culture and morality was one in which there was freedom from toil and that therefore the existence of slavery produced a master class that brought forth a society superior to any possible society that was based upon free institutions. South Carolina's Governor J. H. Hammond asserted this doctrine with his "mud-sill" theory that all societies must be based upon an exploited class in order for humanity to progress, and this kind of reasoning led many southerners, including Calhoun, to become enamored with the notion of the South as a revived "Greek democracy." Surely this was a wildly romantic position for such hard-headed realists to take. There also, of course, were those who attempted to prove "scientifically" that blacks were genetically inferior; unfortunately, neither the Civil War nor the rise of modern science has totally laid such efforts to rest.

Calhoun was not only the foremost spokesman for the South and of the proslavery school, but he is a major figure in American political thought as well. He aspired to be a formal political philosopher in a nation in which they are very few. Because of this, and because of his preeminent position as a representative of the southern position, his thought has commanded attention far beyond that accorded to the thought of all but a handful of Americans. Calhoun has been popular with many political scientists, despite the incredibly reactionary nature of his position, because his method of approach to political questions has a much more modern tone than that of most writers of his day. In many ways he anticipated the fundamentals of contemporary pluralistic thought, and to a considerable extent he also anticipated Karl Marx's analysis of social, political, and economic questions; his conclusions, of course, were at the far end of the spectrum from Marx, whose intentions were essentially humanistic. Richard Hofstadter did not exaggerate and was most perceptive when he described Calhoun as the Marx of the Master Class.[10] Calhoun's reputation as one of the only formal political philosophers in the American heritage plus his undeniably keen insights into the nature of American politics have led many who discuss him to be less critical than they might otherwise have been. Alan Grimes, for example, correctly described Calhoun's principle of the concurrent majority (discussed below) as nothing more than a "euphemistic expression for unanimous consent."[11] Yet four pages later in the same work, Grimes wrote that Calhoun's "system of the concurrent majority ranks as one of the major American contributions to the literature of political thought."[12]

Calhoun's major works are his *Disquisition on Government* and *A Discourse on the Constitution and Government of the United States* (both published posthumously, in 1853). In the *Disquisition* Calhoun set forth his fundamental principles. He rejected natural rights along with state of nature and contract theories. He followed Thomas Hobbes in his pessimistic view of the selfishness of human nature and of the consequent dangers of anarchy, but he rejected Hobbesian individualism. He viewed society as natural and the source of all rights. The numerical majority, he contended, is the source of many ills in society and is destructive of minority rights. To remedy the defect, he proposed that the numerical majority be rejected as a principle of national action, and he offered the "concurrent majority" as a substitute that he believed would be far superior. Each major interest in society, he argued, should have a veto upon governmental policy. He sought in the *Discourse* to propose a practical application of the concurrent majority principle in the United States by suggesting a dual presidency. The South would elect one President, the rest of the nation another, and each would possess the veto. Nevins described this proposal as a "political absurdity,"[13] but Calhoun quite accurately perceived the nature of American society at the time as divided into two significant interests, South and non-South. Moreover, he grasped the difficulties inherent in the notion of what he called the numerical majority far better than have most theorists, including many of those who have been strongest in their advocacy of democracy.

Calhoun did not explain how each interest would determine its own position, nor did he provide a satisfactory explanation of how a government designed to operate as he proposed would avoid deadlock, other than to assert that it would. His scheme was designed to protect the South and its position within the Union. Some analysts have interpreted Calhoun as a liberal because of his efforts to limit the coercive power of government. What they fail to recognize is that Calhoun had no interest in protecting individual rights or in limiting governmental power except as that power might interfere with the self-interest of privileged groups. Individuals as such had no rights except those that society was willing to permit them. He granted full coercive power to the state government, interpreting the state as an organically existing society, whereas he denied organic existence to the nation; the Union was merely the states collectively, no more than the sum of its parts. Like the great conservative thinkers, Calhoun stressed society as a whole, and he rejected notions of equality. In founding his theory upon groups, as opposed to individuals, he foreshadowed the development of institutional pluralism and accurately sensed the direction in which American politics was moving, toward a system of interest group politics with at least a limited veto power exercised by powerful interests (such as labor, bankers, conservationists, etc.). Much of this is hindsight, however; Calhoun sought only to protect a powerful sectional minority, and his institutional scheme was more a rationalization of that effort than a true understanding of what was to become identified as American pluralism with all its implications.[14]

Hofstadter has produced, in his brief essay "John C. Calhoun: The Marx of the Master Class," one of the most insightful of all the studies devoted to Calhoun.[15] Hofstadter noted Calhoun's emphasis upon the class distinction between the rich and the poor and his prediction that there would be an increase in the number of the "ignorant and dependent." He quoted Calhoun to the effect that the South consisted of an aggregate of communities rather than individuals, with each plantation a community whose master represented the common interests of capital and labor, and he stressed Calhoun's conviction that the interests of the *gentlemen* of the North and the South were identical. He rated Calhoun's analysis of America's political tensions as among the most impressive intellectual achievements in American statecraft, and said that the South Carolinian, far in advance of others, predicted the alliance of northern conservatives and southern reactionaries. He concluded, however, that Calhoun, like Marx, miscalculated. Both overestimated the revolutionary potential of the workers, Marx through optimism, and Calhoun through pessimism. Rather than revolt, as both Calhoun and Marx had predicted, laborers were absorbed into the capitalist system. Both thinkers failed to recognize the persistence of capitalism, and Calhoun was doubly misled by the unrest of the Jacksonian period, which he interpreted as imminent social upheaval. In reality, the Jacksonian ferment was an effort to spread capitalism rather than to bring it down.

Hofstadter is among the few critics who recognized the moral implications of Calhoun's thought and doctrine, and he clearly identified their consequences. Calhoun was so "starkly reactionary" that his prescriptions were self-defeating; even the South would have been destroyed by the "mud-sill" theory that all civilization must rest upon a submerged caste, and that southern slaves were better off than the "wage slaves" outside the South. If this were true, there was no reason why all workers should not be enslaved. Although Calhoun did not push his arguments to such an extent, others such as George Fitzhugh did, for such implications were embedded in Calhoun's thought. Regardless of his logical coherence, Calhoun was not morally consistent. To those such as C. M. Wiltse who have written that Calhoun is preeminent as a spokesman for minority rights, Hofstadter, while admitting that Calhoun's thought may have permanent value in formulating the problem of the relations between majorities and minorities, responded that Calhoun was not concerned in the slightest with minority rights, as they would be perceived by the modern liberal mind. Calhoun believed that there were no rights except those granted to the individual by society; he rejected the right of a dissenter to express unorthodox opinions, he consistently upheld the power of the state over the individual, and he certainly cared nothing for any right asserted by an ethnic minority. As Hofstadter made clear, Calhoun was interested in no minority except a propertied minority, and his concern was to protect economic privileges, not rights. He designed the principle of the concurrent majority to protect "a vested interest of considerable power," and it was completely without relevance to the protection of dissent, or to the protection of individual rights against the power of the state. The thrust of his thought clearly was not the protection of rights, regardless of his position in opposition to the growth of national power; any power that he would deny to one level of government, he would grant to another. He desired to build a framework that would protect a privileged minority and that would provide it, not with a proportionate voice, but with a voice in the determination of public policy equal to that of the entire remainder of the polity.[16]

With regard to his position on slavery, Calhoun was merely one among many in the South who wrote and spoke in the same vein. William Harper, a judge of the Court of Chancery in South Carolina, published an essay in 1837 entitled "Slavery," which reflected the southern attitude by attacking the free parts of the nation, and Western Europe and England as well.[17] Harper contended that slavery not only was present wherever civilization had been most advanced, but that slavery was responsible for civilization. Because most persons desire to avoid labor, only slavery is adequate to supply sufficient coercion to require the labor essential to produce property. Since he believed that property was necessary in order to have civilization and that slavery was necessary to have property, he concluded that slavery was prerequisite to civilization. Blacks were especially suited for southern slavery, and because they could not look forward to advancement, they had no ambition and were happier and more contented than paid laborers, whose constant striving for better things was a source of tension and discord. Like most southern writers of the period, Harper attacked the principles of the Declaration of Independence explicitly, arguing that natural rights were minimal and that even they could be interfered with by the state should it be necessary. In addition to denying that the Declaration's truths were self-evident, he denied equality and government by consent of the governed. The strong and the wise should control and would control. Because of his assumptions regarding rights, Harper could advance with enthusiasm the southern argument that black slaves in the South were not only happier but actually better off than were the workers of the North, workers that the South tended to call "wage slaves." What Harper failed to recognize was that, regardless of how undesirable the situation of many northern workers may have been (and southern free workers also, it might be added), they at least could look forward to an improved status for their children if not for themselves, something that slavery prevented. In any case, the condition of the worker at its worst, which at times was deplorable, failed to equal the indignity and the inhumanity of slavery, notwithstanding the fact that there may have been some slaves whose circumstances were better than those of some workers.

Harper based his argument upon the assumption that blacks were naturally inferior to whites and were therefore naturally adapted to slavery. It was not necessary, however, to the southern position to argue that blacks were suited to slavery and that whites were not. In fact, as noted earlier, there were strong implications that slavery might not be limited to blacks, but the typical southerner drew back from pushing the logic of slavery to its conclusion, even though the charge that northern workers were also slaves differing only in detail from those in the South should have been a clear indication of the direction of southern thought.

One of those who did not shy away from the slavery argument's logical conclusion was George Fitzhugh, who wrote *Sociology for the South or the Failure of Free Society* (1854) and *Cannibals All or Slaves Without Masters* (1859). It is interesting to note that Fitzhugh followed in the tradition of those who aspired to be "scientific." That tradition included men such as James D. B. DeBow, publisher of *DeBow's Review* in New Orleans, who, like many of the southern militants, was fascinated with the idea of the "Greek democracy" but based much of his argument upon the new science of statistics (for a time he had been a superintendent of the U.S. Census). DeBow was convinced of black inferiority, and was associated for a time at what was then the University of Louisiana with Dr. Josiah C. Nott, a professor of anatomy who coauthored *Types of Mankind* in 1854 with George R. Gliddon. This book purported to give a "scientific" justification for black inferiority and was consistent with Nott's efforts in helping to edit an American translation of *The Moral and Intellectual Diversity of Races* by Count Joseph Arthur de Gobineau, the French racist whose book became one of the major philosophical underpinnings of Nazi Germany's doctrines of "Aryan" superiority. "Aryan," a term without scientific basis, was in fact originated by Gobineau and his followers. Other writers, such as Dr. Samuel A. Cartwright of Louisiana, attempted to document black inferiority with charges that blacks consumed less oxygen than whites.[18]

Modern science, even in its infancy, was already susceptible to abuse. Many southern laymen, and some outside the South as well, accepted the racist assertions as "proved by science." As Harvey Wish has pointed out, although "popular prejudices, North and South, had long assumed the inherent inferiority of Negroes, the new racial science, at a time of growing humanitarianism, lent its prestige to the lore of the illiterate."[19] Fitzhugh accepted the allegations with enthusiasm. He received Gobineau's works with great favor and added his own notions of the superior racial stock of the "Cavaliers," who were the English ancestors of the southerners, as opposed to the fanatical Puritans, who had sired the Yankees. He proudly wrote that "the gentlemen of the South ... have the lofty sentiments and high morals of a master race."[20] Yet Fitzhugh's prime concern was not to prove black inferiority and certainly not to set blacks apart from the human species, as some writers had done under the guise of science. In *Sociology for the South* he explicitly rejected the "types of mankind" doctrine and conceded that all humankind had descended from common parentage. To deny blacks their humanity, he wrote, would only encourage brutality upon the part of masters. Blacks, Fitzhugh believed, should be treated as "weak, ignorant, and dependent brethren," not as "wicked beasts."[21] His major intent, while justifying and preserving the South's system of slavery and retaining its slave "property," was to encourage a Hobbesian control of all in society and to make clear the total dominance of an elite.

Although there were many southern extremists, and among them several, such as George Frederick Holmes, who advocated slavery from the purported viewpoint of science and sociology, Fitzhugh's writings are the most extreme. Along with other southerners he attacked the notion of natural rights as well as contract and consent theories of government, and he joined the southerners in providing the first concerted onslaught against the liberal traditions that had come from such philosophers as John Locke and Thomas Jefferson. The southerners' concern with the analysis of institutions and with human behavior is considerably more modern in tone, regardless of the substance of their thought, than were the abstractions of the Declaration of Independence, which they never hesitated to criticize as unrealistic.

Fitzhugh was consistent with the other southerners in denying Jeffersonian individualism. Whatever rights existed, he contended, society granted; there were none that were natural. Society was the natural state of humanity, and society therefore forms humankind, not humankind society. There was no such thing as equality. He pushed the argument to its outer limits, however, in asserting that government and freedom were incompatible and that the advance of civilization destroys liberty. The trouble with the world, he contended, was that there was too much liberty, and what was needed for true culture was more coercion and the destruction of liberty.

Fitzhugh thundered against abolition as a surrender to socialism and communism, a surrender that would lead to the elimination of private property, the church, and law and to a society that appeared to terrify him, one with free land, free love, free women, and free children.[22] By contrast, southern slavery was less cruel than the "wage slavery" of the North, because the slave's time presumably was his or her own after working hours, and no slave was burdened by financial cares; even old age presented no hardship, because the master would provide. He called the industrial system "moral cannibalism" because it exploited the worker, whereas the master in the South "works nearly as hard for the Negro, as he for the master." His position was based upon the assumption that citizens were the slaves of their governments, workers of their employers, children of their fathers, and wives of their husbands. As is obvious, he, like Calhoun, was concerned with security and duty; rights meant nothing to him, for there were no rights. Grimes has argued that there is much of Hobbes in Fitzhugh,[23] and so there is in his psychology and in his low opinion of human nature. Unlike Hobbes who was an authoritarian liberal, however, Fitzhugh's orientation is thoroughly conservative in that there is total emphasis upon society and none upon the individual. He goes so far as to compare human society with those of ants and bees in their associative nature; he would have welcomed those modern states that aspire to be totalitarian.

Fitzhugh accurately perceived the exploitation practiced in the industrial system of his time. His solution, though, was not to eliminate the evils of industrialism. He believed that slavery was the lot of all humanity everywhere. He accepted the notion of black inferiority, but also argued that all workers were slaves and that that fact should be recognized by frankly forcing every worker, regardless of color or location, into formal slavery. Because he believed that workers outside the South were slaves without masters, he advocated supplying them with owners, saying that it would be more humane. No capitalist would assume any social obligations to his workers as would a master. In attacking rights he explicitly condemned the First Amendment freedoms and the notion of moral standards apart from the state. He said that all societies had been ruled by a powerful few, all would always be, and that it is better that they be so ruled. One should note the paradox here that so frequently exists in the writings of those who deny the notion of objective moral standards: Fitzhugh, and many who followed him as "realists" adopting a presumably scientific approach, argued at great length that certain courses were "proper" and that others were not. Although such writers admit to no moral standards, their works are saturated with value judgments and moral pronouncements.

The writings of the southern proslavery group as a whole are the most vigorous attacks upon the major traditions of American political thought that have yet surfaced in America, and Fitzhugh's was the most open. He rejected not only the American liberal notions of individualism but even the Aristotelian conception of society as an organic whole within which there was individual volition. His works probably had more impact than even he would have expected, because many outside the South, including Lincoln and abolitionists Charles Sumner and William Lloyd Garrison, interpreted his writings as representative and quoted him extensively. During the slavery debates in Congress during the 1850s, antislavery spokesmen referred more often to Fitzhugh than to any other proslavery propagandist except for Calhoun, although they did not always mention him by name. In 1856, Frémont-for-President clubs distributed leaflets with one of Fitzhugh's most inflammatory statements, "Slavery is the natural and normal condition of the laboring man, whether white or black."[24]

There was very little dissent from the views of Fitzhugh and Calhoun within the South regarding slavery. One southerner, however, Hinton Rowan Helper, who was no friend to blacks or to equality, produced a book, *The Impending Crisis of the South*, that argued for total abolition.[25] Helper bitterly attacked slaveholders and used the southerners' own style of argument—including statistics, biblical citations, philosophical principles, and historical precedent—to condemn the system of slavery, not as a moral evil but as destructive to the South. His North Carolina background and his obvious concern for the South did not prevent the South from banning his book. Essentially he urged small, independent white farmers to reject the leadership of the large slaveholders, gain control of southern governments, and tax slavery out of existence, using the proceeds to colonize blacks elsewhere.

The Position of Moderates

On the issue of slavery the position classed as "moderate" encompassed a number of diverse arguments. Some views advanced as moderate were in the long run as destructive of the rights of man as were the overt attacks of the southerners. One such view was the popular sovereignty argument of Stephen A. Douglas, who held that slavery might or might not expand into the territories, depending upon the vote of the people of the territories. As Lincoln clearly and forcefully pointed out, such an attempt at compromise, at being reasonable, was actually a surrender of basic moral principle. Douglas did not overtly attack the Declaration. Nevertheless, he agreed with Chief Justice Taney that the reference to all men being treated equally pertained only to white men, and this was implicitly as subversive of the spirit of the Declaration as was the explicit rejection of the southerners. Douglas's position in this case was compatible with democracy but not with the rights of man, illustrating that the two not only are not identical but at times may even come into conflict. As Lincoln said in his speech of June 26, 1857, at Springfield during the Lincoln-Douglas debates, the position of blacks in the United States had worsened considerably, and, though at one time the "Declaration of Independence was held sacred by all, and thought to include all . . . now, to aid in making the bondage of the negro universal and eternal, it is assailed, and sneered at, and construed, and hawked at, and torn, till, if its framers could rise from their graves, they could not at all recognize it."[26] Lincoln believed that the authors of the Declaration intended to include all men as equal and in a very definite sense:

> They did not intend to declare all men equal *in all* respects. They did not mean to say all were equal in color, size, intellect, moral developments, or social capacity. They defined . . . in what respects they did consider all men created equal—equal in "certain inalienable rights, among which are life, liberty, and the pursuit of happiness." They did not mean to assert the obvious untruth, that all were then actually enjoying that equality, nor yet, that they were about to confer it immediately upon them. In fact they had no power to confer such a boon. They meant simply to declare the *right*, so that the *enforcement* of it might follow as fast as circumstances should permit.[27]

Lincoln's social conservatism, or perhaps his political acumen, is illustrated as the speech proceeded by his agreement with Douglas that racial intermarriage is wrong. He argued, as he had many times before, for colonization. In the absence of colonization, however, he said that, contrary to the fears that Douglas expressed, free blacks would be less likely to intermarry than slave women were to bear the children of their white masters. "Could we have had our way," he said, "the chances of these black girls, ever mixing their blood with that of white people, would have been diminished at least to the extent that it could not have been without their consent."[28] However much his racial prejudices may have prevented Lincoln from departing from the insensitivity of his white countrymen, his argument is reflective of his understanding of the rights of women and is consistent with his published statement to the editor of the *Sangamo Journal* as early as 1836 that he favored granting women the vote, a right that it took nearly another century for them to achieve.[29] Moreover, there is some ground in his later writings for believing that Lincoln may even have modified some of his racial prejudice in his later years as a result of the valor of black troops in fighting for the Union.

Lincoln's attitude toward government is indicated in brief fragments in which he wrote that government results both from the injustices among men and from the greater potential for accomplishment by collective action. He believed that if all were just, government would still be necessary, although less so. It was here that he wrote the often-quoted statement, "the legitimate object of government is 'to do for the people what needs to be done,' but which they can not, by individual effort, do at all, or do so well, for themselves."[30] Similarly, his fragments on slavery point out that any argument for slavery could result in an argument for the enslavement of a master; if color is the criterion, then any person could be enslaved by any other with a lighter skin; if it is ability, then any more able person could enslave any who was less able.[31] Such themes are frequent in his writings and speeches.

Lincoln had both moral sentiments against slavery and prejudice against blacks, but his prejudice did not extend to the denial of their humanity. His acceptance of natural rights led him to resist the expansion of slavery with all his power. His regard for the Union, his interpretation of the Constitution, and his awareness of political realities led him to assert constantly that he would not, and could not, interfere with slavery in the southern states. Only after the Civil War was in advanced stages, after the Union was broken and public sentiment would accept it, did he issue the Emancipation Proclamation, and even then it freed slaves only in areas in rebellion against the United States. Rarely if ever has any figure in American political history so combined the contradictory qualities of moral fervor and political prudence.

Lincoln has become a symbol not only for America, but for the world. The source of this is less his appeal both to workers and intellectuals than his awareness of the moral dimensions to politics, as uncomfortable as that may make many of us who live in today's scientific culture. His reputation probably has been strengthened paradoxically by his willingness to submerge his own moral sensitivity for practical advantage; therein lies his tragic quality that is the source of such fascination today. Hofstadter's comment that "Lincoln's utter lack of personal malice during these [presidential] years, his humane detachment, his tragic sense of life, have no parallel in political history"[32] sounds as if he must have been overstating the case; he was not.

The Abolitionist Position

The most controversial of the participants to the debate over slavery were the abolitionists. Abrasive they were, and usually unwilling to compromise, but they clearly were the group most strongly devoted to the principles of the Declaration of Independence and its philosophy built upon the rights of man. It seems strange that even today when slavery appears to be universally condemned there remain those who argue that the abolitionists were tragic meddlers who brought about a war solely as a result of their fanaticism. It was their general unwillingness to compromise that has brought them the label of fanatic, but it should be remembered that the principle upon which they refused to bend was that slavery is a moral evil. If there are any principles that today would command complete acceptance, this must be one of them.

As a rule the abolitionists did not aspire to be political philoso-phers, and those who attempted systematic statements of their positions generally fell far short of the sophistication achieved by some of the proslavery adherents, notably Calhoun; nor did they attain the cogency of Lincoln's thought. They were activists, seeking to right a wrong and act upon a moral principle. Their responsibility for the Civil War is open to debate and should be of concern primarily to historians. Their importance to political thought comes from their position as one of the few groups resisting the trend away from a consideration of moral questions and toward a "realistic" approach with foundation in science, the latter approach, as often as not, having misused even the scientific knowledge then available. In this respect the abolitionists are related to the Transcendentalists, and in fact there were overlaps between the two groups.

Prominent in all discussions of the abolitionists is the name of William Lloyd Garrison, the subject of the South's most extreme wrath. He was as roundly condemned outside the South as within it and became a figurehead for the abuse that was everywhere directed at the abolitionists until shortly before the Civil War. V. L. Parring-ton has said that "not since the days of Tom Paine had such unmeasured vituperation been poured out on the head of an Ameri-can."[33] The masthead of his paper, *The Liberator*, read: "Our Country is the World—Our Countrymen are Mankind." It began publication on New Year's Day, 1831, and continued against all odds until the slaves had been freed. Garrison lived up to his first editorial, in which he wrote that he would be as harsh as truth and as uncompromising as justice. He said that he did not wish to speak, think, or write on the subject of slavery with moderation, that he would not retract a single inch, and, he wrote in capital letters, "I WILL BE HEARD."

Garrison accepted pacifism and what has been called "nonresis-tance." The term is misleading. Garrison and his followers strongly resisted slavery, and *The Liberator*'s existence is proof of such resis-tance. They rejected violent resistance, however, as fully as they rejected compromise. Garrison's refusal to compromise led him to reject the Constitution as a proslavery document and therefore also to reject the government based upon it. In 1842 he urged the disbandment of the nation, refusing to accept a state that included slavery. He characterized the Constitution as a "Covenant with Death—An Agreement with Hell," the inflammatory phrase that came to be *The Liberator's* new masthead. Being predisposed to reject the government, he came to reject all government and to adopt the position of John Humphrey Noyes and his Perfectionists that approached anarchism.³⁴ Although there were those, such as the reformer Wendell Phillips, who supported Garrison's efforts to bring about secession from the Union, his zeal matched that of any southern fire-eater and caused a break with many other abolitionists, such as Frederick Douglass, James Birney, and Gerrit Smith, who argued that continued union was the only hope for abolition and that a southern slave nation would simply insure the perpetuation of slavery.

Garrison was concerned more with religion than with politics. Like Roger Williams, however, his religious orientation brought him into the political arena. At its best he considered government to be a punishment from God. He believed that if human beings would cease to be sinful, society would be blessed with freedom from all political restraints. Political institutions, patriotism, and even majority rule he considered to be merely devices to obscure moral issues. He was extreme, but he goaded the nation at its weakest point, its conscience.

One of his greatest antagonists among the abolitionists, one who opposed his secessionist position, was Frederick Douglass. Douglass had been born a slave and escaped in 1838 when he was about twenty-one. He spoke for some years as an agent of the Massachusetts Anti-Slavery Society and became well known for his polished oratorical talents. In 1845 he published his autobiography, *Narrative of the Life of Frederick Douglass, an American Slave, Written by Himself*. It was subsequently revised and published in different editions with different titles. Against Garrison's advice, Douglass published his own newspaper, *The North Star*, later renamed *Frederick Douglass' Paper*.

Douglass argued that the Constitution was not proslavery and that, properly interpreted, it could become a bulwark for human freedom and the rights of man. He received some support in this position even from such radicals as the anarchist Lysander Spooner, whose best-known work is a lengthy book titled *The Unconstitutionality of Slavery* (1845). Spooner's attempt was to prove not only that the Constitution was not proslavery but that it in fact made slavery unconstitutional, and his arguments were detailed and ingenious.

Essentially, the difference between Douglass and Garrison is that Garrison rejected, and Douglass favored, political solutions to political questions.

Because he had lived under slavery, Douglass bowed to no one in his condemnation of the institution. He had served harsh masters and kindly ones, and had seen even the most kindly of persons become harsh under the corrupting influences of absolute power, which he constantly stressed. John Brown confided his Harper's Ferry plans to Douglass, whose belief in political solutions led him to attempt to dissuade Brown.[35] Ultimately, he came to support Lincoln, whose emancipation efforts were painfully slow to most of the abolitionists. He was under no illusions about Lincoln, calling him not "our man or our model. In his interests, in his associations, in his habits of thought, and in his prejudices, he was a white man."[36] Nevertheless, Douglass lauded Lincoln and his efforts for blacks and concluded even that Lincoln's prejudices worked to their advantage. "Had he put the abolition of slavery before the salvation of the Union," he said, "he would have inevitably driven from him a powerful class of the American people and rendered resistance to rebellion impossible." Although Lincoln seemed "tardy, cold, and indifferent" when viewed from the vantage of genuine abolition, when measured "by the sentiment of his country, a sentiment he was bound as a statesman to consult, he was swift, zealous, radical, and determined." Douglass summed Lincoln up with the statement that though he shared the prejudices of his white countrymen, "in his heart of hearts he loathed and hated slavery."[37]

Garrison and Douglass are representative of the two schools of abolitionist thought. As is obvious, the one favored the destruction at least of the government that existed, whereas the other worked for solutions within the existing framework. The one, therefore, quite legitimately could claim the title "radical," while the other could not. Because America tends to be overly sensitive to political labels, however, the term "radical" carries with it great force. All the abolitionists have been lumped together, and all have been termed radicals. The tendency to apply the term indiscriminately has greatly damaged their reputations and probably has damaged the course of black rights in this nation down to the present. It unfortunately is too often true that the choice of a political label can strongly influence the direction of political developments.

Shortly after the Civil War black Americans were left to their own devices, with the southern states being permitted to institute patterns of segregation that were clearly in gross violation of the intent of the framers of the Fourteenth Amendment. The usual explanation for this is that the northern liberals were cynics who cared nothing for their principles. A better explanation is that the situation resulted both from political labeling and from deficiencies of political philosophy. The Radical Republicans, who had attempted to insure rights for the newly freed slaves, before long were rejected partly because they were called "radical." Their program included the Fourteenth and Fifteenth Amendments and civil rights legislation, but these were soon rendered ineffective as protections to black rights by indifference and hostile court interpretations. More important is the theoretical issue. Nineteenth-century liberals defined freedom as the absence of institutional restraint. When the slaves were freed, the liberals thought they had achieved freedom for blacks, as they understood freedom at the time. In the twentieth century freedom has come to take on a different meaning, as requiring positive conditions within which to exercise freedom, if it is to be meaningful; the mere absence of institutional restraint no longer constitutes the liberal notion of freedom.

The North, which left the black to be resubmerged if not reenslaved, can justly be condemned. If interpreted correctly, however, it can be seen that the fault was not ill-will nor lack of conviction. The fault was a theoretical one. It would be difficult to demonstrate more clearly that political philosophy does indeed affect political action.

NOTES

1. Quoted in John P. Roche, ed., *American Political Thought From Jefferson to Progressivism* (New York: Harper Torchbooks, 1967), p. 144.

2. *Free Government in the Making*, 3rd ed. (New York: Oxford University Press, 1965), p. 503.

3. Arthur Zilversmit, *The First Emancipation: The Abolition of Slavery in the North* (Chicago: University of Chicago Press, 1967), pp. 113–115.

4. For the definitive study of abolition outside the South, see Zilversmit, ibid.

5. *Radicalism in America* (New York: Thomas Y. Crowell, 1969), p. 112; see all of chapter 7 for a good discussion of abolitionism.

6. Ibid., p. 115.

7. *American Political Thought*, p. 148.

8. See Alan Nevins, *The Emergence of Lincoln*, vol. 2 (New York: Scribner's, 1950), pp. 464–468.

9. See "The Causes of the American Civil War: A Note on Historical Sentimentalism," *Partisan Review* 16 (1949), 968–981.

10. *The American Political Tradition* (New York: Vintage, 1958), chap. 4.

11. *American Political Thought* (New York: Holt, Rinehart and Winston, 1960), p. 272.

12. Ibid., p. 276.

13. See "The Constitution, Slavery, and the Territories," in Roche, *American Political Thought*, p. 94.

14. The major tenet of the pluralists is that American politics is characterized by a process of compromise among a multitude of competing power centers as opposed to being dominated by a single sovereign power; democratic theory is thus converted into a theory of interest groups. There is considerable variation among pluralist theorists, but among the best and most representative works is Robert A. Dahl's *Pluralist Democracy in the United States: Conflict and Consent* (Chicago: Rand McNally, 1967).

15. *American Political Tradition*, chap. 4.

16. Ibid., pp. 90–91; for an interpretation at variance with the one presented here, see Ralph Lerner, "Calhoun's New Science of Politics," *American Political Science Review* 57 (December 1963), 918–932.

17. Reprinted in E. N. Elliot, ed., *Cotton Is King and Pro-Slavery Arguments* (Augusta, Ga.: Pritchard, Abbott, and Loomis, 1860), pp. 549–571.

18. See his arguments in Harvey Wish, *Society and Thought in Early America* (New York: Longmans, Green, 1950), pp. 514–518.

19. Ibid., p. 518.

20. Quoted in ibid.; the "Cavaliers" were the adherents of Charles I in England, as opposed to the Puritans, who were termed "roundheads."

21. See *Sociology for the South* (Richmond, Va.: A. Morris, 1854), pp. 92–95.

22. See *Cannibals All* (Richmond, Va.: A. Morris, 1857), p. 332.

23. *American Political Thought*, p. 255.

24. Cited in Wish, *Society and Thought*, pp. 516–517. John C. Frémont, known for his efforts in securing California in the Mexican War, was the Whig candidate for President in 1856.

25. (New York: A. B. Bendick, 1857).

26. *The Collected Works of Abraham Lincoln*, vol. 2, Roy P. Basler, ed. (New Brunswick, N.J.: Rutgers University Press, 1953), p. 404.

27. Ibid., pp. 405–406.

28. Ibid., pp. 407–409.

29. Ibid., vol. 1, p. 48.

30. Ibid., vol. 2, pp. 220–221.

31. Ibid., pp. 222–223.

32. *American Political Tradition*, p. 134; however, Hofstadter's interpretation of Lincoln as an opportunist is challenged by Harry V. Jaffa in his excellent essay "Abraham Lincoln," in Morton J. Frisch and Richard H. Stevens, *American Political Thought* (New York: Scribner's 1971), pp. 125–143.

33. *Main Currents in American Thought*, vol. 2 (New York: Harcourt Brace Jovanovich, 1954), p. 349.

34. Noyes and his followers in the Oneida community believed that it was possible to achieve perfection in this life, and that most existing institutions were corrupting influences.

35. See George Ducas, ed., *Great Documents in Black History* (New York: Praeger, 1970), pp. 125–126.

36. "Oration in Memory of Abraham Lincoln," in Herbert Storing, ed., *What Country Have I?: Political Writings by Black Americans* (New York: St. Martin's Press, 1970), pp. 46–56.

37. Ibid., pp. 52–53.

ADDITIONAL READINGS

Coit, Margaret L. *John C. Calhoun, American Portrait.* Boston: Houghton Mifflin, 1950.

Current, Richard N. "John C. Calhoun Philosopher of Reaction." *Antioch Review* III (Summer 1943).

———, ed. *The Political Thought of Abraham Lincoln.* Indianapolis: Bobbs-Merrill, 1967.

Drucker, Peter F. "A Key to American Politics: Calhoun's Pluralism." *Review of Politics* X (October 1948).

Eaton, Clement. *Freedom of Thought in the Old South.* Durham, N.C.: Duke University Press, 1940.

Hartz, Louis. "The Reactionary Enlightenment: Southern Political Thought Before the Civil War." *Western Political Quarterly* V (March 1952).

Heckscher, Gunnar. "Calhoun's Idea of 'Concurrent Majority' and the Constitutional Theory of Hegel." *American Political Science Review* XXXIII (August 1939).

Hofstadter, Richard. "Wendell Phillips: The Patrician as Agitator." In *The American Political Tradition.* New York: Vintage, 1958, chap. 6.

Irish, Marian D. "Recent Political Thought in the South." *American Political Science Review* XLVI (March 1952).

Jaffa, Harry V. *Crisis of the House Divided: An Interpretation of the Issues in the Lincoln-Douglas Debates.* Garden City, N.Y.: Doubleday, 1959.

Jenkins, William S. *Pro-Slavery Thought in the Old South.* Chapel Hill: University of North Carolina, 1935.

Nye, Russel B. *Fettered Freedom: Civil Liberties and the Slavery Controversy, 1830–1860.* East Lansing: Michigan State University Press, 1949.

Spain, August A. *The Political Theory of John C. Calhoun.* New York: Bookman, 1951.

Stampp, Kenneth. *The Causes of the Civil War.* Englewood Cliffs, N.J.: Prentice-Hall, 1959.

ten Broek, Jacobus. *The Anti-Slavery Origins of the Fourteenth Amendment.* Berkeley: University of California Press, 1951.

Williams, T. Harry. "Abraham Lincoln: Principles and Pragmatism in Politics." *Mississippi Valley Historical Review* XLI (June 1953).

Wiltse, Charles M. *John C. Calhoun.* 3 vols. Indianapolis: Bobbs-Merrill, 1944–1951.

Wish, Harvey, ed. *Ante-Bellum.* New York: Capricorn, 1960 (includes Helper's *Impending Crisis*, Fitzhugh's *Sociology for the South* and *Cannibals All*, etc.).

Woodward, C. Vann. "John Brown's Private War." In *The Burden of Southern History.* New York: Vintage, 1960, chap. 3.

Wright, Benjamin F. *American Interpretations of Natural Law.* Cambridge, Mass.: Harvard University Press, 1931.

10

Industrialism: The Age of Individualism

The years following the Civil War were characterized by a tremendous strengthening of nationalism, the growth of urbanism with its rush from rural areas to the cities, and the transformation of America into an industrial state dominated by a relatively new form of social and economic organization, the corporation. Industrialism created private power undreamed of by the Founding Fathers, and the corporation permitted concentrations of the new power to an extent that often rivaled, and sometimes appeared to exceed, that of government itself. Corporate industrialism brought with it material advantages never before equaled, but also social, economic, and political difficulties with which the Constitution had not been designed to deal.

In truth the Civil War marked a turning point not only in American history but in American thought. As the first modern war engaged in by Americans, it signaled the increased importance of technology and symbolized the dwindling of the old order. Although the arguments of the southerners had been discredited, their mode of thought reflected the years to come rather than America's past. It might be an exaggeration to say that the new industrialism caused a turning away from the consideration of ethical absolutes that had been predominant in the early years and an acceptance instead of the new and glamorous principles of science, but surely the rapid rise of industrialism and the popular fascination with and acceptance of scientific developments were at least reflections of the ferment taking place within American culture. The same factors that predisposed Americans to welcome industrialism, with as a rule only a vague uneasiness that they seemed to associate less with industrialism than with political corruption or foreign influences, led them also to a preoccupation with science. Science had become a major influence upon American thought, including American political thought, with the result that the society as a whole moved, perhaps unconsciously, to become and to remain largely a scientific culture. It is no exaggeration, in fact, to say that since the Civil War science, or what passed for science at the moment, has occupied much the same position in American thought that religion had occupied earlier. In the last quarter of the nineteenth century, the search began in earnest for that science of humankind that would reveal laws of behavior and permit perfect prediction and control. The laws have not been revealed, but scientific prediction has become highly sophisticated, and the search continues today.

Social Darwinism and Its Advocates

Any society must have justifications for its basic institutions. In the late nineteenth century it was clear to all that the disparity between the rich and the poor in America was growing rapidly. A society that is essentially religious will tend to justify its institutions by religion, as the Puritans did. Similarly, a scientific society tends to justify its institutions by science. The rise of the industrial state coincided roughly with the publication of a scientific theory that Americans seized upon to prove the correctness of the new institutions, however much those institutions were working to the disadvantage of individual citizens (as they did before meliorative measures softened some of the harshness of their impact). The theory was biological evolution, and the book was Charles Darwin's *Origin of Species*, published in 1859. Darwin's American impact, however, was indirect, and his writings certainly never gave any indication that he would have anticipated the form that his ideas would take in American thought.

An English sociologist, Herbert Spencer, had already coined the phrase "survival of the fittest" before Darwin wrote. Spencer had produced his first book, *Social Statics*, in 1850, and believed that Darwin's biological theories supported his own views of social evolution. According to Alan Grimes, Spencer had an astonishing influence on American thought: "No visiting philosopher before or since has received such a reception as was accorded Spencer in his triumphant visit to America in 1882. The only plausible explanation seems to be that his writings told many Americans the very sort of thing which they wished to hear."[1] Spencer wrote prolifically, and succeeded in substituting his own notion of "survival of the fittest" for Darwin's "natural selection," while popularizing Darwin's theories of biological evolution as applicable to the development of human societies and the rise and fall of individual members of those societies.

Spencer believed that natural laws predestined the human race to progressive improvement. He admitted that the process he outlined, that of struggle between all persons, was bitter and cruel, but he contended that in the long run it was for the best. Spencer spoke of liberalism and defined it in terms of the principle of laissez faire. Because action by the state would interfere with the struggle that was the natural order, he would have confined the function of the state to an absolute minimum. Any kind of state action, whether public health law, relief to the poor, or public education, was in his view "illiberal" and could only harm society by perpetuating the unfit. Those who were fit would survive, regardless; those who were not, would, and moreover *should*, perish.[2]

Spencer's thought was widely accepted and became known as Social Darwinism. American political rhetoric, despite the great change in basic principle, changed little. Whereas the Founding Fathers had meant by equality that all human beings were equal in their humanity and deserved to be treated with equal dignity and to be equal before the law, the Social Darwinists spoke of equality only as the equal right of each to compete with and best those of inferior ability, while being bested by anyone superior. The founders thought of natural law as guaranteeing human rights; the Social Darwinists thought of natural law as scientific law whose essence was combat. Therefore, though the Social Darwinists used words very familiar to Americans, such as "equality," "natural law," and many others, their meanings were totally different from those to which Americans had become accustomed; nevertheless, the words continued to sound familiar. This demonstrates the value of the study of political language and illustrates the degree to which changes in language usage, whether deliberate or unconscious, may influence politics. Certainly Social Darwinism was more effective on the American scene than it would have been had the Social Darwinists discarded the customary American mode of expression for one that was alien to American ears.

The most prominent Spencerian in the United States was Yale sociologist William Graham Sumner. Sumner had been educated as a clergyman, and this apparently was a major reason for his appointment as professor in 1872. President Noah Porter of Yale had been concerned with the growing loss of religious faith in American society and no doubt believed it safe to entrust the chair in the new discipline of political economy to one with Sumner's background. He was aghast when Sumner not only rejected his belief in religion, but taught the works of "the archinfidel, Herbert Spencer." Porter even ordered Sumner to cease exposing his students to such subversive influences, but Sumner resisted despite a protracted effort by the university to silence him.[3]

Sumner was one of the earliest American social scientists. He purported to be a pure scientist, applying the principles of science to the study of humankind without emotion, prejudice, or personal value. He distinguished between scientific ideals and those of ethics, justice, liberty, or others that he considered mere dogmatism. Sumner's classic *Folkways*, written in 1906, is in fact still often studied in classes in sociology. Sumner represented the American academic beginnings of the position that attempts rigidly to distinguish between fact and value in the social sciences; his aim was to achieve a value-free social science. Such an approach dates from the theories of the French sociologist August Comte, whose theory has been given the name "positivism." The force of such an idea is well documented by the fact that many political scientists as late as the 1960s came only reluctantly to the conclusion that a value-free social science is impossible to achieve, still disagreeing with those of their colleagues who contended that it would be undesirable were it possible. Sumner unwittingly demonstrated the futility of the search. His writings, despite his honest intent and his earnest efforts, reeked with value judgments, as did Spencer's; he accepted the judgments not as values, however, but as scientific truths.

Sumner was avidly devoted to the principle of laissez faire and extraordinarily limited government. Nor was he a friend to private efforts to relieve social ills. Those who should survive would do so on their own, and those who could not, would not. "Root hog or die" was his principle. In *What Social Classes Owe to Each Other*, written in 1883, he concluded that they owed precisely nothing. His *bête noire* was socialism or any effort even within a capitalist system on behalf of those he considered to be weak and therefore undeserving.

Sumner was not merely a follower of Spencer and did not share Spencer's optimistic view of the inevitability of human progress. His purpose seemed more simply to be to acquaint his hearers with the inescapable nature of strife and struggle and to convince them that any effort to relieve this "natural" order would only make things worse. Like most American followers of Spencer, though calling himself liberal, Sumner was intensely conservative, and his adaptation of biological theory to conservative social and political thought was widely read. His synthesis was less grand than Spencer's, but, according to Richard Hofstadter, "bolder in its stark and candid pessimism."[4] He fitted well the conservatism of the age, when the predominant feeling among Americans appeared to be that there had been more than enough political agitation before the Civil War and that it was important merely to support and sustain the status quo.

As a whole, Social Darwinism, with its attacks upon reform and its denial that social matters were susceptible to improvement as a result of conscious human action, was one of the strongest conservative movements in the history of American thought and certainly overshadowed all others for a considerable period of time. It was greatly different, however, from more conventional conservative thought. Its strongest appeal was to secular, not religious, minds, and its deemphasis of the state was so complete as to border upon anarchism, thus dispensing with the traditional reverence for the state and for central authority that was the hallmark of most conservative thought. Moreover, Social Darwinism was rationalist and rejected the appeals to emotion and symbol that are so characteristic of most conservative systems. It shared with conservatism in general a revulsion at attempts to change socioeconomic and political conditions and a rejection of notions of equalitarianism and natural rights. But in their attitudes toward religion, rationalism, and the traditions of the past they differed profoundly. Sumner and the Social Darwinists were intensely individualistic, as traditional conservatives were not, and they seem uniquely reflective of the social conditions of the American scene in the late nineteenth century, rather than displaying the timeless appeal of conservatism. Few schools of thought illustrate more clearly the difficulties in assigning precision to the terms "liberal" and "conservative" in the American setting. The American right, with its devotion to property and suspicion of the people, has had many representatives who were known for innovation and change, figures such as Alexander Hamilton, Andrew Carnegie, and John D. Rockefeller. Many of the left, on the other hand, have sought to restore what they considered to have been a previously more democratic order. Only with Franklin Roosevelt and the New Deal did there come to be a fairly clear-cut identification of the American liberal with innovation in social and economic matters.

Interestingly, although Social Darwinism was largely secular in nature, like communism, it sometimes took on a different character for its followers. Many contend that the secular philosophy of communism has produced in practice a religion of the state. Similarly, as Hofstadter noted, the "social Darwinism of the hard-bitten sort represented by men like Sumner, expressed a kind of secular piety that commands our attention." It presents a sort of "naturalistic Calvinism" that holds the relation between man and nature to be much the same as that between man and God in the Calvinist system.[5] There is additional irony in the fact that the conservative system Sumner and his followers advocated brought with it some of the most radical and profound changes in the history of social and economic development.

It would be incorrect merely to dismiss Sumner as an apologist for an aristocracy of wealth. In fact, although his doctrines tended to be warmly received by the "captains of industry," he was sufficiently independent that he received attacks from those quarters as well as from those favoring social action. Upon the few occasions when his conclusions differed from the conventional wisdom, he stood his ground. He favored free trade, or removal of tariffs, as fully as free enterprise on the domestic scene, and he strongly condemned American imperialism at the turn of the century. He criticized the wealthy as favoring protectionism and corruption and praised those portions of Jeffersonian democracy that encouraged weak and decentralized government, despite his disdain for democracy in general. He was, and he considered himself to be, a spokesman for American middle-class values, but they were values carried to extremes. Protection of property to him was the most important principle, and the only liberty that he considered to be meaningful was the liberty that property provided and the liberty to pursue acquisition. Sumner's Social Darwinist essays, with titles such as "The Absurd Effort to Make the World Over," appear today to be dated and are of interest primarily to historians and students of social and political thought. As noted above, however, his later sociological works have survived.

Sumner's thoroughgoing pessimism worsened throughout his life. Ultimately, he had lost all hope for America, saying that he had lived through the best period and that the nation had in store for it only war and social calamities. He said that he was glad that he did not have to live through them.[6]

The influence of men like Sumner and Spencer should not be underestimated. The period following the Civil War saw no outstanding thinkers in public office who produced lasting contributions to American political thought, but academicians and journalists did take up the themes of Social Darwinism and apply them to politics. Although it is difficult to determine the degree to which the popular mind was affected, it seems that the new intellectual currents, the new orientations in politics, science, and social considerations, did attract public attention. Hofstadter remarked that Spencer's writings were widely known by those who were partly educated or self-educated and by thousands in small towns who were drifting or pulling away from religious orthodoxy; this is suggested, he said, by the casual references of many who later achieved prominence to the impact that Spencer had upon them when they were young. He cites the economist John R. Commons as saying that every one of his father's cronies had been a follower of Herbert Spencer and that they all talked politics and science. During that time in eastern Indiana, Commons said, everyone had a background similar to his, and he had been "brought up on Hoosierism, Republicanism, Presbyterianism, and Spencerism."[7]

Part of the reason for this is that Social Darwinism was simply verifying the prejudices of the middle class; moreover, the academicians and journalists who were foremost among the Social Darwinists were able publicizers.[8] Among those who called themselves liberals were, in addition to Sumner, many contributors to *The Nation*, including its editor, E. L. Godkin. Godkin had come to the United States from England, where he had been strongly influenced by the liberal thought of the utilitarians, such as John Stuart Mill and Jeremy Bentham, who argued that usefulness determines what is good and that actions in general may be judged good if they lead ultimately to pleasure rather than to pain. Politically the utilitarian doctrine translated into the notion that governments should pursue policies that produce the greatest good for the greatest number. In America Godkin became fully convinced by the arguments of the Social Darwinists. The character of the American followers of the English utilitarians became vastly more conservative than that of their models. *The Nation*, for example, first endorsed suffrage for the newly freed blacks, then reversed itself because of fears that propertyless masses would corrupt the political process. It followed the same course with regard to rights for women. Its writers saw many of the ills of society but concluded that they resulted from excesses of democracy. It was an age of get and grab, and one that produced such "robber barons" as Jim Fiske and Jay Gould, noted for their shady and even outrageous financial manipulations. Politically, the late nineteenth century was a distressing period. Corruption prevailed throughout the country, not just in the Reconstruction governments in the South. It was probably the time of the lowest political morality in American history. Mark Twain caught the spirit of the time when he called it the "Gilded Age," a name that symbolizes the surface glitter of the period hiding a baser foundation.

True to its skepticism regarding democracy, when *The Nation* advocated reform, it was not intended to provide more popular control. It favored split tickets and independent voting in order to enable the enlightened elite, which it deemed to be much in the minority, to exercise a balance of power, and it worked for the passage in 1883 of the Pendleton Act establishing the civil service system that it hoped would insure merit in government employment. Godkin favored popular election of senators, not because he favored extending democracy but because it would change a system that was demonstrably corrupt. Those in *The Nation*'s camp as a whole followed Sumner's example in opposing socioeconomic reform and expected the courts to be a bulwark of the status quo. The Supreme Court did not disappoint them, especially in the numerous decisions written by Justice Stephen Field. The doctrine of laissez faire during the chaotic growth of American industrialism could not have been better calculated to benefit the powerful at the expense of the whole.

Wealth and Social Darwinism

In an age in which individual fortunes were developing to an extent hardly dreamed of before, there were many apologists for unlimited accumulation. The doctrines of Sumner and others provided a "scientific" basis, but many felt the need for some ethical support. Those attempting to provide such support developed what came to be called the "Gospel of Wealth." The first efforts were to find religious justifications, and such persons as Mark Hopkins, president of Williams College, went to considerable effort in his *The Law of Love and Love as Law*, published in 1868; he contended that acquisition of property is required by love because property is a means of benefiting others. He cautioned against a selfish accumulation of property, which was not to be encouraged, although even that would be better than indolence or wastefulness. Hopkins favored the Social Darwinists' rugged individualism, and he accepted the sanctity of private property, but he also, contrary to such hard-nosed Social Darwinists as Sumner, preached the duty of stewardship, recognizing as many did not some form of social responsibility.[9]

On a vastly cruder level were the "Acres of Diamonds" speeches by Russell H. Conwell, a Baptist minister and the founder and first president of Temple University. Conwell gave the same speech more than 6,000 times and spread his gospel to countless numbers of eager listeners, thereby illustrating the thirst of the middle class for such justifications. Religion demanded that one get rich, he said; it was not a privilege, but a duty. The foundation for the speech was a tale of a man who sold his land to seek riches, only to wander unfulfilled for a lifetime of disappointment and finally to learn that the world's richest diamond mine had been discovered on what had been his own land. Riches, therefore, said Conwell, are in one's own backyard. Even the poorest person in the United States, he urged, could get rich both quickly and honestly. Money was the key to a successful Christian life, because it permitted one to assist in spreading the gospel—the Christian gospel, that is. He dismissed the role of politics and charged that only the small-minded person holds office in a democracy; his support was totally for laissez faire. He urged that it was a Christian and godly duty to attain riches, that ninety-eight out of a hundred rich men in America were honest, and in fact that honesty was the reason for their being rich! Similarly, he said, there was not a poor person in the United States who was not poor because of his or her own shortcomings, or those of someone else. It was, he taught, a sin to be poor, and it was therefore a sin to sympathize with or to help a person whom God had made poor as a punishment.[10]

Despite the cruel unreality of such assertions, they were inordinately popular. It is tempting to describe them as reflecting, briefly, the errors of an unsettled period, but Conwell is read even today in some quarters. There are popular courses in leadership training that adopt arguments similar to those in "Acres of Diamonds," and at least one college president as late as the early 1970s kept a copy on his nightstand. It would be a mistake to dismiss the effect of such arguments out of hand even today.

The unmitigated "robber barons," of course, followed Sumner in disclaiming all social responsibility. But even among the "captains of industry" there were those who accepted some responsibility to the public and sought to justify their actions. The most articulate spokesman for this point of view was steel tycoon Andrew Carnegie. In 1889, after he had become one of the wealthiest persons in American history, Carnegie published an article titled "Wealth" in the *North American Review*.[11] The *Review*'s editor wrote that Carnegie's article was the finest ever published in that journal.[12]

Carnegie admitted that the new industrial order had brought with it some disadvantages. The growth of large concentrations of economic power had engendered class conflict, there were sharper class distinctions than before, and the rise of the large employer had eliminated the previous face-to-face contact between employer and employee. Nevertheless, the advantages outweighed the disadvantages. Even the poor had become able, he believed, to purchase things that the rich themselves had been unable to afford before. Such a result followed from the four underpinnings of modern capitalism: individualism, private property, the "Law of Accumulation and Wealth," and the "Law of Competition." Unrestrained selfishness, Carnegie was quick to admit, was an evil and should not be a part of the capitalistic system. People should be free to accumulate the utmost that their talents allow, but wealth brought with it responsibility. Carnegie condemned the hoarding of family wealth from one generation to another as incompatible with republican institutions and unhealthy for children who should work for their own fortunes, not inherit them. He approved confiscatory inheritance taxes and considered them to be compatible with a Darwinian struggle for existence, a struggle that he contended would produce in the long run the strongest persons and the best society. His answer to the great inequality of wealth was that the wealthy should treat their riches as a trust to be used for the good of society. In his book *The Gospel of Wealth*, written in 1900, he said that men of wealth had the duty to live simply and unostentatiously, to provide moderately for those who were dependent upon them, and to use the surplus for worthy and unselfish purposes.[13] He lived up to his principles by actions, such as the construction of public libraries, the endowment of numerous philanthropic foundations, the establishment of educational institutions and the support of others, and the founding of the Carnegie Endowment for International Peace. Carnegie ably and articulately presented both a justification for the system that existed and a proposal to remedy some of its worst features. He condemned the search for wealth for its own sake but exalted it as a means to improve society.

As may be imagined, many of the millionaires rejected out of hand the notion that they had a duty to use their funds for social purposes. But some agreed with Carnegie and followed his example. John D. Rockefeller, for example, established the Rockefeller Foundation, which made major breakthroughs in public health measures in the South, and he created the University of Chicago. He had hoped that the university would grow into a great Baptist institution but did not interfere with its secular development. In fact, the contributions of the "captains of industry" to colleges and universities probably assisted in the development of strong state support to state institutions. Many of the muckrakers in years to come, journalists intent on exposing the nation's social and economic ills, would charge that tainted money from big business controlled private institutions. Upton Sinclair's *Goose Step*, written in 1923, is a case in point. Whether accurate or not, such criticisms very likely strengthened the state schools as counterbalances.[14]

Meliorist Social Darwinism

It should not be thought that Social Darwinism led inevitably to the conclusions of Sumner or the advocacy of the Gospel of Wealth. The example of Lester Frank Ward illustrates that, far from requiring conclusions supporting laissez faire, Social Darwinism could also bring about advocacy of governmental action. Ward was largely self-educated but published widely in the fields of biology, paleontology, and geology. His scientific knowledge was enormous, and he developed an international reputation. Ward was strongly influenced by the positivism of August Comte and by Spencerian evolutionary theory. He contended, however, that societal evolution depended more upon psychology than upon biology. He argued that the crude Social Darwinism of those such as Sumner was inappropriate; biological evolution, he pointed out from his scientific experience, is incredibly wasteful. If society permits itself to follow nature in this regard, it repeats nature's mistakes.

Ward advocated affirmative governmental action to shape social evolution. In 1883 he published *Dynamic Sociology*, in which he asserted that civilization was the result not of a Sumnerian neglect but of refusing to let nature take its course.[15] Throughout his writings he pointed out that capitalists had never been reluctant to take government aid and that they tended to oppose government only when it attempted to regulate them. He denied the allegation that social matters were beyond the power of human intelligence to direct and urged society to plan wisely for its future. Government itself, he believed, was the product of human intelligence, not accident. Its purpose was protection, accommodation, and control, but its likely origin was in the desire for a few to control rather than in the desire of the many for protection. Ward maintained that it is important not only to plan wisely but to keep the common good uppermost in mind and to eliminate control and repression for the benefit of the few, or even of the many, when their interests are separate from the whole.

Ward, no less than Sumner, sought to develop a science of man. Sharing Sumner's faith in science, he purported to be completely objective, yet there is a strong element of utopianism in his thought. There is no denying his erudition. Ralph Gabriel remarked that no other American social thinker was so well versed in the natural sciences, and that, in comparison with Ward, William Graham Sumner "was a sophomore."[16] But not even scientific knowledge can produce freedom from values in the study of society. It is to Ward's credit that he attempted to humanize a science of man and that he rejected the crude naturalistic determinism prevalent during the age. His thought was in advance of his time and no doubt was as fully in keeping with the attitudes of the people as they developed as Sumner's was when he wrote. Although Sumnerism lingers in some quarters, Ward's thought not only prevailed but went on to become the philosophical basis for much of Franklin D. Roosevelt's New Deal.

Assisting Ward and others in their efforts to found a science of man and to formulate scientific bases for politics was the pioneering anthropological work of Lewis Henry Morgan, who published his *Ancient Society* in 1878. Morgan's studies of ancient societies led him to conclude that humanity has progressed through three stages: savagery, ending with the invention of pottery; barbarism, ending with the invention of the alphabet; and civilization. Gabriel wrote that Morgan's Americanism was apparent in his discussion of representative democracy, which he considered to be the highest stage of civilization to date, with people moving from class to class as permitted by their individual merit. Despotism, imperialism, and monarchy, he thought, were older patterns that had been destroyed in America by the Revolution. Thus, according to Gabriel, "Morgan put the American folk beliefs, the democratic faith, and the gospel of wealth at the top of his evolutionary sequence," and he restated the old doctrine of America as the savior of the world in the new language of naturalism.[17]

When America did succeed in saving the world, Morgan contended, the ultimate plane of democracy would be reached. He thus accepted a naturalistic determinism, which in his case was a law of inevitable progress, as with Spencer. Because of his determinism and his recognition of certain contradictions in the institution of private property, Marxists found Morgan's writings to be highly congenial, but Morgan always considered his conclusions to be tentative, not the final truth.[18]

Reform Movements and Reformers in the Late Nineteenth Century

Despite the popular and intellectual appeal of Social Darwinism in the last quarter of the nineteenth century, there were those who searched for social justice outside the confines of a framework that resulted from a misapplication of scientific findings to social matters. Some were workers who were building what finally came to be the great labor unions of the United States. Some were agrarian protestors, who sought through third-party and other actions remedies for their oppressions. The period saw the rise of the influential Grangers, formally named the Patrons of Husbandry, a movement that was related to the development of farmer-labor parties, the Greenback party, and the strong southern and midwestern Populist party that died only with its absorption into the Democratic party in 1896.

At the same time that the farmer-labor groups were organizing to express their displeasure with the status quo that placed them outside of groups benefiting from social and economic developments, there were strong efforts to encourage a popular recognition that denying political participation to women was unjust. Under the leadership of such figures as Susan B. Anthony and Elizabeth Cady Stanton, the women's movement gained in strength. In 1890 a merger created the National American Suffrage Association, reflecting growing unity among advocates of women's political rights. Many in the South feared the women's movement as having implications for the status of blacks as well, although among the women's leaders themselves there was considerable racism, along with resentment against those who were working for black civil rights. The first solid gain came in 1890 when Wyoming was admitted to the Union as the first state permitting women to vote, but the general belief still seemed to be that the husband's vote adequately represented the entire family's interests and that women themselves were not competent to participate in politics.

One of the most potent attacks upon laissez-faire attitudes came from an economist and ardent reformer, Henry George. George became enormously popular, and although his ideas were not widely adopted, he was a splendid social critic whose writings directed needed attention to reform. American philosopher John Dewey considered him to have been among the world's great social thinkers, saying that "it would require less than the fingers of the two hands to enumerate those who from Plato down rank with him."[19] His reputation was not limited to the United States. Russian novelist Leo Tolstoy admired his work and praised him as the one who had suggested an immediate solution of the Russian land problem. He wrote that George's work was "alone in the literature of science," and that by demolishing "the whole scientific web of Spencer-Mill [it] enlightened the conscience of mankind."[20] Nor was George merely an academic reformer; he actively entered politics, and once ran a strong race for the mayoralty of New York City, polling more votes than one of his major opponents, Theodore Roosevelt.

George's *magnum opus* was *Progress and Poverty*, published in 1879, which sought to deal with the paradox of increasing poverty along with material progress. He concluded that the answer lay in land values. The three elements of production are land, labor, and capital, and "that part which goes to land owners as payment for the use of natural opportunities is called rent; that part which constitutes the reward of human exertion is called wages; and that part which constitutes the return for the use of capital is called interest."[21] He defined rent narrowly, in the technical sense, to include only "that part of the produce which accrues to the owners of land or other natural capabilities by virtue of their ownership."[22] "Rent" for buildings or improvements he classed as interest on invested capital. Among the three kinds of return, he justified both interest and wages as resulting from contributions to production; rent, he said, was unjustified. No person has a right to land exclusively. The land belongs to all. George accepted Locke's labor theory of value, which asserts that the value of an object is directly related to the labor that it takes to produce it, and contended that land was God-given, not man-made. As for rent, he accepted the "law of rent" as formulated by the English economist David Ricardo that "the rent of land is determined by the excess of its produce over that which the same application can secure from the least productive land in use." In economic terms land has no value until it is capable of yielding rent. He pointed out that he might possess rich land, but that it could produce no rent if other land as rich were available without cost.[23] Nevertheless, vast returns from landownership were common, although mere ownership contributes nothing to production. Rent, therefore, results only from monopoly.

George's proposal was the single tax; that is, the taxing of all rent. He contended that this tax would require that all land be used productively, and it would recognize that it is the presence of society and civilization that increases land values, not individual effort. Improvements upon the land, in other words, would continue to profit the "owner," but an increase in the value of the land itself would be confiscated by taxation. The person who farmed or who built a factory upon a piece of land would receive the profits therefrom, but the increase of the land value would be taxed. The person who purchased a plot of ground far from a city, he would argue, should not profit from the value created by the city when it expands to include that land.

George was not a socialist, and he did not propose the confiscation of land. Legally, land would be publicly held, but it would be leased back to its current holders, if they wished to retain it. He did not advocate public ownership of the means of production and distribution. He did advocate the confiscation of unearned gain, gain from the land values created by society.

Groups throughout the United States formed Single-Tax Clubs to support George's ideas. By 1905 the estimate is that *Progress and Poverty* had sold more than 2 million copies in numerous languages.[24] He introduced a humanistic theme into a world dominated by Social

Darwinism, and his proposals, although radical, accepted the basic structure of the society and the economy. There were single-tax communities that based their local institutions upon George's scheme, and some, such as Fairhope, Alabama, still exist along with organizations devoted to propagating his ideas. His greatest lasting influence, however, was on the burgeoning reform movement. He was unexcelled as a social critic.

Related to the single-tax phenomenon was that produced by the "nationalism" of Edward Bellamy. Bellamy's *Looking Backward*, a novel published in 1888, aroused immense enthusiasm. The story is that of a young man, Julian West, who was placed into a deep sleep in 1887 and awoke in the year 2000. He conducted a dialogue with a Dr. Leete, who described the new society, a complete socialism. Each person was to work from the age of twenty-one to forty-five, with equal pay. The job was to be determined by the good of the state and society. Strife no longer existed, nor did poverty. The sharp contrast of the new society with that existing in Bellamy's day was a clear call to action, and Bellamy's book affected the imagination of many as few books have.

Bellamy was not at all hostile to industrialism; on the contrary, the new society was the result of a total industrialization and such increasing monopolization that all producers had merged into one. The state then naturally assumed control. There had been a revolution, but no violence. Bellamy was quite unconcerned about the political process and gave little attention to individual freedoms. Politics were to be minimal, with experts administering the state; as with many schools of thought, Bellamy's "nationalism" placed a premium upon administration, naively considering it to be a neutral function, and denied that in the perfect state there would be sufficient disagreement on policy as to require politics. Of course, when one eliminates politics, one eliminates the people's control. Bellamy merely assumed that there would be no difficulty. Only those who had retired would vote, so that there would be no "intrigue" among the workers.[25]

The success of *Looking Backward* no doubt is attributable partly to Bellamy's skill at creating what was for the time an able and unusual view of a fanciful future; he accurately predicted many modern conveniences that were not to come for years. The greatest factor contributing to his success, however, was his contrast between the two societies, with his piercing descriptions of the injustice then existing. To him nineteenth-century society represented a coach to which the masses were harnessed and which was being driven along a hilly, sandy road:

The driver was hunger, and permitted no lagging. . . . Despite the difficulty of drawing the coach at all along so hard a road, the top was covered with passengers who never got down, even at the steepest ascents. These seats on top were very breezy and comfortable. Well up out of the dust, their occupants could enjoy the scenery at their leisure, or critically discuss the merits of the straining team. Naturally such places were in great demand and the competition for them was keen, everyone seeking as the first end in life to secure a seat on the coach for himself and to leave it to his child after him. By the rule of the coach a man could leave his seat to whom he wished, but on the other hand there were many accidents by which it might at any time be wholly lost.

If one fell from the seat, he immediately was required to grab hold of the towline. There was some compassion felt by the riders for the toilers, for they frequently would call down words of encouragement to the workers.[26] Such a bitter picture of the America ruled by Social Darwinism clearly was more influential than Bellamy's denigration of the potential of the political process as a whole, but there were thousands who joined Nationalist Clubs to advance his ideas. His more didactic and less literary novel, *Equality*, published in 1897, was considerably less popular but is a clearer statement of his views. In it his socialism is better formulated and more doctrinaire, and his attitude toward politics fully as disdainful.

These and other currents prominent in the late nineteenth century were parts of the milieu that was to result in the Progressive Movement, a movement that effectively marked the end of one era and the beginning of another. Thus the twentieth century began with a burst of reform that foreshadowed the tremendous changes that were to come.

NOTES

1. *American Political Thought* (New York: Holt, Rinehart and Winston, 1960), p. 302.

2. See Herbert Spencer, *Social Statics* (New York: D. Appleton, 1864), esp. pp. 79–80 and 414–415.

3. See Ralph Henry Gabriel, *The Course of American Democratic Thought*, 2nd ed. (New York: Ronald Press, 1956), pp. 227–228.

4. *Social Darwinism in American Thought*, rev. ed. (Boston: Beacon Press, 1955), p. 51.

5. Ibid., pp. 5–10; quotation from p. 10.

6. See Perry Miller, *American Thought: Civil War to World War I* (New York: Holt, Rinehart and Winston, 1965), p. xxxviii.

7. Quoted in Hofstadter, *Social Darwinism*, p. 34.

8. For insights into the temper of the period, see Cynthia Eagle Russett's excellent study, *Darwin in America: The Intellectual Response, 1865–1912* (San Francisco: W. H. Freeman, 1976).

9. See Gabriel, *American Democratic Thought*, pp. 157–158.

10. See ibid., pp. 158–169.

11. 148 (June 1889), 651–664.

12. Quoted in Gabriel, *American Democratic Thought*, p. 153.

13. Andrew Carnegie, *The Gospel of Wealth and Other Timely Essays* (Cambridge, Mass.: The Belknap Press of Harvard University Press, 1962).

14. See Harvey Wish, *Society and Thought in Modern America* (New York: Longmans, Green, 1952), p. 184.

15. (New York: D. Appleton, 1883).

16. *American Democratic Thought*, pp. 217–218.

17. Ibid., p. 177.

18. See ibid., pp. 173–178.

19. Quoted in George R. Geiger, *The Philosophy of Henry George* (New York: Macmillan, 1933), p. 4, note.

20. Quoted in Wish, *Modern America*, p. 335.

21. Henry George, *Progress and Poverty* (New York: Robert Schalkenbach Foundation, 1940), p. 162.

22. Ibid., p. 165.

23. Ibid., pp. 166–168.

24. Gabriel, *American Democratic Thought*, p. 212.

25. Edward Bellamy, *Looking Backward* (Boston: Houghton Mifflin, 1966), pp. 114–115.

26. Ibid., pp. 6–7.

ADDITIONAL READINGS

Adams, Henry. *The Education of Henry Adams.* Boston: Houghton Mifflin, 1961 [1918].

Arnold, Thurman W. *The Folklore of Capitalism.* New Haven, Conn.: Yale University Press, 1937.

Barker, Charles A. *Henry George.* New York: Oxford University Press, 1955.

Bowman, Sylvia E. *Edward Bellamy Abroad: An American Prophet's Influence.* New York: Twayne, 1962.

Cochran, Thomas C., and William Miller. *The Age of Enterprise.* New York: Macmillan, 1942.

Commager, Henry Steele. *The American Mind: An Interpretation of American Thought and Character Since the 1800s.* New Haven, Conn.: Yale University Press, 1950.

Corwin, Edward S. *The Twilight of the Supreme Court.* New Haven, Conn.: Yale University Press, 1934.

Cravens, Hamilton, and John C. Burnham. "Psychology and Evolutionary Naturalism in American Thought, 1890–1940." *American Quarterly* XXIII (December 1971); a discussion of the continuing effect on American thought of the orientation that led to Social Darwinism.

Dunne, Finley Peter. *Dissertations by Mr. Dooley.* New York: Harper, 1906.

Fine, Sidney. *Laissez-Faire and the General Welfare State.* Ann Arbor: University of Michigan Press, 1967.

Goldman, Eric. *Rendezvous With Destiny: A History of Modern American Reform*. New York: Knopf, 1952.

Hacker, Louis W. *The World of Andrew Carnegie: 1865–1901*. Philadelphia: Lippincott, 1968.

Hays, Samuel P. *The Response to Industrialism: 1885–1914*. Chicago: University of Chicago Press, 1957.

Hofstadter, Richard. "The Spoilsmen: An Age of Cynicism." In *The American Political Tradition*. New York: Vintage, 1958, chap. 7.

Josephson, Matthew. *The Robber Barons*. New York: Harcourt, Brace, 1934.

Kirkland, Edward C. *Dream and Thought in the Business Community, 1860–1900*. Ithaca, N.Y.: Cornell University Press, 1956.

Mason, Alpheus T. "American Individualism: Fact and Fiction." *American Political Science Review* XLVI (March 1952).

McClosky, Robert G. *American Conservatism in the Age of Enterprise: A Study of William Graham Sumner, Stephen J. Field and Andrew Carnegie*. Cambridge, Mass.: Harvard University Press, 1951.

Morgan, Arthur E. *The Philosophy of Edward Bellamy*. New York: King's Crown, 1945.

Persons, Stow. *American Minds: A History of Ideas*. New York: Holt, Rinehart and Winston, 1958, pp. 342–62; excellent treatment of Social Darwinism.

Prothro, James W. "Business Ideas and the American Tradition." *Journal of Politics* XV (February 1953).

Rhodes, Harold V. *Utopia in American Political Thought*. Tucson, Ariz.: Institute of Governmental Research—Political Theory Studies No. I, University of Arizona Press, 1967; deals with George and Bellamy, among others, as well as with American utopian thought in general.

Twiss, Benjamin R. *Lawyers and the Constitution: How Laissez-Faire Came to the Supreme Court*. Princeton, N.J.: Princeton University Press, 1942.

Wall, Joseph Frazier. *Andrew Carnegie*. New York: Oxford University Press, 1970.

11

Into the Progressive Era

Although there had been hope on the part of some that blacks freed by the Civil War would join with workers, small farmers, and other low-income groups to form an irresistible political force, the hope was soon shattered. Rather than enshrining radicalism, the postwar period brought the entrenchment of capitalism built upon the industrial corporation. Just as white Americans turned their backs upon the newly freed blacks, so also did they work to remove the Indian from their path as they swept across the continent. The efforts of whites to force Indians onto reservations were met with fierce resistance, which usually ended with a massacre of Indian bands because of the white man's superior firepower and technology. Even the Indians who had settled on reservations were constantly moved about when it became clear that the waste land onto which they had been moved had value for whites; neither a promise of perpetual title to the land nor an assurance of safe conduct for a tribe was honored. Many of the massacred tribes, in fact, had sworn allegiance to the United States and had been promised protection. The record is one of broken promises and atrocities often characterized by the brutal murder of women and children and the mutilation of their bodies.[1]

There was violence within white society as well. With the beginnings of labor unions and the protests against the economic conditions of workers, employers frequently moved against strikers with private armies hired to crush any resistance. There was violence on both sides, but the workers tended to be no match for the power of the employers and their Pinkerton agents. Such conditions brought out some sentiment both for socialism and for anarchism.

American Socialists and Anarchists

Socialism received some encouragement in the United States because of the availability of the writings of Karl Marx, but it never succeeded in capturing the imagination of American workers as it had those in Europe. Both the moderate socialism of Eugene V. Debs and the more militant version advocated by Daniel De Leon played a part in the development of American unions, politics, and political ideas, but neither managed to become a major force. Much of their influence, in fact, resulted from negative reactions to socialism in any form.

De Leon was a dogmatic Marxist with a flair for political invective. He advocated the overthrow of the existing political system, to be replaced by one with representatives of trades, not geographic areas, but he opposed the use of force. He believed that ballots were the weapons of civilization.[2] Debs rose to fame as a leader of the American Railway Union in the great Pullman strike in Chicago in 1894, which was crushed by federal troops. He was sentenced to six months in jail and went on to become the most prominent voice of moderate American socialism of his day.[3] He imparted a distinctively American flavor to the socialist movement, whereas De Leon's tone had been essentially European. Daniel Bell has cited the period from 1902 to 1912 as the "Golden Age of American Socialism," but socialism rapidly dwindled in influence.[4] There are many explanations for this, most centering upon the relative affluence in this country, but Bell contends that the cause was a "set of ideological blinders" that prevented American socialists from understanding American society adequately. He has written that American socialists tended to be too Marxist in orientation, and were too dogmatic either to understand or to be effective in an American setting.[5]

From a theoretical point of view, one of the most influential socialists was Laurence Gronlund, who lectured and published widely. His book *The Cooperative Commonwealth* (1884), sought to achieve acceptance of German socialism in America and attacked the wage and profit system. He distinguished socialism from anarchism, contending that socialism viewed the state as the whole of organized society; the state was not merely the government, separate from society and serving as its agent, as would be the view of an individualist. His organic view of society accepted it as a natural entity, and not a voluntary, deliberate creation of human beings. Society, not individual rights, was the datum upon which to found politics. He argued that the natural rights theory had been a good method to destroy previous notions of the state but that it was not adequate to serve as the foundation of the new system. He departed from orthodox Marxism, which held that the state ultimately would wither away, in his insistence that it must continue to exist, because it was synonymous with organized society.

Gronlund rejected a pure communism, advocating only collective control of production and distribution, not common ownership. He contended that this would result in a classless society in which the state would work for the good of all its constituent members. Like Edward Bellamy, he was hostile to the political process and favored instead appointive administrators, or a rule by experts, with referenda upon major questions among those who were immediately affected.[6]

In the late nineteenth century there were also anarchist appeals, some related to socialism, some not. Johann Most, a German immigrant, advocated violence and bombing, and became associated with the movement known as the "Black International."[7] In the public mind, the Haymarket incident in Chicago in 1886 was synonymous with violent anarchism, but there is no evidence that the anarchists were responsible, although they had urged the workers to arm themselves. Police had fired into a group of strikers at the McCormick Harvester works, and there was a protest meeting in front of the Haymarket the next day. Someone threw a bomb that killed seven policemen, and with no evidence whatsoever, eight anarchists were arrested and convicted of murder. Staughton Lynd has written that the obvious injustice "shocked reform-minded Americans much as Elijah Lovejoy's murder in the 1830's electrified abolitionists."[8] It would be difficult to demonstrate such long-term effects, but, as Lynd contends, the Haymarket episode probably did shape the radical convictions of such persons as Emma Goldman and William Haywood.[9]

There was also a group of pacifist anarchists on the American scene at the time, including Lysander Spooner, Benjamin Tucker, and Josiah Warren. These men denied the necessity of any coercion in society and argued that the state had no right to authority over the individual. Spooner, who earlier had sought to prove the unconstitutionality of slavery, was a strong and articulate spokesman for his views, going so far as to send a tightly reasoned letter to President Grover Cleveland upon his inauguration that condemned the foundations of the American state. Spooner had concluded that the Constitution had no authority at all because no one had signed it or agreed to it as a contract. Moreover, he thought that the Constitution as it was written was far different from the claims that had been put forth for it; even had it been a binding contract, it would not only have failed to justify the nineteenth-century American state, but in fact was designed to prevent it from developing as it did.[10]

Warren and Tucker were two of the most prominent of the individualist anarchists. Warren's best-known work was his 1863 book *True Civilization*. He apparently converted Tucker to anarchism after they met in 1872; Tucker previously had been a reformer, speaking for the eight-hour day, prohibition, and women's rights. Subsequently, he edited the magazines *Radical Review* and *Liberty*, and translated the writings of the Russian anarchists into English. His arguments essentially were that crime was caused by the state and that the state's coercive function was not necessary to protect society. Government, therefore, was a danger not only to freedom but also to security.[11]

Rise of the Social Gospel

Both anarchism and socialism sometimes took the form of religiously based political philosophies. Adin Ballou, for example, offered nonresistance as a basis for Christian anarchism.[12] Near the end of the century religion and socialism mingled in America in the form of the Social Gospel.[13] From the beginning American Protestantism had contained, along with its major emphasis upon individualism, currents of ethical concern and criticisms of materialism. Such currents took religious and philosophical form in the rational liberalism of Universalism and Unitarianism, on the one hand, and the more intuitive liberalism of Transcendentalism, on the other (see pp. 104–107). Many of the Transcendentalists were significant political thinkers, but in general they shied away from political involvement. It was not until the rise of the Social Gospel that the currents produced explicit political and economic programs.

Amidst the chaotic swirl of ideas and patterns of economic growth following the Civil War, a Congregational minister, Jesse H. Jones, founded the Christian Labor Union in 1872 and began a monthly journal called *Equity*. *Equity* ceased publication in 1875, but during its existence it advocated education for workers, labor reforms, and the frankly socialistic public ownership of the means for producing and distributing goods. Such a position brought Jones intense criticism, socialism being then, as later, a political swear word in the American lexicon. In 1876, however, a young minister named Washington Gladden brought out a book under the imprint of the Congregational Publishing Society entitled *Being a Christian*. Gladden was a follower of Horace Bushnell, whose efforts to humanize Calvinism brought him international fame in the middle of the century. Gladden rejected communism, or total socialism, because of his emphasis upon the individual, but he favored a limited socialism in the form of public ownership of utilities; even this was radical for the time. He rejected equally the extremes of individualism, which he compared to a pile of sand, and of socialism, in which there would be too little individual identity. He proposed a middle way consisting of the "socialized individual," who, following religious dictates, accepted social responsibility. Along with other advocates of the Social Gospel, he criticized the Social Darwinists' view of natural law as being simply greed and strife; he said that such was not the law of nature, but a crime against nature.

In 1887 William Dwight Porter Bliss, with Episcopal Bishop F. D. Huntington of New York, established the Church Association for the Advancement of the Interests of Labor (CAIL). Earlier, Bliss had organized a church for workers in South Boston, the Mission of the Carpenter; the Brotherhood of the Carpenter met there regularly to discuss labor difficulties. Bliss also founded, the same year as CAIL, a Society of Christian Socialists, with assistance from the Reverend Francis Bellamy, a cousin of the author of *Looking Backward*, and in 1895 he was instrumental in establishing the American Fabian Society. Other such groups were beginning simultaneously in California and Washington under Gronlund's influence. In 1897 Bliss edited the *Encyclopedia of Social Reform* and contributed an article on Christian socialism in Europe and America. He saw the true goal of Christianity as that of leading humanity into a truly cooperative society and away from individualistic capitalism. In America, he wrote, Christian socialism demanded that the individual practice brotherhood and that the state reform politics; moreover, the state must extend democracy by broadening the suffrage to include women, adopting initiative and recall measures, and reforming labor conditions. He favored the adoption of the eight-hour day so that workers would have more time to spend at home, in church, and in libraries. He stressed both religion and a full-fledged socialism, but the socialism of the Social Gospel emphasized cooperation rather than class conflict and gradualism rather than revolution.

Similar themes continued to be advanced by others, such as George D. Herron of the First Congregational Church of Burlington, Iowa. His famous paper, "The Message of Jesus to Men of Wealth," castigated the rich for living off of the fruits of society without contributing to it. He called for the law of love to replace the law of selfishness, thereby arguing in a fashion directly opposite to that of the Gospel of Wealth. Because of his oratorical abilities, he convinced many that the way to a better society was through individual sacrifice for the common good. In 1900 he joined the Socialist party.

Probably the best known of the advocates of the Social Gospel was another minister, Walter Rauschenbusch, who wrote *Christianity and the Social Crisis* in 1907. In this, and a series of other books and messages, he argued that industrial capitalism was the primary cause of American social evils. He urged that competition be ended as the foundation of the economy because it was a denial of brotherhood. He saw business as the last stronghold of autocracy and condemned the profit motive. Rauschenbusch did not advocate complete communism, but he favored public ownership of the more important economic resources because he considered social justice to depend upon the abolition of unjust privileges and the socialization of economic power.

The Christian socialists shunned the Marxist notions of class conflict and dialectical materialism. Their program, as Ralph Henry Gabriel wrote, "was the Christian counterpart of that humanism which, in America, began with the Enlightenment, modified evangelical Protestantism, was the core of transcendentalism, became militant in the religion of humanity and late nineteenth-century neo-rationalism, and which found its supreme expression in the democratic faith." The Kingdom of God, Gabriel continued, as seen by the advocates of the Social Gospel was simply the democratic dream.[14]

Black Civil Rights:
The Debate over Direction

The treatment accorded to American blacks in the post-Reconstruction period was altogether inconsistent with the democratic dream. In a direct repudiation of the Fourteenth Amendment, the Supreme Court in *Plessy* v. *Ferguson* declared in 1896 that "separate but equal" was permissible, thereby establishing a total legal justification for racial segregation. The southern states were thus given approval for their efforts to require racial separation, regardless of the spirit of the Constitution as amended following the Civil War. Segregation, or "Jim Crow," thus became firmly fixed in the legal system of the South, reflecting in law the popular attitudes that had long existed. It was adopted, according to C. Vann Woodward, as a result not so much of a conversion as "a relaxation of the opposition."[15] It was left largely to blacks themselves to fight their way into pàrticipation in the American system, and blacks did play a major role in the slow development of civil rights, a far greater role than they had played in the movement for abolition.[16] A split developed over tactics, however.

Among the first efforts were those directed at playing the white man's game and accepting separate and inferior status. The black man who did most to popularize this approach was Booker T. Washington, a former slave who came to serve as a mediator between blacks and whites and long was the most prominent spokesman for America's blacks. Part of Washington's approach no doubt was based upon his need to gain the favor of white southerners, but part also was a reflection of his firm convictions regarding what was practical under the circumstances. Washington argued that it was fruitless, and even tragic, to educate blacks in the classics and the liberal arts; because most jobs open to blacks were agricultural, he contended that the majority of a black's education should be agricultural training. To this end he worked for the founding of Tuskegee Institute in Alabama and in 1881 became its first president. Tuskegee was devoted to providing agricultural and vocational training to black youth. Washington condemned black cries for immediate equality, saying that equal rights must be earned, and he frankly accepted social separation. He believed that southern blacks had the power to make themselves so important to the economic life of the South that the black "will not have to seek privileges, they will be freely conferred upon him."[17] As a part of his emphasis upon rejecting protest, accepting menial trades and purely vocational training, and remaining separate from the dominant whites, Washington stressed the necessity for individual effort to better oneself. The Puritan ethic of work and individual responsibility that he preached was so American, and his avowal of the existing patterns of race relations was so complete, that the South as well as the rest of the nation acclaimed him a great man; southerners saw him as an honored leader of American blacks, yet one who presented no threat to the status quo, one who not only was no radical but whose influence would help keep blacks "in their place."

So great was Washington's reputation among whites that he was invited to address the Atlanta Exposition in 1895, an indication that the white community would respect economic success in one who had risen from poverty, even if he were black, if that person were sufficiently conservative and could be seen as valuable in preserving the status quo. It was in this address that Washington made his famous comment that in all things purely social blacks and whites could be "as separate as the fingers, yet one as the hand in all things essential to mutual progress." He pointed out to southern whites that blacks constituted one-third of the South's population and were an invaluable resource. He praised the coming of what he termed "a new era of industrial progress" and asked only that blacks be given a chance in the commercial world. Southern blacks, he said, were the rock upon which southern industrial prosperity would be built, and he called upon the South not to recruit immigrant or northern workers but to make use of the blacks, who, he pointed out, had labored long without strikes or labor wars. Betraying no aspirations for the masses of blacks to live other than by their hands, Washington said that blacks would prosper in proportion as they learned to dignify and glorify common labor and put intellect and skill into life's common occupations. In closing, he stressed that the wisest of the black population understood that agitation for social equality would be the greatest of follies, and that there could be no progress as the result of, as he put it, "artificial forcing." He put forth his program as best for blacks, best for southern whites, and best for the blotting out of sectional differences as well as of racial animosities.[18]

Despite his platform of accommodation, Washington's program contained glimmerings, albeit the faintest of glimmerings, of some of the black power proposals of the 1960s. He based his approach, as did the black power advocates, upon separate status, black pride, and the development of economic power. From the point of view of political philosophy, his most interesting insights were in his recognition that racial discrimination was even more injurious to whites than to blacks. In an address delivered in Brooklyn in 1896, he said that blacks could more easily afford to be wronged than whites could afford to wrong them and that unjust laws merely inconvenienced blacks, whereas they injured whites. "No race," he wrote, "can wrong another race simply because it has the power to do so without being permanently injured in morals. The Negro can endure the temporary inconvenience but the injury to the white man is permanent."[19] As "realistic" as Washington was, and as much as he was devoted to the "practical" aspects of human affairs, such an argument would have been most congenial to the Transcendentalists.

From the latter part of the nineteenth century until his death in the second decade of the twentieth, no other American had a following among both blacks and whites to rival Washington's. There were, however, severe criticisms of his policies of accommodation, although the criticisms were heavily outweighed by public praise. One of the most bitter critics was the first black to have become a member of Phi Beta Kappa at Harvard, Monroe Trotter. Trotter founded and edited the best known of the anti-Washington newspapers, the Boston *Guardian*, which castigated Washington's servility to white prejudices. Washington even had words of approval for the new southern state constitutions that effectively disfranchised blacks, saying that they encouraged the qualities he contended were necessary for blacks to develop, such as thrift, intelligence, property ownership, and character. Such an acceptance brought harsh words from Trotter, who denied that disfranchisement contributed anything to the betterment of blacks, and who accused Washington of being among the worst enemies of his race by having accepted without complaint a situation that denied to one race what it granted to another. He called for a black Patrick Henry to save his people from the stigma of cowardice.[20]

Trotter's criticisms of Washington went beyond questions of race relations. He did not ignore the implications of Washington's repeated statement that blacks had never disturbed the country by strikes or lockouts and had performed "peaceful, faithful, humble service." He said that this was a doubtful compliment, because strikes and lockouts are sometimes necessary, and that those who brag that they never resort to them are not always to be commended. To Washington's contention that individual effort would bring more benefits to blacks as a race than anything else could, Trotter wrote that it was "mere claptrap" and pointed out that all the wealth, skill, and intelligence acquired by blacks before the Civil War did not do half so much toward bringing freedom as the agitation by Frederick Douglass, William Lloyd Garrison, Wendell Phillips, and the black abolitionist Samuel Ringgold Ward. It was agitation, he said, that brought freedom, and Washington's constant belittling of the very thing that had made him free was the height of stupidity.[21]

Washington's best-known opponent, however, was a young Harvard Ph.D. named W. E. B. Du Bois. Du Bois attacked Washington's Atlanta Exposition speech as the "Atlanta Compromise" and followed in the tradition of Douglass in calling for ceaseless action to achieve black rights, which he saw as natural rights. In 1903 he published his famous work on race relations, *The Souls of Black Folk*, and in 1905 he met with other black leaders at Niagara Falls, Canada, to draw up a program of action. The Niagara movement was an important development that led to the formation of the National Association for the Advancement of Colored People (NAACP) in 1910.[22]

At first, Du Bois had been friendly with Washington, but he had totally rejected the Tuskegee attitude by 1903. Du Bois was a professor of sociology at Atlanta University; as Herbert Storing remarked, he also was a poet, a propagandist, and a revolutionary who at various times professed "Washingtonianism, racism, integration, Pan-Africanism, individualism, and Marxism."[23] Part of the reason for his changes in position was that times changed; he lived past ninety years of age and was active throughout his life. His break with Washington came because his historical and sociological studies indicated to him that Washington's approach gained nothing for blacks and even permitted a worsening of conditions. Moreover, Washington's emphasis upon industrial and agricultural training diverted resources from liberal arts institutions such as Atlanta University.[24]

Du Bois had influence from his writing, speaking, and his long tenure as the editor of the NAACP publication, *The Crisis.* His piercing analyses of Washington's arguments were devastating and set the tone of the civil rights movement for years to come. He pointed out the materialism that was the basis for Washington's position and noted that Washington had thoroughly learned the speech and thought of triumphant commercialism. Du Bois, too, called for race pride, but he also argued that it was wrong to relegate blacks to menial positions and that it was as necessary to provide sound liberal education to blacks as to whites. A university, he wrote in his essay "The Talented Tenth," was an institution designed by human beings to transmit knowledge and culture from generation to generation. Nothing else could do this, not even the trade and industrial schools that Washington advocated. He disagreed with Washington's emphasis upon the mass and said that not all could go to college, although some must. In every race—white, black, or other—and in every society, he asserted, progress would come from "the talented tenth," or the few exceptional persons who would lead the way for the others to follow. Du Bois criticized the Tuskegee program as calling for at least temporary acceptance of a lack of political power, civil rights, and higher education for black youth. The results, he said, far from being progress, were black disfranchisement, a status of legal inferiority, and the withdrawal of aid from black institutions of higher education; Washington had not caused these developments, but his policies encouraged them.

Du Bois stressed the political. No worker or property owner could protect his or her rights, he asserted, without the vote, and no person subjected to constant civil inferiority was likely to be able to develop the self-respect that Washington demanded. Education, civil equality, and the vote were essential to black development, and blacks could not therefore wait for them until they were "earned." He did urge blacks to judge the South gently, saying that southerners were not responsible for their ancestors and that racial prejudice was more the result of inadequate or faulty education than anything else. There was much good will, he pointed out, even in the South. He admitted that blacks needed to help themselves but said that Washington's doctrines led all whites, North and South, to ignore the race question and to shift the entire burden to black shoulders. Du Bois followed a long tradition of natural rights thought, a kind of thought that had become less and less in evidence as the movement toward scientific social thought progressed. Urging that Americans at the beginning of the twentieth century turn to the truths of their fathers, truths that they were forgetting, he argued from the principles of the Declaration of Independence that "all men are created equal; that they are endowed by their Creator with certain unalienable rights; that among these are life, liberty, and the pursuit of happiness."[25] Du Bois wrote with feeling and with power. In 1920 he published *Darkwater: Voices from Within the Veil*,[26] which not only presented his thought but also described his life and heritage. It conveys as few things could a sense of what it was like to be black in America.

Progressive Thought

The motivating spirit at the turn of the century appeared to be reform, and those who advocated reform adopted some of the suggestions of the radicals, yet worked to avoid radical solutions by remaining within the system. This was the Progressive period. The violence of previous years led to appeals for governmental action from all quarters. Such conflicts as the railroad strike of 1877, the Homestead battle in 1892, and the Pullman strike in 1894 brought about calls for reform from many of those who had been active in farmer and debtor causes, such as the Granger and Greenback movements and the Populist party; they also led businessmen and industrialists to depart from even a theoretical devotion to laissez faire and to insist that the government stifle labor unrest. The result was a growth in governmental regulation.

Even before the Progressive movement had strongly influenced the national government, there were beginning steps. There had been considerable effort to end such abuses of railroad power as rate structures that discriminated against small farmers. The Interstate Commerce Act had been passed in 1887 and the Sherman Antitrust Act in 1890. The culmination of the pre-Progressive ferment was the Populist party, which called for direct election of senators, the progressive income tax, strong economic regulation, and many other reform measures. Populism was especially strong in the Midwest and the South, and by 1892 it had become a strong third party at the national level. In 1896, however, the Populists joined with the Democratic party to support the presidential candidacy of William Jennings Bryan and thereafter quickly lost their separate identity.

The Progressives, following closely upon their heels, were similar to the Populists in many ways, but there was one striking difference. The Populists tended to be workers and farmers and to represent low-income groups. The Progressives were staunchly middle class and had a strong appeal to intellectuals that the Populists, with their reputations as "hayseed reformers" and "wild-eyed uneducated radicals," could never achieve. The Progressives, therefore, had more long-range impact upon the political system, although much of their program had been lifted intact from the Populists. The wave of reform as represented by both groups affected both the national and the state governments and strongly influenced many in both major parties. The Progressives, in fact, never formed a separate party, as had the Populists, but exerted their greatest impact as Republicans during the administration of Theodore Roosevelt and as Democrats during Woodrow Wilson's term of office.

Progressives were most evident in three separate groups. There were, of course, Progressive politicians and officeholders who shaped the course of legislation and administrative policy, but the Progressive spirit was also manifest in journalism and in academic quarters. Despite Roosevelt's reputation as a "trust buster" and his desire for moderate reform, he was no friend to critics of the fundamental system itself. Those journalists and novelists who came to prominence as social critics, he allegedly charged, were merely "raking in the muck." The description stuck, and they have since been known as the muckrakers.

Journals such as *McClure's Magazine* and *Atlantic Monthly* gave the muckrakers their forum. Even before Roosevelt identified the group, Henry Demarest Lloyd had attacked the Standard Oil Company. In 1881 he wrote an *Atlantic Monthly* article on the subject that required the *Atlantic* to go through several printings to keep up with sales. In 1894 he continued the theme in his book *Wealth Against Commonwealth*, in which he argued that monopolistic tendencies worked in a fashion precisely opposite to that claimed by the Social Darwinists; that is, they permitted the unfittest economically to survive. He exposed the practices of price fixing and economic pressures that drove those who disagreed out of business. Lloyd's theme was picked up in a series of articles in *McClure's* at the turn of the century by Ida Tarbell, who wrote a corporate biography of Standard Oil and reached a much wider audience than Lloyd because of a new revolution in the publishing of popular periodicals. The managing editor of *McClure's* at that time was Lincoln Steffens, whose articles on urban corruption were republished as *The Shame of the Cities* (1904) and *The Struggle for Self-Government* (1906).

The socialist writer Upton Sinclair published some articles about filth in the meat-packing industry in *Collier's*, but his novel on the subject, *The Jungle*, catapulted him to national prominence and attracted the attention of a large part of the nation, including President Roosevelt. His book was instrumental in the passage of the Meat Inspection Act of 1906, and he and other writers encouraged the adoption of the Pure Food and Drug Act the same year. David Graham Phillip's articles on "The Treason of the Senate" probably had considerable influence on the adoption of the Seventeenth Amendment providing for direct election of senators.[27] The muckrakers exposed fraudulent business practices and unethical activities throughout the large industries of the United States, especially the railroads and the oil and insurance industries, and they documented an unholy alliance between government and big business that worked to fleece the public. Rather than placing American business in a position of honor and condemning governmental corruption, as most writers had done previously, the muckrakers suggested that business corruption was the cause of much of the corruption in government. They thus supported the socialist thesis of the connection between economics and government, but the general influence of their writings was in the direction of reform within the system, not the radical revisions of the system suggested by socialists.

Less striking at the time, but in the long run fully as influential, were innovative currents in the academic world. Among the new scholars was Josiah Royce, who joined the Harvard faculty in 1884 and became a prominent figure in American philosophy. Royce rejected Social Darwinism, but he accepted the general thesis of evolution, saying that it was a great truth but not the entire truth. Royce feared the loss of individuality inherent in a mass society and dealt with ways to prevent it. His solution was a glorification of loyalty and the development of a philosophy based upon loyalty. The highest goal, as he put it, was loyalty to loyalty, a dedication to some cause external to one's self. This notion formed the basis of his book *The Philosophy of Loyalty*, published in 1908, and also underlay a scheme that he outlined for an international relations system built upon hierarchies of loyalty. The structure would be built upon loyalty to family, to a province that would provide for local escape from standardization, to the nation, and ultimately to the human family. Royce was an idealist in a world that was reacting against idealism. As such, his effort to reconcile Christianity and science in a philosophy of loyalty that was to bring about a world order based upon voluntary cooperation was virtually ignored; *The Hope of the Great Community* was in press in 1916 when he died, and the age of cynicism that followed World War I was not one that would welcome idealism.[28]

Both Royce and Charles S. Peirce helped shape the course of American philosophy largely because of their influence upon William James. Peirce was a philosopher and mathematician whose work was little known during his life, but his conclusion that the truth of an idea is to be found in its consequences was the foundation upon which James built his characteristically American philosophy, pragmatism. James was a physician, philosopher, and psychologist who was also a religious thinker. His work *The Varieties of Religious Experience*, published in 1902 as the compilation of lectures that he had given at Edinburgh, suggested that God is finite and evolves along with the universe; not even God knows how it will all end. But although this denies the possibility of inevitable progress, it also heightens the dignity of human beings, who, in an indeterminate world, have at least some effect upon the future. He expressed the same regard for human dignity and rejected any form of determinism, natural or otherwise, in all his works, including *Principles of Psychology* (1890) and *Pragmatism* (1907). James was enormously influential, both directly and through the subsequent works of John Dewey.

In the social sciences the new scholarship was represented by such persons as Richard T. Ely and Thorstein Veblen in economics; Lester Frank Ward, E. A. Ross, and Charles Cooley in sociology; and Frederick Jackson Turner, Charles A. Beard, and Vernon L. Parrington in history and political science. Veblen's *Theory of the Leisure Class* (1899) was a classic piece of economic criticism, arguing that the productive talents of those such as engineers were subverted by the sloth, "conspicuous waste," and "conspicuous consumption" of those who were interested only in pecuniary matters and had no pride of workmanship. Veblen later argued for a technocratic society based upon the engineer's instinct of workmanship, but his significance within the Progressive movement was to question the practices and values of the business system. Turner's frontier thesis (see p. 128) revolutionized American historical thought, and its emphasis on the influence of the environment was compatible with Parrington's treatment of the impact of property upon politics and with Charles A. Beard's theme, summarized in his great work, *An Economic Interpretation of the Constitution of the United States*, published in 1913 (see p. 62).

The Progressives' Impact on Politics

The Progressive period was not radical in any true sense, and the motivating spirit was one of reform and of seeking to make industrialism compatible with human values within the existing system. The Progressives attacked the notion of laissez faire as a fraud and clearly documented the role of politics within the economic system as well as the effect of economics upon politics. They argued that government had never been divorced from economic activity and that it should continue to be involved, but on the side of the people rather than that of special interests. They recognized the political power of the newly developed economic concentrations and therefore worked to bring economic power under public control, a task that the Founding Fathers had not been aware would be needed. The growth of corporate industrialism had permitted such a strengthening of private power that democracy was being subverted and popular rule was becoming a facade. Nevertheless, the Progressives generally worked for the preservation of capitalism; they merely sought to make it compatible with popular democracy by regulating private power. As a whole, they did not seek to adopt socialism, although there were those among them who became socialists.

Herbert Croly, a long-time editor of *The New Republic* and author of *The Promise of American Life* (1909) and other works, argued for what he called the "New Nationalism." Croly urged that humankind must not become slave to science, but must exercise "social virtue." According to Croly, collectivism in government, unions, and corporations was the order of the day, and a new Hamiltonian program of governmental action should replace the older notions of equal rights and no special privileges. In other words, there should be national discrimination, but it should be exercised to control the powerful and aid the weak. All was to be based upon the public interest, and the emphasis was to be upon a national moral pattern that would allow various special interest groups to merge and establish altruistic national policies that would counter selfish national economic tendencies. Croly urged the national recognition of unions and the control of corporations, but he accepted industrial bigness, saying that it should be turned to the public, rather than selfish, interest. One of Croly's followers was Theodore Roosevelt, whose 1912 Progressive platform, the "New Nationalism," was influenced strongly by Croly's writings.

Walter Weyl, a colleague of Croly's and an associate editor of *The New Republic*, also had influence upon Roosevelt and subsequently upon Woodrow Wilson. Weyl's book *The New Democracy* (1912) exploded the simplistic assumption that freedom was a negative quality (the absence of restraints) and that government activity inevitably restricted liberty. He pointed out that laws forbidding certain practices may enhance freedom by preventing private power from exploiting the weak to the detriment of their liberty.

Early in the Progressive period American intellectuals such as Mark Twain argued forcefully and bitterly against American imperi-

alistic ventures in the Philippines and elsewhere. They condemned
the assumption of the inferiority of nonwhites upon which such
policies were based and the violence and torture to which they led. It
was impossible, they argued, for a nation to preserve democratic
ideals at home if it worked to subvert them elsewhere.

At the same time the women's movement was seeking trade
unions for women and also the vote. Many of the Progressives
favored women's suffrage, assuming that women would be more
predisposed to reform than were men and that a women's vote would
aid small business and farmers and help them to keep from being
consumed by big corporations. There were demonstrations, and
there was violence. Opposing the women were the Roman Catholic
Church, southern whites, political bosses, big business, and the
liquor interests, but the movement at least won the suffrage with the
adoption of the Nineteenth Amendment in 1920.[29] Subsequently
there was little gain until the 1970s.

In the Progressive years numerous associations brought together social workers, such as Jane Addams and Grace and Edith
Abbott, with influential figures such as Eleanor Roosevelt, Newton
D. Baker, Louis Brandeis, and John R. Commons encouraging their
reform efforts. One of the most militant reform organizations was
Florence Kelley's National Consumers' League, and another, the
Women's Trade Union League, conducted a long and hard fight
against the exploitation of industrial workers. The American Association for Labor Legislation, headed by John B. Andrews and his
wife, brought about the beginnings of workmen's compensation laws
in many states. At the time there had developed between reformers
and many government officials at all levels a spirit of cooperation.
The reformers considered the defeat of Theodore Roosevelt in 1912 a
severe blow to their cause, but they found that they were able to
work with the Wilson administration until World War I destroyed the
reform impulse by redirecting popular concern and associating many
reform programs with pro-German sympathies.[30]

Woodrow Wilson's "New Freedom" was based upon the idea that
society should work to eliminate the institutions that had frustrated
popular rule, some since the beginning of the nation. Wilson professed admiration for Jeffersonianism, but sought often the adoption
of Hamiltonian programs, thereby attempting to achieve Jeffersonian
ends through Hamiltonian means. He opposed the view that bigness
is good and should merely be regulated for the public interest, calling
as early as 1912 for competition rather than regulation of monopo-
lies.[31] The growth of bigness overwhelmed the individual and forced
workers to depend upon an employer rather than themselves. Under
a more personal system, according to Wilson, human beings had felt

responsibility for their own acts, but within the corporation employers often lost their ethical sense, producing a heartless economic
system.[32] He favored governmental action, but only as necessary to
insure the control of private power, thus rejecting the "New Nationalism" proposals.

Unfortunately, Wilson suffered from some personality flaws
that inhibited him from working consistently for his program. He
had a huge ego and reacted poorly to disagreement. This led him to
approve massive assaults upon individual liberty during the war in
the name of national security. Whereas he threw himself wholeheart-
edly into the achievement of actions based upon the broad principles
that he advocated, he was often inconsistent in detail. For example, in
addition to approving the Sedition Act of 1917 and the infamous
"Palmer raids" conducted by his Attorney General, Wilson accepted
the institution of racial segregation in the District of Columbia, a
practice that persisted until after the Supreme Court's decision in
Brown v. *Board of Education of Topeka* in 1954.

Wilson, therefore, was a tragic figure. His fame as a reformer is
justly great, but he acted frequently in ways that were inconsistent
with his humanitarian principles. Moreover, his greatest principles,
summarized in his Fourteen Points, went down to defeat when he
was unable to persuade the United States Senate to approve his
policies in international affairs, a situation that certainly contributed
to the developments that led ultimately to World War II.

World War I not only frustrated Woodrow Wilson and dealt a
blow to political and economic reform, but it also led to cynicism and
disillusionment at home. In the words of Roger Baldwin, a conscien-
tious objector who later became the first president of the American
Civil Liberties Union, American pacifists were subjected to "a punishment longer and severer than that of desperate criminals."[33] Jane
Addams of Hull-House found herself forced into a radical position in
opposition to the state because her society had totally shut her out. A
person's primary allegiance, she wrote, is not to the state but to his or
her vision of the truth.[34] Of course well-known radicals suffered.
"Big Bill" Haywood, who had been active in the International Workers of the World (IWW) and the Socialist party, was arrested for
sedition in 1917 because he opposed the war. He had long advocated
syndicalism, in which workers would control industries and direct
action to insure the enforcement of laws when political action failed;
indeed, he was skeptical of the efficacy of purely political action.[35]
During the wartime period even citizens who held mainstream ideas
were suspect; the nation was in no mood to tolerate any dissent.
The war to "make the world safe for democracy" brought the
consequences that its critics had predicted: all over postwar Europe,

nations were seeking not peace and brotherhood, but spoils and self-interest.

One of the most interesting of the critics is very little known today. Randolph Bourne bitterly hated war and castigated liberals and intellectuals for rushing to its call at the behest of the state.[36] He dealt insightfully and brilliantly with the state in an unfinished essay in which he traced the historical development of the nation-state and analyzed the circumstances that brought about war.[37] He wrote that the republican state almost vanishes in a period of prolonged peace, but that war brings it again into its own. "War," he said, "is the health of the State." As such, leaders and elites often welcome war, for no longer are citizens indifferent, and the "large element of pure filial mysticism" that exists in their feelings toward the state are intensified. At such times there arises conflict within the state and the "pursuit of enemies within outweighs in psychic attractiveness the assault on the enemy without."[38]

Persons rule the government, but the mystic notion of the state behind them sanctifies their every action. Bourne's discussion of state symbolism, military achievement, and the flag is among the most perceptive in all of political literature.[39] Nations organized only for internal administration or lacking the political centralization of a dynasty, he contended, would be powerless to wage war. Only in a system such as exists today, a system of competing nation-states, could modern wars occur; they are a function of such a system.[40]

Bourne possessed a trenchant style and a keen mind. In addition to his other writings, he was a literary critic; his critical essays outline his beliefs regarding cultural leaders, and may also be read with profit for their implications for political philosophy.[41] He died before the 1920s but was a hero of the age among many intellectuals in that decade. Curiously, Bourne was not persecuted as were many others who spoke out against the war.

America thus closed out one of its most vigorous periods, the Progressive years, with a war that succeeded in destroying some of its accomplishments and suppressing many others. Regardless of the justification for the war, the effects of the war upon the United States were devastating. It killed not only many persons of numerous nations, but also the spirit of a generation.

NOTES

1. See, for example, the testimony of white soldiers regarding the Chivington Massacre in *Reports of the Committees*, 39th Congress, Second Session, Document No. 156, (Washington, D.C.: Government Printing Office, 1867), pp. 53 and 73–74; an excellent

account is Stan Hoig's *The Sand Creek Massacre* (Norman, Okla.: University of Oklahoma Press, 1961), which includes an extensive bibliography.

2. See Daniel Bell, *Marxian Socialism in the United States* (Princeton, N.J.: Princeton University Press, 1967), pp. 32–36.

3. Ibid., pp. 48–53.

4. Ibid., p. 55.

5. Ibid., p. viii.

6. See Laurence Gronlund, *The Cooperative Commonwealth* (Boston: Lee and Shepard, 1884).

7. See Bell, *Marxian Socialism*, pp. 25–26.

8. *Nonviolence in America: A Documentary History* (New York: Bobbs-Merrill, 1966), p. 109.

9. Ibid.

10. See the selections from *No Treason* in Merle Curti et al., ed., *American Issues: The Social Record*, vol. 1 (New York: Lippincott, 1971), pp. 569–574.

11. Benjamin Tucker, "The Relation of the State to the Individual," an address delivered in 1890, in Lynd, *Nonviolence in America*, pp. 111–118.

12. See the selection from his *Non-Resistance and Government*, in Leonard Krimerman and Lewis Perry, eds., *Patterns of Anarchy* (Garden City, N.Y.: Doubleday/Anchor Books, 1966), pp. 140–149.

13. The following discussion of the Social Gospel draws to a considerable extent upon Ralph Henry Gabriel, *The Course of American Democratic Thought*, 2nd ed. (New York: Ronald Press, 1956), chap. 20.

14. Ibid., p. 280.

15. For the development of Jim Crow legislation, see C. Vann Woodward, *The Strange Career of Jim Crow* (New York: Oxford University Press, 1957); the quotation is from p. 51.

16. Ibid., p. 110.

17. See Booker T. Washington, *The Future of the American Negro* (Boston: Small, Maynard, 1899).

18. Booker T. Washington, "The Atlanta Exposition Address, September—1895," in his *Up from Slavery* (New York: Doubleday, 1901), pp. 218–225.

19. In *Selected Speeches of Booker T. Washington*, E. Davidson Washington, ed. (New York: Doubleday, 1932); reprinted in Herbert Storing, ed., *What Country Have I?: Political Writings by Black Americans* (New York: St. Martin's Press, 1970), pp. 65–74.

20. Editorial in the Boston *Guardian*, December 20, 1902, reprinted in August Meier, Elliott Rudwick, and Francis Broderick, eds., *Black Protest Thought in the Twentieth Century* (New York: Bobbs-Merrill, 1965), pp. 32–35.

21. Editorial in the Boston *Guardian*, April 4, 1903, reprinted in ibid., pp. 35–36.

22. See John Hope Franklin and Isadore Starr, *The Negro in Twentieth Century America* (New York: Vintage, 1967), pp. 90–91.

23. *What Country Have I?*, p. 75.

24. See Meier, et al., *Black Protest Thought*, p. 37.

25. See W. E. B. Du Bois, "Of Mr. Booker T. Washington and Others," in *The Souls of Black Folk* (Chicago: A. C. McClug, 1903), pp. 41–59; reprinted in ibid., pp. 37–47.

26. (New York: Schocken, 1969).

27. See Harvey Wish, *Society and Thought in Modern America* (New York: Longmans, Green, 1952), pp. 353–356; for excellent treatments of the period, see Richard Hofstadter, *The Age of Reform* (New York: Vintage, 1955), and David W. Noble, *The Paradox of Progressive Thought* (Minneapolis: University of Minnesota Press, 1958).

28. See Gabriel, *American Democratic Thought*, chap. 22.

29. See Barbara Deckard, *The Women's Movement* (New York: Harper & Row, 1975), pp. 276–284.

30. Max J. Skidmore, *Medicare and the American Rhetoric of Reconciliation* (University, Ala.: University of Alabama Press, 1970), pp. 40–41.

31. Address at Buffalo, New York, September 1912, reprinted in E. David Cronon, ed., *The Political Thought of Woodrow Wilson* (New York: Bobbs-Merrill, 1965), pp. 174–181.

32. *The New Freedom* (New York: Doubleday, 1913), pp. 4–10.

33. See statement reprinted in Lynd, *Nonviolence in America*, p. 177.

34. "Personal Reactions During War," in ibid., pp. 178–191.

35. See "Testimony Before the Industrial Relations Commission," 1915, in ibid., pp. 217–241.

36. See "The War and the Intellectuals," in *War and the Intellectuals: Collected Essays 1915–1919*, Carl Resek, ed. (New York: Harper Torchbooks, 1964), pp. 3–14.

37. In ibid., pp. 65–104.

38. Ibid.; quotations are from pp. 71, 74, and 77.

39. See ibid., pp. 87ff.

40. Ibid., p. 80.

41. See ibid.

ADDITIONAL READINGS

Auerbach, Jerold S., ed. *American Labor: The Twentieth Century.* Indianapolis: Bobbs-Merrill, 1969, part I.

Blum, John Morton. *Woodrow Wilson and the Politics of Morality.* Boston: Little, Brown, 1956.

Clor, Harry. "Woodrow Wilson." In Morton J. Frisch and Richard G. Stevens, eds. *American Political Thought.* New York: Scribner's, 1970.

Daugert, Stanley M. *The Philosophy of Thorstein Veblen.* New York: King's Crown, 1950.

Diamond, William. *The Economic Thought of Woodrow Wilson.* Baltimore: Johns Hopkins University Press, 1943.

Egbert, Donald D., and Stow Persons, eds. *Socialism and American Life.* Princeton, N.J.: Princeton University Press, 1952.

Filler, Louis. *Crusaders for Americal Liberalism.* New York: Harcourt, Brace, 1939.

Fine, Sidney. "Richard T. Ely, Forerunner of Progressivism, 1880–1901." *Mississippi Valley Historical Review* XXXVII (March 1951).

Hays, Samuel P. *The Response to Industrialism, 1885–1914.* Chicago: University of Chicago Press, 1957.

Hicks, John D. *The Populist Revolt: A History of the Farmer's Alliance and the People's Party.* Minneapolis: University of Minnesota Press, 1931.

Hofstadter, Richard. *The American Political Tradition.* New York: Vintage, 1958, chaps. 8, 9, and 10.

Lerner, Max, ed. *The Portable Veblen.* New York: Viking, 1948.

Link, Arthur S. *Woodrow Wilson in the Progressive Era, 1910–1917.* New York: Harper Torchbooks, 1954.

Mowry, George E. *The Era of Theodore Roosevelt, 1900–1912.* New York: Harper, 1958.

Nye, Russel B. *Midwestern Progressive Politics: A Historical Study of Its Origins and Developments, 1870–1958.* East Lansing: Michigan State University Press, 1959.

Pollack, Norman, ed. *The Populist Mind.* Indianapolis: Bobbs-Merrill, 1967.

———. *The Populist Response to Industrialized America.* New York: Harper, 1962.

Resek, Carl, ed. *The Progressives.* Indianapolis: Bobbs-Merrill, 1967 (diverse collection of readings).

Waldo, Dwight. *The Administrative State.* New York: Ronald, 1948 (for Progressivism's effect on public administration).

Westin, Alan F. "The Supreme Court, the Populist Movement, and the Campaign of 1896." *Journal of Politics* XV (February 1953).

Woodward, C. Vann. *The Burden of Southern History.* New York: Vintage, 1960, chaps. 4–8.

12

Postwar Malaise

The years following World War I were characterized by political apathy and reaction. Weary of almost two decades of reform and disillusioned by the results of the war, Americans tended to turn inward. The most prominent features of the 1920s were dominance by business and commerce and relaxation of some of the more rigid standards of personal conduct. Prohibition brought with it extensive lawbreaking. In addition to encouraging a large segment of the population to break the law, it led to the beginnings of modern organized crime. Socially, with the spreading use of the automobile and the radio, the culture was changing rapidly.

Politically, on the other hand, the mood was to reject new programs, to be hostile to change, and to be content to permit business to run the nation. The voters overwhelmingly chose in turn Warren G. Harding, Calvin Coolidge, and Herbert Hoover to represent them. The "Jazz Age," for many a time of frenetic activity, was for others a time of "normalcy." The average person probably viewed the 1920s as a relatively pleasant time, and yet there were ominous portents. The decade had begun with a "red scare," in which the government violated civil liberties in a wholesale fashion and encouraged a fear of anything radical or foreign. In 1919 there were numerous strikes, some extremely serious. Motivated by fearful reaction to the Bolshevik Revolution in Russia, the press overlooked the workers' great grievances and was quick to charge that such strikes were inspired by communists. Many believed that organized labor was seeking violent revolution, and the hysterical reaction in part was fostered by prevailing sentiments of racism and fear of all things foreign. The dominant American union, the American Federation of Labor (AFL), was philosophically opposed to organizing unskilled workers, and this lent support to the revolutionary Industrial Workers of the World (IWW), which had been in existence for some two decades. The IWW prospered for a time, but soon dissolved as the government, reflecting the temper of the time, waged war upon it and other radicals.[1] The U.S. House of Representatives refused to seat a socialist elected from Milwaukee, Victor Berger, and the New York legislature expelled five socialist members.

The diminution of the red scare owed more to government action that shattered radical organizations and discouraged dissenters than to a growth of tolerance. At the same time there were strong indications that all was not well with the economy. In the later years of the decade, community relief sources began to show strain as a result of rising unemployment. The sociologists Robert and Helen Lynd in 1929 wrote a famous study of Muncie, Indiana, entitled *Middletown*, which documented the prevailing attitudes as well as the inadequacies of the economy. The long slump of unemployment there had begun as early as March 1924, and the Lynds concluded that the sentiment of the business class was summed up in a statement by the wife of a prominent businessman, who said that persons often came to her home claiming they could not get work, but that she did not believe them because anyone who "really tried" could get work of some kind.[2] There was a surface prosperity, but unemployment and other conditions requiring relief increased substantially throughout the 1920s. Many social workers expressed concern at the phenomenon of unemployment in the midst of prosperity. In 1928 the Belgian economist Henri de Man declared that as industrialism produces more goods, it also produces more unemployment. The same year the National Federation of Settlements found unemployment to be the "prime enemy of the American family." Although there are no welfare data for the nation or for entire cities prior to 1929, they do exist for some public welfare departments and some private relief agencies. They indicate that there was a uniformly rapid increase in relief costs during the presumably prosperous 1920s.[3]

Bigotry in the Postwar Years

In 1920 an event occurred that set the tone for the decade, and indeed the episode was drawn out for seven years. There had been an armed robbery of a South Braintree, Massachusetts, factory by two men who killed the paymaster and a guard. Shortly afterward the police arrested two Italian immigrants, Nicola Sacco and Bartolomeo Vanzetti. Sacco and Vanzetti were individualist anarchists, had gone to

Mexico during the war to evade the draft because of their pacifist beliefs, and could speak English only poorly. Although the evidence against them was flimsy, they were convicted in 1921. The judge in the case, Webster Thayer, was notably and admittedly prejudiced against anarchists, but the judicial system in Massachusetts permitted him to assess his own impartiality. Judge Thayer refused to permit a new trial when further evidence was uncovered, and the two were executed on his order in 1927 after prolonged motions and appeals.

The furor surrounding the case attracted the attention of Felix Frankfurter of the Harvard Law School, who was appalled at the trial procedures. After reading the entire 6,000-page trial record, he wrote an article in the March 1927 issue of the *Atlantic Monthly* condemning the conduct of the court and the prosecution; shortly thereafter he expanded his study into a book entitled *The Case of Sacco and Vanzetti* (1927). His involvement with the case and his failure to affect the outcome strengthened his concern for civil liberties, a concern that clearly influenced his later career as one of the most prominent Associate Justices ever to serve on the United States Supreme Court.[4]

Public sentiment undoubtedly was against Sacco and Vanzetti, but many liberals and intellectuals were convinced that they had been executed for no crime other than their opinions and that they were the victims of judicial murder. In 1939 the Massachusetts law was revised to take from a trial judge the sole authority as to the reopening of a case. Writers replayed the case in various forms. Upton Sinclair's *Boston* (1928), James T. Farrell's *Bernard Clare* (1946), and *The Big Money* (1936) by John Dos Passos were novelistic treatments; Maxwell Anderson based his play *Winterset* (1935) upon the theme; and many other novelists, poets, and playwrights found inspiration from the case.[5]

The years of the Sacco-Vanzetti appeals were also years of a nationwide resurgence of an organization that had nearly died out and had previously been limited to the South, the Ku Klux Klan. The Klan opposed all foreign groups, Jews and Catholics, blacks and Orientals, and labor unions. It was responsible for lynchings and mutilations, and played upon the worst prejudices of the people, having a special appeal to many prohibitionist, rural, and fundamentalist groups.

On a presumably more sophisticated level was the cult of eugenics. Many of the eugenicists asserted the superiority of Anglo-Saxon peoples and their right to rule "lesser races." They founded their attitudes largely upon works that had inspired some of the southern racists prior to the Civil War and upon the large body of purportedly scientific literature that had followed in the same vein since. Even such respected figures as the psychologist William McDougall and the geneticist Edwin East, both of Harvard, assigned superiority to "Nordics" and inferiority to all others.

Such teachings had a major impact upon the American legal system, even disregarding the support that they gave to segregationist and other racist laws and practices permeating the South and existing to a lesser extent elsewhere. In 1921 President Harding signed into law the Johnson Act, which established quotas for the number of immigrants from a particular nation allowed on the basis of the number of nationals from that country already settled here. In 1924 the Immigration Act replaced the Johnson Act and perpetuated quotas, making them even more restrictive, particularly for those whose origins were elsewhere than in western Europe. The same year the Japanese Exclusion Act closed any immigration from Japan. These acts proclaimed American racism to the world and openly evaluated a potential immigrant's worth on the basis of race and nationality, not personal factors. Various state statutes calling for the sterilization of "mental defectives," a practice that Hitler's Germany demonstrated could easily be turned against entire populations, also reflected the doctrines of the eugenicists. The Supreme Court in 1927 upheld compulsory sterilization in the case of *Buck* v. *Bell*, in which Justice Oliver Wendell Holmes delivered the court's majority opinion, the heart of which was that the state might call upon its best citizens for their lives, and that it might therefore call upon those "who already sap the strength of the state for these lesser sacrifices . . . in order to prevent our being swamped with incompetence." It is better, he wrote, to prevent those who are "manifestly unfit from continuing their kind. The principle that sustains compulsory vaccination is broad enough to cover cutting the Fallopian tubes. . . . Three generations of imbeciles are enough."

As C. Herman Pritchett wrote, there has seldom been so much questionable doctrine compressed into a few sentences of an opinion by the Supreme Court. Citing the court's acceptance of a completely unacceptable standard of legislative action, he pointed out that if it were indeed true that society could demand any sacrifice just because it may upon occasion demand the supreme one, then any protection established by the Constitution could be disregarded at will. As for precedent, he quoted Walter Berns to the effect that it is a broad principle that sustains both a needle's prick and an abdominal incision when one considers the results: "no smallpox in one case and no children in the other." Even beyond these arguments, and more significant as Pritchett recognized, "was Holmes's apparent failure to realize that there could be any question as to the scientific theories on which this legislation was based." He pointed out that it could be shown that state legislatures, in passing such laws, had been responding to the propaganda of small but active groups that advocated doctrines based allegedly upon scientific eugenic principles, doctrines that reputable scientists denied were actually valid.[6] Most significant of all is the question whether any such doctrine, even if it were universally accepted as valid, would be justified; a universally accepted doctrine may be in error. Moreover, is it ethical, or indeed is it even truly scientific, to apply scientific findings about groups to individuals?

Franz Boas, of Columbia University, was the most forceful adversary of those who advocated Nordic supremacy. His efforts were strengthened by revulsion toward the Hitler regime in Germany during the 1930s, when it became clear to many thinking persons just how dangerous racial doctrines were and to what degree they contradicted the basic traditions that Americans presumably revered. Boas argued that eugenics was a two-edged sword and that it was futile to expect to breed a race of supermen. He pointed out that the very idea of race superiority was pernicious and concluded from his anthropological studies that physical differences between human beings bore no relationship to cultural or mental differences.[7]

Political Statements in Literature in the 1920s

Frequently the political thought of a period is reflected at least as accurately in the works of its artists as in explicitly political writings. In the 1920s many Americans turned their attention away from politics and became preoccupied solely with making a living. Although he could hardly be called an artist, an advertising man named Bruce Barton captured the attention of Americans with an enormously popular book titled *The Man Nobody Knows* (1924). Barton's book told the people that businessmen were the true heirs of Jesus and that in fact Jesus, who picked twelve men from the bottom ranks of business and created with them an organization that conquered the world, was the true founder of modern business. Religion was thus welded onto the system which accepted President Coolidge's famous words, "the business of America is business."

In a more artistic vein were novelists such as Ernest Hemingway and F. Scott Fitzgerald. Both prolific writers, they produced a series of books and stories that captured the spirit of the times, most notably in Fitzgerald's 1925 novel *The Great Gatsby*, with its nervous and empty activity, and Hemingway's *The Sun Also Rises* (1926). Hemingway's protagonist in that work was Jake Barnes, an expatriate, as was Hemingway himself, whose impotence as a result of having been hurt in the war spoke to, and of, an entire age of Americans. Closer to Main Street than Hemingway's Americans in Europe or Fitzgerald's characters of great wealth were those created by Sinclair Lewis. In *Main Street* (1920) and even more so in *Babbitt* (1922), Lewis portrayed the narrow intolerance of middle-class and small-town America, devoted entirely to boosterism and business. In 1925 he emphasized a similar theme in *Arrowsmith*, that of a society in which medical research meant little and was socially less acceptable and vastly less rewarding than high-society medical practice, and in 1927, in *Elmer Gantry*, he illuminated the commercialism of much of modern religion. Lewis, however, did not jeer; although he frequently presented stereotypes, he did not lack sympathy for his subjects or for his society.

One who did jeer and who scornfully assailed democracy, yet who loved it because it was a great circus, was the Baltimore journalist H. L. Mencken. As newspaper columnist and magazine editor first of *The Smart Set* and later of *The American Mercury*, he took great delight in deflating all forms of windbags, whether in politics, religion, or business. He professed to be a follower of Friedrich Nietzsche, the German philosopher who believed in a rule by the superior, but his barbs, vicious though they often were, were sufficiently good natured as to call his devotion to the "superman" into question. His greatest target was Puritanism, which he defined as the haunting fear that someone, somewhere, may be enjoying himself. He exposed to ridicule the state of Tennessee and its ad hoc special prosecutor at the Scopes Trial in 1925, William Jennings Bryan, for defending the law that made it a crime to teach the theory of evolution in the public schools. He jabbed unmercifully at the rings and ribbons, the turbans and gold braid of American lodge members and military officers. And he noted, partly in sorrow and partly in glee, that a democracy's first reaction, when it is at all threatened or when it considers itself to be threatened, is to abandon its entire philosophy and engage in the most despotic of actions.[8] Mencken became the center of a cult among many intellectuals who hung upon his every word and experienced vicarious thrills as he aimed his verbal shafts at organized religion, the wealthy, and the commercialism and lack of taste of the 1920s. Although he remained a columnist for the Baltimore *Sun* well into the 1940s, his influence waned sharply in the 1930s, when Americans no longer were inclined to laugh at democracy; the times had become too serious.

Another figure prominent in the 1920s, Walter Lippmann, also continued his career for decades. Clinton Rossiter and James Lare wrote that Lippmann was one of the truly "essential" persons of modern times not in public office, and they ranked him with John Dewey, Thorstein Veblen, Frank Lloyd Wright, Charles Beard, H. L. Mencken, Eugene O'Neill, Robert Frost, Lewis Mumford, Roscoe Pound, and Reinhold Niebuhr "as a major contributor to the American way of life and thought." They classed him first and foremost as a political thinker and called attention also to the great volume of his work as a columnist, editorial writer, author of articles, and author of dozens of books.[9] Lippmann considered the dilemma of democracy to be that, although it is a more satisfactory form of government than others yet devised, its dependence upon majority rule is no guarantee of right action. Some writers ignore the problem, others degenerate into counsels of despair, and yet others retreat into a positivist social science in which they ignore values completely. Lippmann, on the contrary, dealt with values and with ways to make democracy viable. His answer was the "public philosophy." He was among the first to direct systematic attention to public opinion and to its role in democratic societies.

In an article in *Harper's Magazine* in 1926, Lippmann referred to the Scopes Trial in an effort to examine why the majority should rule. He noted that upon occasion the majority may act most unwisely, as it did at Dayton, Tennessee, and that even education is inadequate to assure that it will always be correct. He contended that majority rule is justified, not by its ability to discern the truth, but by a primitive intuition from which is derived a democratic view of life that gives rise to a feeling of fellowship and of ultimate equality with all other creatures. Behavior is too poor a thing upon which to base the judgment of a human being's worth; it is "not good enough to endure a cold and steady analysis." Majority rule is justified by a mystic sentiment, and as a political convenience; but all human decisions should remain tentative in recognition of possible error. We do not know of a less troublesome method than majority rule of arriving at political decisions, he maintained but "it may easily become an absurd tyranny if we regard it worshipfully, as though it were more than a political device." The majority does not, in fact, represent the whole.[10] He noted as early as 1922 in *Public Opinion* that democratic theory is faulty in failing to take account of the fact that self-centered opinions are not adequate to produce good government and that it is therefore involved in continuing conflict between theory and practice.[11]

Lippmann echoed Mencken's criticism of democracy's tendency to abandon its principles in time of crisis in his 1925 book *The Phantom Public*. He easily documented such a tendency in wartime, but asked why it existed in peacetime as well. He answered by calling international affairs and industrial relations the two greatest centers of anarchy in society. "Out of the national state with its terrifying military force, and out of great industry with all its elaborate economic compulsion, the threat against personal security always arises." These issues he believed sufficient to pursuade a people to adopt extreme measures to deal with them, and democracy as yet had arrived at no answers to the dilemma. He proceeded to question the existence of a "public" that directs the course of events. Anticipating pluralist thought, with its emphasis upon the clashing desires of interest groups, he defined the public only as "those persons who are interested in an affair and can affect it only by supporting or opposing the actors."[12] Professing an intellectual debt to his Harvard professors William James and George Santayana, Lippmann called for a new humanistic faith that would deal with the public interest. This was the burden of his *A Preface to Morals* (1929) and was an outgrowth of his contention that self-interest must not be allowed to dominate the "true public."[13] In any case Lippmann, with his emphasis upon the mystic and upon the obligation to the past as well as the future, was one of the few truly conservative political influences in the American tradition.

Protest Before the Depression

To describe the 1920s as a period of political apathy and one with little challenge to the status quo is not to argue that there was none. In 1924 Robert M. La Follette ran for President on a third-party ticket that he called "Progressive." La Follette had been a reform-minded leader in the Senate, reflecting the political climate in his native Wisconsin. His running mate was a Democrat, Burton Wheeler, from Montana. La Follette carried only Wisconsin, but he won 16.5 percent of the popular vote and ran ahead of the Democratic candidate, John W. Davis, in eleven states. His strength was essentially agrarian and reflected at least a strong minority of disenchantment. The Republican cry was "Coolidge or Chaos," and La Follette was portrayed as a radical, which by prevailing standards he was, although his program anticipated much that later came in the 1930s in the New Deal.[14]

Also important was A. Philip Randolph, coeditor with Chandler Owen of *The Messenger*, which proudly described itself as "The Only Radical Negro Magazine in America." Randolph organized the Brotherhood of Sleeping Car Porters in 1925 and long remained active in civil rights and labor affairs. One of his prime achievements was his contribution to the great March on Washington in 1963.

Randolph rejected racism and separatism, and urged black and white workers to combine for the same reasons that individual workers combine: to increase their bargaining power. He said that labor history demonstrated that employers recognized no race lines and were as ready to exploit a white worker as a black worker. Pointing to the existing abuses of child labor, he charged that capitalists were concerned only with profit. Every nonunion worker, white or black, he said, is potentially destructive of the standard of living of union members because a nonunion worker who is out of a job cannot be expected to refuse an offer that will improve his or her situation, even if that offer is on terms that unions would reject as unsatisfactory. In 1919 he applauded the efforts of the IWW to enlist blacks along with whites into one big union and noted that the AFL had recently set aside its "infamous" color line, not because of a change of heart but because of fear that blacks would become organized elsewhere.[15]

The phenomenon of lynching was directly attributable, Randolph believed, to capitalism.[16] The legacy of slavery, he said, was that blacks had been elated by their new freedom yet distrustful of their former masters and were not inclined to work. Because of the great need for labor, the South desired to make blacks work, and work cheaply. It therefore adopted vagrancy laws that resulted in unemployed blacks being jailed and then contracted them into the custody of employers who compelled them to work and to trade at company stores. Peonage of this sort, he said, applied to poor whites as well as to blacks. But in order to prevent black and white workers from recognizing their common interests and combining to present a united front against unfair practices, those in charge of the South's economy specifically encouraged race prejudice, which in turn led directly to lynching. Political parties chose the elected officials and the parties were financed by the ruling class; there was therefore no hope within the system as then structured, he contended. The tools that he saw as effective in controlling workers were the schools, to keep them uneducated; the churches, "to preach the Christianity of lynch law profits"; and the press, to foment race hatred.[17]

Randolph believed that socialism was the only hope. It would reduce lynchings because persons would no longer possess the power to make fortunes from the labor of other persons and would have no more incentive to encourage racial tensions. He admitted that not every case of lynching was traceable to economic causes but argued that the underlying economic issues conditioned southern psychology to the extent that they invited lynching, thus making them at least indirectly responsible. Socialism, on the other hand, he believed would provide education and the ballot for all; vagrancy, child labor, and peonage would no longer exist. Until it could be achieved, he urged that blacks practice self-defense. Despite his professions of pacifism, he argued that blacks should use both economic power and physical power, including armed resistance, to protect themselves.[18] As was consistent with his beliefs, Randolph condemned W. E. B. Du Bois for failing to emphasize the need for unions and for rejecting revolution.[19]

Although his concern was for the masses, Randolph was a middle-class intellectual who spoke and wrote largely to a middle-class audience. He organized railway porters into a union in spite of powerful opposition, some from other black leaders, but he had little success in projecting his message to slum dwellers. Far more effective, for a time, in arousing enthusiasm in the black ghetto was Marcus Garvey, with his Universal Negro Improvement Association (UNIA). Garvey spoke of black pride, an honorable past, and a glorious future for blacks. He sometimes spoke disparagingly of the light skins of such leaders as Du Bois, and he anticipated some of the program of the Black Muslims in advocating black businesses and economic nationalism. Garvey attracted numerous followers, hundreds of thousands of them in thirty cities. His downfall came in 1925 because of his Black Star Steamship Line, which was organized both to promote trade between American and African blacks and to facilitate his major goal, colonization and the formation elsewhere of a nation of American blacks.[20] He was charged with fraud, convicted, jailed, and eventually deported to his native Jamaica.

Because of race prejudice, Garvey argued, blacks could achieve progress only within their own nation. He professed friendship with whites and said that the principles of UNIA were consistent with white desires and black improvement. He had kind words for Booker T. Washington's refusal to seek social equality, and criticized other American black movements whose policies, he thought, would lead to "race destruction." Each race, he taught, should grow and develop by itself, and not frustrate nature's plan by introducing "mongrel types." He granted that blacks were constitutionally entitled to positions of political leadership in America but condemned Du Bois and others for advocating that blacks work to achieve them because such attempts would only lead to bloodshed. Africa was the place for blacks, not white society, and the NAACP and other integrationist associations he believed would destroy blacks in America.[21]

Garvey's program in many ways was indistinguishable from the racist programs of some white Americans. In fact, he received support from the Ku Klux Klan and, incredibly, invited the Grand Cyclops of the Klan to address a convention of his followers. This brought a blast from other black leaders, including Du Bois, whom he had severely criticized. Du Bois wrote in 1923 that Garvey had flown South to consult the Grand Cyclops after the Black Star Line had folded, UNIA's West-Indian membership had dropped, and his American supporters had become increasingly critical. He said that no one knew who initiated the trip but that the Klan probably had invited Garvey, indicating the worth of Garvey's policies. Du Bois noted that criticism finally drove the Klan-Garvey alliance under cover but that Garvey had advertised the Klan's program as demonstrating that it was impossible for blacks to remain in America, and that the Klan had issued circulars supporting Garvey and charging that his opposition was from the Catholic Church.[22]

In a friendly commentary on Garvey, John Henrik Clarke has written that blacks needed a Moses, and he had to be black. Du Bois, he said, had tried to rationalize the situation, not to appeal to the masses. Moreover, he had "gone overboard" on the war effort and become further estranged from the people. Blacks settled for racism rather than radicalism. Clarke quoted Adam Clayton Powell, Jr., to the effect that Garvey was one of the greatest mass leaders of all time, that he had been maligned and misunderstood, but that he brought to the Negro people for the first time pride in being black.[23]

Du Bois, on the other hand, pointed to Garvey's inconsistencies. Garvey had sensed, said Du Bois, that his emphasis upon color was driving away lighter blacks; indeed, he had protested that his organization included mulattoes and those of all colors. Du Bois admitted that it did, but said that Garvey's propaganda remained all-black because it was the color emphasis that brought him cash from Jamaican peasants. Blacks, said Du Bois, needed liberty, brotherhood, and equality. They had often been misled:

> And yet the world's Garveys are not solely to blame, but rather every worshiper of race superiority and human inequality. On the other hand back of all this lurks the quieter more successful, more insistent, and hopeful fact. Races are living together. They are buying and selling, marrying and rearing children, laughing and crying. They are fighting mobs and lynchers and those that enslave and despise, and they have not yet failed in that fight.[24]

Their fight had been a lonely one, however, and was to remain so for years to come.

NOTES

1. See Harvey Wish, *Society and Thought in Modern America*, (New York: Longmans, Green, 1952), pp. 415–417; also see Paul F. Brissenden, *The IWW: A Study of American Syndicalism* (New York: Russell and Russell, 1957).

2. See Max J. Skidmore, *Medicare and the American Rhetoric of Reconciliation* (University, Ala.: University of Alabama Press, 1970), p. 10.

3. Ibid., p. 11.

4. See Joseph P. Lash, *From the Diaries of Felix Frankfurter* (New York: Norton, 1975), pp. 37–40.

5. See G. Louis Joughin and Edmund M. Morgan, *The Legacy of Sacco and Vanzetti* (New York: Harcourt, Brace, 1948), pp. 375–454; this volume presents a detailed legal, social, and artistic history of the case and its effects.

6. *The American Constitution*, 2nd ed. (New York: McGraw-Hill, 1968), pp. 662–664.

7. See the excellent discussion of the 1920s in Wish, *Modern America*, chap. 18.

8. Mencken's works are numerous, but the best available sampling is that compiled by Alistair Cooke, *The Vintage Mencken*, (New York: Vintage, 1955).

9. See Rossiter and Lare's "Introduction" to *The Essential Lippmann* (New York: Random House, 1963).

10. Reprinted in ibid., pp. 6–14; quotations are from pp. 8, 9, and 13.

11. Reprinted in ibid., p. 20.

12. See portions reprinted in ibid., pp. 52–53 and 89–93; quotations are from pp. 53 and 89.

13. See Wish, *Modern America*, p. 469.

14. See V. O. Key, Jr., *Politics, Parties, and Pressure Groups*, 5th ed. (New York: Thomas Y. Crowell, 1964), pp. 259–262; see all of chap. 10 for an excellent discussion of the role of minor parties in the United States.

15. "Our Reason for Being," editorial in *The Messenger* (August 1919); reprinted in August Meier, Elliott Rudwick, and Francis Broderick, eds., *Black Protest Thought in the Twentieth Century* (New York: Bobbs-Merrill, 1965), pp. 81–84.

16. See "Lynching: Capitalism Its Cause; Socialism Its Cure," in *The Messenger* (March 1919); reprinted in ibid., pp. 85–91.

17. Ibid., p. 89.

18. "How to Stop Lynching," editorial in *The Messenger* (August 1919); reprinted in ibid., pp. 95–100.

19. "Du Bois Fails As A Theorist," editorial in *The Messenger* (December 1919); reprinted in ibid., pp. 91–94.

20. Ibid., pp. 100–101.

21. See *Philosophy and Opinions of Marcus Garvey*, Amy Jacques Garvey, ed., (New York: Universal Publishing House, 1923), selections of which are reprinted in ibid., pp. 101–109.

22. "Back to Africa," reprinted in John Henrik Clarke, ed., *Marcus Garvey: The Vision of Africa* (New York: Vintage, 1974), p. 117.

23. Ibid., p. 9.

24. From *The Century* (February 1923); reprinted in ibid., pp. 105–119; the quotation is on pp. 118–119.

ADDITIONAL READINGS

Auerbach, Jerold S., ed. *American Labor: The Twentieth Century*. Indianapolis: Bobbs-Merrill, 1969, part II.

Bernstein, Irving. *The Lean Years, A History of the American Worker, 1920–1933*. Boston: Houghton Mifflin, 1960.

Chambers, Clarke A. *Seedtime of Reform.* Minneapolis: University of Minnesota Press, 1963.

Franklin, John Hope, and Isidore Starr, eds. *The Negro in Twentieth Century America: A Reader on the Struggle for Civil Rights.* New York: Vintage, 1967.

Hicks, John D. *Republican Ascendency, 1921–1933*, New York: Harper and Brothers, 1960.

Leuchterburg, William E. *Perils of Prosperity, 1914–1932.* Chicago: University of Chicago Press, 1958.

May, Henry. *The Discontent of the Intellectuals, A Problem of the Twenties.* Chicago: Rand McNally, 1963.

Schapsmeier, Edward L. and Fredrick H. *Walter Lippmann, Philosopher-Journalist.* Washington: Public Affairs Press, 1969.

Stearns, Harold E. *Civilization in the United States: An Inquiry by Thirty Americans.* New York: Harcourt, Brace, 1922.

Storing, Herbert J., ed. *What Country Have I? Political Writings by Black Americans.* New York: St. Martin's Press, 1970.

Warne, Colston E., ed. *The Steel Strike of 1919.* Boston: D. C. Heath, 1963.

13

The Great Depression and Its Aftermath

Just as Jacksonianism brought to a close the formative period in the nation's history and inaugurated another, so the Great Depression marked the end of one era and the beginning of contemporary America. As the most severe economic catastrophe ever to strike the nation, the depression painfully demonstrated that earlier approaches to politics and economics were inadequate to deal with the new and complex conditions brought about by corporate industrialism. The depression period presents a fertile field for study, not only because it began many of the practices that characterize modern America and revived others dating from the days of Progressivism, but also because it illustrates the effects of three separate and fairly clear-cut approaches to the role of government: first, the nineteenth-century individualism of Herbert Hoover; second, the early New Deal with its emphasis upon aiding business and providing it with a key position in rebuilding the nation; and third, dating from 1935, the so-called second New Deal aimed essentially at increasing competition and controlling the power of private interests not responsible to the public. Part of the reason for the shift in the New Deal is that Franklin D. Roosevelt, the prime mover of reform and recovery, was guided more by a spirit of experimentation than by a definite political philosophy. This opened the way for the direct influence of pragmatism upon political action. Assessment of New Deal approaches is complicated not only by the complexity of the conditions themselves but also by the influence of America's anticipation of, and entry into,

World War II, which brought about changes of its own in American political and economic structures and practices.

However vague the conclusions may be regarding the two foremost orientations of the New Deal years, there is little doubt that the days of nineteenth-century individualism were gone forever, and that attempts to perpetuate them had brought only disaster. Yet many of the attitudes that brought about the crisis of the depression had been at one time accepted almost universally; in fact, to some extent they persist even today, despite our completely contrary practices and the vast evidence that today's interrelated world is too complicated for the older attitudes of individualism to be realistic, if indeed they ever were.[1]

The Thought of Herbert Hoover

Perhaps the person most reflective of America's basic political philosophy in the 1920s was Herbert Hoover. Hoover was an engineer by training and had built a considerable reputation for himself as director of the American Relief Administration, which distributed food in Europe after World War I. He was also one of the major architects of European economic recovery. He accomplished extraordinarily difficult tasks with astonishing efficiency and was Secretary of Commerce in the Harding and Coolidge administrations. He followed them, winning election to the presidency in 1928. Hoover may well have been the most competent administrator ever to serve as an American President, but he was inept politically and adhered dogmatically to a political and economic philosophy that was manifestly unsuited to the conditions that were to develop. His doctrinaire resistance to proposals that he believed to be incompatible with what he termed the "American System"—a relatively unregulated free-enterprise, profit-based economy—led to his downfall and the destruction of his previously unparalleled reputation.

Hoover believed that the greatest enemy facing the American people was socialism. In his book *American Individualism* (1922), published while he was Secretary of Commerce, he praised individualism as the basis for the American industrial system and the high standard of living that it had provided. He accepted some governmental regulation, but very little, and only that which he perceived to be consistent with free enterprise. In Hoover's opinion government must never become involved in the production or distribution of goods or services within the United States and must always encourage initiative and equality of opportunity. He denied that what he favored was laissez faire, but he feared that any significant growth in national power would bring alien practices and ultimately socialism.

"Confidence" was Hoover's greatest tool in dealing with economic difficulties. After the Great Depression had hit, he consistently maintained that a restoration of confidence in the business community was the cure. The basic principles of the economy were sound, he believed and although speculation had contributed to the depression, the major causes were from outside American borders. He continued to hold that only minimal regulation of business was permissible or necessary; anything further would add to the weakening of confidence and worsen the situation. He granted the need for regulation of utilities, banking, and finance, but nevertheless argued bitterly after he had lost the presidency that the New Deal's regulatory measures would lead the United States into a European totalitarianism.

Hoover issued a stream of incredibly optimistic forecasts during the early years of the depression, but it is clear that these were for the purpose of restoring confidence and that he was aware of the seriousness of the situation. He worked diligently with business and industrial leaders to persuade them to maintain wage levels, which they generally did voluntarily until the early 1930s. They could not maintain production and wage levels indefinitely when there was no market, however, and conditions steadily worsened. Hoover did exercise leadership but refused to call for coercion of the economy. He was enslaved both by his overoptimism and his acceptance of American individualism, and never did he recognize how the purchasing power of the American people had been overshadowed by their huge productive capability. He was an able man entrapped by a rigid ideology inappropriate for the complex world in which he lived. He always insisted that his policies represented true liberalism, as opposed either to laissez faire or to the "false liberalism" of his opponents.[2] The term was preempted by the New Deal, which he hated, and came to apply to policies that he considered to be the ruin of the nation.

Hoover was not a heartless man, as some of his critics charged when he continued to insist that poverty and unemployment were essentially local and, beyond that, were personal and individual. He was, however, dogmatic and inflexible, unable to understand the changes that had come to the world in which he lived. Unfortunately, he held power not in an earlier time but as the changes came; his inability to deal with them brought not only personal bitterness but national and international tragedy.

Part of the tragedy was that Hoover failed to understand the nature of modern corporate capitalism in certain key respects, and his failure was shared by most persons at the time and by many today. Not only had industrialism created power that could never have existed before, but the corporation had enabled that power to become concentrated in private hands with virtually no public responsibility. In fact, as economists Adolph A. Berle and Gardiner C. Means of Columbia University pointed out in their book *The Modern Corporation and Private Property* (1932), the modern corporation had become a form of nonstatist, or nongovernmental, socialism. Such an institution presented social and economic implications that had not been acknowledged by governmental policies or even basic theories. Corporations were great economic concentrations that were widely owned, but the owners had surrendered control of their wealth to a managerial elite. They were, in fact, quasi-public entities, and as such should be subjected to public control.

By developing an institution of such power, the "captains of industry" had changed the basic form of American society. No longer were Americans largely self-employed. The corporation had become the dominant institution in American life. It was innovative also in that it resulted in a divorce of ownership and control of wealth. No avowed radical or group of radicals could possibly have achieved such a revolution in the structure of American institutions. The industrialists ironically brought about radical changes while insisting that things should remain as they always had been. Berle and Means called into question the traditional logic of property and of profits, and they pointed out that "public" and "private" no longer had the same meanings that they once had. A. T. Mason has remarked that the book by Berle and Means was a "fitting prelude, perhaps even a prerequisite," to the New Deal and to the age of Franklin Delano Roosevelt.[3] In this he did not exaggerate.

A Conservative Critique of the American System

Most of the critics of American institutions had been liberals, but there was one group at the time that recognized the direction of corporate industrialism, yet called not for liberal programs to control change but for a turning back to a past that they assumed had been idyllic. The group produced one of the few truly conservative documents in the American tradition, and, significantly, its members had their roots in the South. Writing as the "Twelve Southerners," they produced a collection of essays in 1930 called *I'll Take My Stand: The South and the Agrarian Tradition.*

At the center of the group were four poets—John Crowe

Ransom, Allen Tate, Robert Penn Warren, and Donald Davidson—who had previously been among the "Nashville Fugitives," those who had published in a little magazine called *The Fugitive.* Also part of the Twelve were poet John Gould Fletcher, novelists Stark Young and Andrew Nelson Lytle, and historians Frank Lawrence Owsley and Herman Clarence Nixon. In addition there were Lyle Lanier, a psychologist, Henry Blue Kline, a journalist, and John Donald Wade, a professor of English. Most had been associated with Vanderbilt University. They proclaimed their agrarian manifesto just as the Great Depression was getting fully under way.[4]

The Twelve believed that the South, backward though it was, had created an admirable society which was based upon tradition, leisure, religion, aesthetics, and honor. The pursuit of economic gain was threatening its basic institutions. Nevertheless, the South still had the power potentially to avoid the course of industrial development that had overtaken the rest of the nation, or at least to humanize it.

The book consists of twelve essays, one by each of the Twelve. Varying considerably in subject, quality, and mood, the essays range in tone from benign good humor to vicious bitterness. They agree in stressing tradition, religion, and agrarianism. As a whole they are strongly racist; Robert Penn Warren's essay "The Briar Patch," for example, was a justification for segregation, although admittedly mild in tone and attempting a spirit of good will. Warren has spent the rest of his career trying to live down this early position and has rejected it totally. As economists, historians, and political philosophers, the Twelve failed miserably. They were the victims of some of the most stereotyped southern attitudes regarding race, the past, and the North. They sentimentalized history and distorted it; they oversimplified economics and sectionalism in America; and they failed to recognize the moral questions implicit in racism, even while they based their appeal upon a system that they alleged to be morally superior to others.

The value of their work, therefore, does not lie in their prescriptions or their preferences but rather in their criticism of corporate industrialism. They saw themselves as Jeffersonian agrarians, not recognizing the implications of their position in modern times and the essential conflict between Jeffersonian individualism and an emphasis upon tradition and formal religion. Nevertheless, they, like many liberals and radicals whom they would have despised, recognized the dehumanizing factors present in a modern mechanized and scientific civilization. Although the system that they praised was destructive to human values in its own way, it would be wrong to dismiss their critical evaluation of the direction of modern industrial society. The Twelve are important both for the substance of their criticism and for a lucid statement of a conservatism rare in American political thought.

New Deal Pragmatism

The Great Depression shattered American self-confidence for a time, and it wiped out much of the sentiment for laissez faire and the reverence for the wisdom of the business community. President Hoover, previously praised for his humanitarianism and his policies of cooperation between business and government, became an object of scorn, as were his optimistic forecasts. Americans, even those who desperately wanted to work and many who had been outstanding workers, were unable to find jobs; unemployment rose to unprecedented levels as the national income plummeted. So severe were the difficulties that the national government had to step in. The people rejected Hoover and his reluctance to make use of governmental power and turned to Franklin Roosevelt and his New Deal. The New Deal had no consistent and coherent political philosophy except that of experimentation; Roosevelt did not fear innovation, and he was not wedded to specific courses of action. He was therefore temperamentally suited to a program of trial and error, to applying new programs and solutions, and revising or rejecting them as the situation appeared to require.[5]

Roosevelt was not only the dominant figure of the New Deal but probably of the whole of American politics since Lincoln. He had long experience in government prior to becoming President, having been Assistant Secretary of the Navy under Wilson, the Democratic candidate for Vice President in 1920, and Governor of New York from 1929 until 1933. He was a pragmatic, humanitarian liberal who was undoubtedly far ahead of his Democratic party, which he led into the New Deal.

At first there was considerable cooperation between Roosevelt and the business and industrial community, and his early campaign was for a balanced budget. Nevertheless, his practical temperament brought him quickly to recognize that traditional remedies were inadequate to deal with the severity of the crisis. The imposition of governmental controls, along with the newly developed friendship of the New Deal for organized labor, ended the honeymoon between business and government and brought bitter and personal criticism of the President. Many persons and groups flung reckless charges of "socialism" and "communism" at Roosevelt, despite his explicit avowal and "tirelessly reiterated" aim of saving capitalism.[6] In truth his policies were middle-of-the-road. Certainly there was some move leftward from previous administrations, but it was more a move from the right to the center than to a "leftist" point of view. The increased popular acceptance of governmental action hardly qualified as "socialist" sentiment. Socialists, in fact, are among the first to recognize Roosevelt's goal of saving capitalism, and they generally have criticized him for his success. It is true that Roosevelt recognized that "a financial element in the larger centers has owned the Government ever since the days of Andrew Jackson,"[7] and he campaigned hard against "economic royalists." But although many of the privileged considered him to be a "traitor to his class," the New Deal was in no sense a revolution against capitalism or against the fundamental American political system as it had developed through the course of a century and a half. The only sense in which it was truly revolutionary might be its impact upon governmental practice.

The nondoctrinaire, innovative, and experimental approach of the New Deal was consistent with the temper of the time, and the nation had long been prepared for it by the development and growth of the American philosophy of pragmatism. As noted previously, William James at the turn of the century had taken a seminal idea advanced twenty years earlier by Charles Saunders Peirce and attempted to apply it to religion. Peirce had suggested that beliefs are really rules for action, and that the meaning of a thought lies in the conduct that it will produce.[8] James offered pragmatism as a philosophy that, in his words, could remain religious, like the rationalisms, but preserve the richest intimacy with facts, like the empiricisms.[9] Pragmatism as James defined it was an approach, a method. It was "the attitude of looking away from first things, principles, 'categories,' supposed necessities; and of looking towards last things, fruits, consequences, facts."[10] It was a philosophy of experience and experiment, and its essence was openness and opposition to closed systems and final judgments. Rather than arguing over principles, pragmatism encouraged concentration upon results of particular courses of action.

James was intensely individualistic, but pragmatism came to take on more of a social emphasis in the thought of John Dewey. Dewey refined pragmatism into a system that he called "instrumentalism." The thought of both men has been criticized because of their denial that there is a preexisting relation between ideas and truth. The critics charge James and Dewey with providing a philosophical system that is nothing other than a justification for expedience. James, in particular, often wrote using such terms as "cash value," a practice that encouraged some to misinterpret his views, which certainly never were intended to provide a philosophical framework for commercialism. Dewey defended himself and James from such criticism, admitting that all philosophies to some extent reflect the cultures within which they originate and that pragmatism and instrumentalism were not exceptions. Nevertheless, he argued, they also criticized their culture and contributed as a lasting legacy the idea of a universe that is not all closed, that in some respects remains indeterminate and in the making, that is adventurous and exciting. Instrumentalism, he suggested, should imply that technology and science are tools and that they should be used to shape the conditions of life.[11]

Dewey more than James emphasized the application of the scientific method to the solution of social problems. Along with James he rejected closed systems and notions such as natural law, as well as any form of determinism, including both Social Darwinism and Marxism. He stressed that human beings were not slaves to the environment but that they could apply intelligence to mold their surroundings and bring about consequences that were superior to those that otherwise would result. Dewey was a confirmed advocate of democracy and accepted its value framework. Instead of deducing liberal values from general principles or from natural law, however, he accepted them because he concluded that they produced socially beneficial consequences. He argued both for equality and for individuality as possible only within democratic systems. To obtain them, he would support democratic principles with scientific techniques. Science, to Dewey, was not the "art of accepting things as they are," as it was to the ancient Greeks, but rather "an art of control."[12]

It would be difficult to overemphasize Dewey's influence. He participated in numerous reform movements, his ideas revolutionized American education, and they strongly flavored American political thought. His greatest emphases were upon the development of a truly international community, greater equality in education and economics, and the use of public power to achieve socially desirable goals. Pragmatism's direct relationship to the New Deal is obvious; indirectly, its relationship to jurisprudence as it developed during the 1920s and 1930s is equally significant to the New Deal.

One of the first jurists to bring pragmatism to bear upon the law was Oliver Wendell Holmes, Jr., an Associate Justice of the Supreme Court from 1902 until 1932. Holmes had been associated with Peirce and James in the Metaphysical Club in Cambridge in the 1870s during the time that the ideas were developing that led to pragmatism. He brought to the court pragmatism's opposition to closed systems and rejection of the notion that constitutional principles are fixed and irrevocable regardless of changing conditions. He conceived of the Constitution as an instrument that permitted, and was conducive to, social development. It was not a written reflection of absolute and unchanging Truth that provided an exact rule for settling every case. He stressed that judges interpreted the Constitution and that this was unavoidable. In interpreting the Constitution their own attitudes toward social, economic, and political thought inevitably influenced their conclusions, however much they may have thought that they were being impartial, objective, and merely applying absolute standards. He did not object to this because he concluded that it could not be otherwise, but he did consider it vital that judges recognize their own prejudices and not be deluded into believing that their decisions were completely nonpolitical.

Throughout his tenure on the Supreme Court, Holmes was noted for the quality of his decisions, especially those that dissented from the position of the majority; he was known, in fact, as the "Great Dissenter." The courts had frustrated reform from the late nineteenth century into the first few years of the New Deal, and as the Supreme Court began to change its opinions during Roosevelt's second term, after 1936, it frequently turned to opinions by Holmes as a basis for its reasoning.

Holmes has been praised as a champion of liberty and a defender of the rights of the individual as opposed to the power of the state. His record in this regard, however, is inconsistent; in general, his position was to uphold the power of legislatures at any level— national, state, or local—to experiment as they desired. As H. L. Mencken pointed out in a witty and characteristically intemperate essay, Holmes often issued reactionary opinions that infringed liberty, as in cases dealing with prostitution, Prohibition, or espionage, including the case of Eugene V. Debs, in which "one finds a clear statement of the doctrine that, in war time, the rights guaranteed by the First Amendment cease to have any substance, and may be set aside summarily by any jury that has been sufficiently inflamed by a district attorney itching for higher office."[13] Although Mencken applauded Holmes for his decision in *Buck* v. *Bell* favoring compulsory sterilization, his ruling in that case also certainly supported the violation of an individual by the state. There may be some justification for Mencken's gibe that the liberals of the 1920s were so frantically eager to find at least one judge who was not violently and implacably against them that they seized upon certain of Holmes's opinions for comfort without examining the rest. At any rate his arguments did assist the court in its adoption of the principles of pragmatic jurisprudence.

Holmes outlined many of his principles as early as 1881 in his study *The Common Law*. His thought is contained in numerous writings and judicial opinions. His greatest contributions to jurisprudence and to American political thought were his adaptation of the pragmatic idea that the past should not completely determine decisions for the future and his recognition that the law was far from an exact and impartial science. These ideas were not new in America and would have been congenial to Jefferson; Holmes's achievement was in calling them to the attention of a legal system that had become increasingly rigidified in the late nineteenth century.

Although there were differences among the supporters of pragmatic jurisprudence, they all opposed a reverence for the past that disregarded consequences, favored experimentation with social programs, and opposed inflexible and closed systems in general. Despite inconsistencies noted earlier, the thrust of their decisions also tended to favor civil liberties and minority rights, at least in contrast with most earlier decisions. Roscoe Pound founded the "sociological" school of jurisprudence and produced in his works a general theory of law. Pound was Dean of the Harvard Law School for twenty years, until 1936, and his criticisms of the mechanical approach to the law that sought to infer decisions from natural law or absolute principles had considerable influence. Law was neither an absolute science nor the applied will of the state, but rather a process of compromise among various competing interests. Joining Pound in the sociological school was Justice Benjamin Cardozo. "Legal realism" was a school notable in the 1920s and 1930s, and was closely related to the sociological school and to Holmes. The realists, such as Thurman Arnold and Jerome Frank (the lawyer, not to be confused with the psychiatrist of the same name), dealt with the values of any given situation and attempted to derive a science of the law that was related to observed reality. They considered judicial behavior to be of prime importance because they held that the actions and decisions of judges *were* the law, in practice, and not merely interpretations of it. They stressed that a judge's preconceptions and prejudices influenced his actions and his decisions, and therefore colored the law itself. The realists attacked the notion that law implied a certain decision, inevitably derived from logic in all cases; they argued that to understand the law it was necessary to understand the factors that influenced legal decisions and that these factors could be understood only by applying the insights of sociology, psychology, economics, and political science. Although the phrase "science of law" was popular among them, "social science as applied to law" would have been more appropriate. The name of Justice Louis Brandeis must also be included among the great adherents of pragmatic jurisprudence.

The acceptance of pragmatism both in the legal realm and in the explicitly political world of Franklin Roosevelt was crucial to the New Deal. The willingness to experiment, the spirit of innovation, and the recognition of the necessity for change and active government that characterized the New Deal would have been impossible under the political system as constituted without similar developments in the judiciary. In many ways the New Deal, which was pragmatism applied to politics in the American setting, and pragmatic jurisprudence were two manifestations of a single strain of thought that had begun in the Progressive era. The strain continued into the Fair Deal of the late 1940s and the years of John Kennedy's New Frontier and the early part of Lyndon Johnson's administration, the "Great Society" years. In the judiciary it culminated in the Warren Court of the 1950s and 1960s and led to such revolutionary changes in the system as the elimination of legally prescribed racial segregation and judicially protected malapportionment in electoral districts.

In addition to his legal writings, Thurman Arnold is also important for his theoretical work on modern democracy and his trust-busting activities as Assistant Attorney General under Franklin Roosevelt. In *The Symbols of Government* (1935) and *The Folklore of Capitalism* (1937) Arnold dealt with the role of language in modern industrial societies and with the need to rationalize policies in terms of a "folklore" in order to achieve popular acceptance. He reflected pragmatic principles but had a low opinion of the mass of people, believing that it was necessary to manipulate them for their own good by appealing to them in terms of the symbols that they accept. The leaders, in contrast, were to be "fact-minded," while the mass remained essentially irrational. Arnold was witty and devastating in his writings, but his pessimism shines through the wit and leaves little room for hope.

Critiques of the New Deal

The most bitter challenges to the New Deal tended to be challenges to democracy itself. There were many on both the left and the right who contended that democracy had failed, that it was unable to deal with the conditions of the modern world. Those on the far left turned to the example of the Soviet Union, which was performing economic miracles and was in the process of adopting a new constitution that allegedly was to insure freedom. They could not have been aware of the impending Moscow trials, which, along with the Hitler-Stalin nonagression pact that unleashed Germany against its western neighbors, were to destroy the illusions of all but the most dogmatic. Those on the far right were attracted by the example of Hitler's Germany. Germany, too, was performing economic miracles and was the strongest power in Europe, if not in the world. Both leftists and rightists agreed upon the inability of democracy to cope with the crisis and pointed out that it could not even guarantee jobs or feed its people. Roosevelt came forth to inspire confidence and to argue that democracy had not yet been proved unworkable; he brought courage not only to many Americans who were in despair, but to many throughout the world as well. Before the nation began to pull out of the economic depths, however, there were powerful forces working to undermine democracy and turn the people to authoritarian solutions. Under such conditions the New Deal, innovative though it was, must be considered to have represented mainstream American policies.

From the right came such movements as those of Father Charles Coughlin, the "radio priest" who founded the National Union for Social Justice and whose anti-Semitism became an embarrassment to American Catholic leaders, the similar racist and anti-Semitic crusades of the Reverend Gerald L. K. Smith, Fritz Kuhn's American-German Bund, William Dudley Pelley's Silver Legion with its troops, the Silver Shirts, and numerous others.[14]

The most powerful movement was that of Senator Huey Long, whom President Roosevelt considered one of the two most dangerous men in America, until Long was assassinated in 1935.[15] Long had truly been a dictator in Louisiana and aspired to the same position in the nation. His "Share-the-Wealth" and "Every Man a King" programs forced Roosevelt to become more active in advocating social reforms, and Long and Roosevelt became strong political enemies. Long was probably one of the two major demagogues of the 1930s, the other being Charles Coughlin, who espoused a program strongly resembling a native American fascism; Long has also been categorized as close to fascist, although his proposals contained strong leftist and humanitarian elements that make them difficult to classify. After Long's assassination his movement fell apart, but Gerald L. K. Smith attempted for a time to carry it on. Smith remained active on the rightist fringe of American society until his death in 1976.

Another important critic of Roosevelt was Dr. Francis Townsend, who headed a movement for old-age pensions. Townsend called for a national sales tax to finance a $200 monthly payment to every older person, with the stipulation that the amount had to be spent each month; $200 was a significant monthly wage in the 1930s. Townsend's popularity played a role in encouraging the passage of the Social Security Act in 1935, after which his influence dwindled. On the far left were numerous varieties of communists and other Marxists.

The only American on the far right who is notable for his theoretical formulations was Lawrence Dennis, who formally advocated fascism for the United States. That there were some fears for the direction in which the nation was moving is evidenced by the popularity of Sinclair Lewis's 1935 novel *It Can't Happen Here*, depicting a fascist takeover of the country. Dennis rejected Marxism's humanitarian goals and its hope for a classless society. He contended that all politics require a ruling elite and an obeying mass. There were no objective standards of right and wrong, and the elite was to determine social policy according to its preference. The ruling elite would, and should, be all powerful, and it achieved its position by superior power; might, therefore, made right.

Dennis would have eliminated all restraints upon the rule of the elite. His scheme provided no place for federalism, a constitution, bills of rights, or separation of powers. Only a Fascist party was to be permitted to exist, and that only as a tool of the elite. He exalted the typical values of the fascist: power, discipline, and national unity. The elite had a responsibility only to itself, not to the ruled. Dennis shared his emphasis upon success with the pragmatists, and his worship of power and moral relativity recalled the Social Darwinists and other advocates of a science of man.

Dennis published prolifically, including three books of theory: *Is Capitalism Doomed?* (1932), *The Coming American Fascism* (1936), and *The Dynamics of War and Revolution* (1940). Like all fascists, Dennis stressed the role of the emotions. He contended that the intellect was merely the tool of the will and of the drive for power. Essentially, he viewed the human race in a Hobbesian fashion and prescribed a Hobbesian form of totalitarian rule. For Hobbes the purpose had been to protect the citizens; Dennis, on the contrary, was concerned with national glory. His concerns, despite his professions of realism, were strongly mystical, and his criticisms of liberalism, capitalism, and democracy were ethical criticisms. This was quite in opposition to his own viewpoint that ethics consisted solely of the will of the ruling class, not by virtue of superior wisdom or virtue, but entirely on the basis of their power.

Just as Dennis was the most articulate spokesman for the far right, so Paul Sweezy was his counterpart for the far left. Sweezy was an articulate spokesman for philosophical Marxism, not a Communist party activist. His writings began in the 1930s and spanned more than two decades. Sweezy sought to provide the Marxist academic criticism within the American system that European scholars had long supplied to continental nations. He criticized the usual reform movements as being mere palliatives that failed to relieve the true causes of distress. Fully accepting and applying

Marxist principles, Sweezy attempted to produce a complete analysis of American economic, governmental, social, and political institutions and trends. He stressed the internal contradictions of capitalism that would cause it to decay and agreed with Marxists of all persuasions that democracy could not exist within a capitalistic economic system, which would insure instead a dictatorship of the bourgeoisie. Class distinctions would become increasingly great, and capitalism would ultimately be destroyed by class conflict, which would bring socialism. His analyses provided no better prediction of the future than those by other Marxists. In fact, developments have often differed from Marxist expectations, not only within capitalist countries but on the international scene as well; nationalism, rather than class consciousness, has become the dominant force.

Representative of criticisms of the New Deal from American Communist party members was that of the party's General Secretary, Earl Browder, who alleged that only communists, not New Dealers, followed the principles of the Declaration of Independence.[16] In general the American communist activists have contributed little to American political thought; not even the many conflicts between those of one persuasion and those of another have theoretical relevance. As a whole Marxist communism in the United States has been too dogmatic to adjust its theory to native conditions, and Marxist activists have been more concerned with doctrinaire issues than with adapting an essentially alien philosophy to a far different situation from that in which it was born. Nevertheless, Marxism is a powerful force in world affairs, and it has strongly affected America, if only by America's reaction to it both internally and elsewhere. It would be imprudent to dismiss Marxist criticism out of hand simply because Marxism has not been shown to be adequate as a complete system. Certainly developments within many Marxist countries have shown that early capitalist critics demonstrated a conspicuous lack of perception when they denied the possibilities of Marxist vitality.

There were, however, socialists who were not dogmatic Marxists and who developed a specifically American socialism. Democratic socialism in the United States is most fully typified by Norman Thomas, who ran as the Socialist party's presidential candidate in every election from 1928 until 1948. Thomas was a critic of the New Deal for doing too little and too late. He accused Roosevelt of borrowing from the socialists because the situation forced him to act, yet of not borrowing enough and of being more concerned with saving capitalism than with true reform. Thomas first and foremost opposed war and poverty. His pacifism led him also to oppose the Marxist notion of inevitable class war, and he advocated policies more in the spirit of the individualism of Henry David Thoreau and Mohandas Gandhi than of Marxist collectivism.

As a socialist Thomas advocated a considerable amount of state ownership of the means of production and distribution, but he rejected economic determinism, whether Marxist or otherwise, and he called for cooperation between classes rather than class conflict. He favored a democratic, pragmatic approach to social and economic planning. Long before they were adopted by the New Deal, he urged the enactment of social security and collective bargaining, and he called for a governmental health care program that was not adopted until 1965, and then only minimally. Thomas viewed Marx as having provided many great insights, and he admired many of the accomplishments of Marxist societies. He strongly opposed much of Marxism, however, and viewed with horror the tyranny adopted in the name of communism.

The most prominent quality exhibited by Thomas was his humanitarianism. He helped to make respectable many of the programs that might otherwise have been rejected as "communist," and his pragmatism and flexibility rivaled those of the New Deal itself. In fact, the "liberal left" that has developed since World War II has carried on much of his spirit as well as many of his programs. His concern was for the people, not for the details of an economic or political dogma. His moderate tone was explicit in an article that he wrote in 1954, in which he said that the primary issue was not the economic system, not capitalism or socialism, but the political system and the way that it treats the people; the major concern was democracy versus totalitarianism.[17] Thomas was a democratic socialist, with the emphasis upon "democratic."

The discussion of criticism directed at the New Deal should not obscure the fact that the New Deal retained the firm support of most Americans and was immensely popular. There were within it the beginnings of socially and politically significant movements that flowered later and enhanced some aspects of democracy. Out of the 1930s came citizens' movements that worked to advance the interests of the consumer. Such groups as Consumers' Research and Consumers' Union have grown to have impact on public policy, and their reasoned criticism of industry and consumer products paved the way for such prominent individual reformers as John Banzhaf III and Ralph Nader. Nader's activities are well known, and Banzhaf's successes have included the removal of smoking commercials from radio and television, and piercing investigations of credit and sales abuses. As a professor of law at George Washington University, Banzhaf has encouraged the development of public-interest law practice to force both government and corporations to consider the interests of consumers. His rallying cry, and a very effective one, has been "Sue the Bastards!"[18]

The end of the 1930s brought with it the beginnings of World War II and the development of the modern American wartime state. The Great Depression had required a vast expansion in the size and powers of the central government, and the war required even more. After the war, with the intensification of international suspicions and the fact of the "cold war," came growth in arms manufacture and stockpiling, regimentation of Americans including peacetime conscription, and the creation of the "imperial presidency" along with pervasive security and intelligence forces both domestically and internationally. Not until the 1960s was there significant criticism of these tendencies, and not until the malaise and disillusionment produced by the Vietnam War and the exposure of police-state tactics in the Watergate affair was it possible to voice severe criticism without being condemned as "unpatriotic." It remains a question whether it will ever be possible to control the forces unleashed by corporate industrialism, by technology, and by the political concentration of power resulting from the Great Depression and World War II.

NOTES

1. See Max J. Skidmore, *Medicare and the American Rhetoric of Reconciliation* (University, Ala.: University of Alabama Press, 1970), esp. chap. 1, "The American Ideology."

2. See "Herbert Hoover and the Crisis of American Individualism," in Richard Hofstadter, *American Political Tradition* (New York: Vintage, 1958), pp. 283-314.

3. A. T. Mason, *Free Government in the Making*, 3rd ed. (New York: Oxford University Press, 1965), p. 701.

4. See "Introduction to the Torchbook Edition," by Louis D. Rubin, Jr., in Twelve Southerners, *I'll Take My Stand* (New York: Harper Torchbooks, 1962) pp. vi-xviii.

5. For an excellent documentary history and critique of the New Deal, see Howard Zinn, ed., *New Deal Thought* (New York: Bobbs-Merrill, 1966).

6. See Skidmore, *Medicare*, p. 8.

7. Letter to Edward M. House, November 21, 1933, in *Franklin D. Roosevelt: Selected Speeches, Messages, Press Conferences, and Letters*, Basil Rauch, ed. (New York: Rinehart, 1957), p. 121.

8. See William James, *Pragmatism* (New York: Meridian Books, 1965, p. 43 (originally published in 1907).

9. Ibid., p. 33.

10. Ibid., p. 47.

11. See John Dewey, "The Pragmatic Acquiescence," *The New Republic* 49 (January 5, 1927), 186-189.

12. See *The Quest for Certainty* (New York: Capricorn, 1960), pp. 99-100 (originally published in 1929).

13. "Mr. Justice Holmes," in *The Vintage Mencken*, compiled by Alistaire Cooke (New York: Vintage, 1955), pp. 189–197.

14. See the review essay by Leo Ribuffo, "Fascists, Nazis and American Minds: Perceptions and Preconceptions," *American Quarterly* 26, no. 4 (October 1974), 417–432; Daniel Bell, *The Radical Right* (New York: Doubleday, 1963); and Richard Hofstadter, *The Paranoid Style in American Politics and Other Essays* (New York: Vintage, 1967).

15. T. Harry Williams, *Huey Long* (New York: Knopf, 1969), p. 640; the other was General Douglas MacArthur.

16. Earl Browder, "Appendix" to *What Is Communism?* (New York: Vanguard, 1936).

17. "Our Welfare State and Our Political Parties," *Commentary* 17, (April 1954), pp. 342–351.

18. See Jarol B. Manheim, *Déjà Vu: American Political Problems in Historical Perspective* (New York: St. Martin's Press, 1976), chap. 6.

ADDITIONAL READINGS

Anderson, Sherwood. *Puzzled American*. New York: Scribner's, 1935.

Auerbach, Jerold S., ed. *American Labor: The Twentieth Century*. Indianapolis, Bobbs-Merrill, 1969, part III.

Bell, Daniel. *Marxian Socialism in the United States*. Princeton, N.J.: Princeton University Press, 1967.

Bodenheimer, Edgar. *Jurisprudence, the Philosophy and Method of the Law*. Cambridge, Mass.: Harvard University Press, 1962.

Calkins, Clinch (pseud.). *Some Folks Won't Work*. New York: Harcourt, Brace, 1930.

Frisch, Morton J. "Franklin Delano Roosevelt." In Morton J. Frisch and Richard Stevens, eds. *American Political Thought*. New York: Scribner's, 1971, pp. 219–235.

Fusfeld, Daniel R. *The Economic Thought of Franklin Delano Roosevelt and the Origins of the New Deal*. New York: Columbia University Press, 1956.

Geiger, George R. *John Dewey in Perspective*. New York: Oxford University Press, 1958.

Greer, Thomas H. *What Roosevelt Thought: The Social and Political Ideas of Franklin Delano Roosevelt*. Ann Arbor: University of Michigan Press, 1958.

Hofstadter, Richard. *The American Political Tradition*. New York: Vintage, 1958, chaps. 11 and 12.

Holtzman, Abraham. *The Townsend Movement: A Political Study*. New York: Bookman, 1963.

Hugh-Jones, E. M., and E. A. Radice. *An American Experiment*. London: Oxford University Press, 1936.

Ickes, Harold L. *The Secret Diary of Harold L. Ickes*. New York: Simon and Schuster, 1953, II and III, 1954; fascinating diary of Franklin Delano Roosevelt's Secretary of the Interior.

Konefsky, Samuel J. *The Legacy of Holmes and Brandeis*. New York: Macmillan, 1956.

Leuchtenburg, C. E. *Franklin Delano Roosevelt and the New Deal, 1932–1940.* New York: Harper & Row, 1963.

Lynd, Robert S. and Helen M. *Middletown in Transition.* New York: Harcourt, Brace, 1937.

Perkins, Frances. *The Roosevelt I Knew.* New York: Viking, 1946; account by FDR's Secretary of Labor.

Rauch, Basil. *The History of the New Deal, 1933–1938.* New York: Capricorn, 1963.

Rogat, Yosal. "Mr. Justice Holmes: A Dissenting Opinion." *Stanford Law Review* XV (December 1962) and XV (March 1963).

Rossiter, Clinton. "The Political Philosophy of Franklin Delano Roosevelt." *Review of Politics* XI (January 1949).

Sabine, George H. "The Pragmatic Approach to Politics." *American Political Science Review* XXIV (November 1930).

Schlesinger, Arthur M., Jr. *The Age of Roosevelt.* 3 vols. Boston: Houghton Mifflin, 1957, 1959, 1960.

Tugwell, Rexford G. *The Democratic Roosevelt.* Garden City, N.Y.: Doubleday, 1957.

Tull, Charles. *Father Coughlin and the New Deal.* Syracuse, N.Y.: Syracuse University Press, 1965.

Wecter, Dixon. *The Age of the Great Depression.* New York: Macmillan, 1948.

Wener, Philip P. *Evolution and the Founders of Pragmatism.* Cambridge, Mass.: Harvard University Press, 1949.

White, Howard. "The Political Faith of John Dewey." *Journal of Politics* XX (May 1958).

White, Morton G. *Social Thought in America: The Revolt Against Formalism.* New York: Viking, 1949.

Woodward, C. Vann. "The Populist Heritage and the Intellectual." In *The Burden of Southern History.* New York: Vintage, 1960, chap. 7.

14

Currents and Crosscurrents in Contemporary America

Contemporary political thought in the United States has drawn upon deeply rooted American traditions as well as innovations that developed as a part of, or in reaction to, the Great Depression and World War II. In addition there have been significant contributions in the past two or three decades that have come about in response to rapidly changing conditions in the modern world, changes that have been most prominent in the realms of society, technology, and politics.

With the growth of population, the increasingly organized and pervasive nature of institutions, and the newly created powers of invading privacy and even total destruction, the individual human being in the modern world has come to have progressively less control over the influences upon his or her life. Such conditions have led to both intensified justifications of the system and criticisms of it. The predominant political philosophy in recent decades, as reflected in such diverse programs and movements as Progressivism, the New Deal, the Fair Deal, the New Frontier policies of John Kennedy, and Lyndon Johnson's programs for the Great Society, has been liberalism. Modern liberalism has become so pervasive since the New Deal, in fact, that it represents mainstream American political thought. This is not to deny that much of modern conservatism can also be identified as mainstream, but it clearly has been secondary to the dominant current of liberalism. Recently, however, the term "liberal" has taken on a measure of unpopularity, and there is widespread disillusionment with many of the approaches that once excited the nation.

Criticism of contemporary liberal political assumptions has come from both conservative and leftist-oriented thinkers. Examination of these criticisms provides insight into the substance of much modern political thought. Before turning to these, however, it is useful to look at some of the evaluations of today's society provided by writers in such diverse fields as theology, psychology, and sociology. Indeed, a plausible claim can be made that these thinkers have contributed as much to contemporary political theory as those whose concerns are more explicitly political.

Political Thought from Nonpolitical Writers

Among those who have contributed to an understanding of contemporary political phenomena, Reinhold Niebuhr, utilizing an essentially theological approach, has had considerable influence on American political thought. Niebuhr in his early years was an exponent of the Social Gospel of Walter Rauschenbusch and others but became more influenced by Marxism in the 1930s. In his early years as the minister of a church in Detroit, he had become concerned with the dehumanizing effects of industry, particularly the assembly line, on his working-class parishioners. He moved to the faculty of Union Theological Seminary but retained his social consciousness and his concern for the power relationships that he saw as dominant in society. He moved into, and out of, Marxism in the early 1930s, with his political thought increasingly influenced by his conservative theology.

Niebuhr joined the Socialist party and supported Norman Thomas, but unlike John Dewey, who was also a socialist, he was not optimistic. He rejected Dewey's contention that science and reason can bring about improvement in the human condition, and he argued that human beings in groups are even more immoral than as individuals and that therefore the prime consideration in any political system is pure power. As groups grow in size, they grow in power but become less cohesive, finding it increasingly more difficult to achieve self-consciousness except in conflict with other groups. Groups are also less governed by moral restraints than are individuals.[1] The implications for international relations are obvious.

Niebuhr's pessimism, however, was not complete. Just as humankind has the capacity for evil and requires restraint, he believed, so also it has the capacity for good and requires freedom. Evil does not result from human institutions but is rather a part of human nature, though not the whole of it. Because of ego involvement human beings can never achieve objectivity and can never apply an impartial science to human affairs; science can be valuable, but it cannot provide final answers. Recognizing the duality of human nature, Niebuhr divided humankind into two parties: the "children of light," those who believe that self-interest should be subjected to a higher law, and the "children of darkness," those who know no law beyond their own will and interests. The children of light are virtuous but usually foolish because they fail to recognize the power of willfulness, including their own; the children of darkness are wise because they do understand that power, but they are evil. Niebuhr believed in freedom and in democracy, but he did not accept natural law as their base, setting forth instead a tragic view of humanity that recognized both virtue and evil in human affairs. Democracy is not perfect, nor are people perfectible; they must be subject to authority, yet control that authority.[2] There are no final answers on earth, and democracy must not preclude criticism of any principle or idea. It is significant that his 1944 book *The Children of Light and the Children of Darkness* bears the subtitle "A Vindication of Democracy and a Critique of Its Traditional Defense."

In his later years Niebuhr mellowed somewhat in his criticism of what he considered to be sentimental or utopian thought and its consequences. His emphasis upon both the good and evil in human nature remained. The law of love he conceded to be the basis of moral life, but people are too self-concerned, he believed, to obey it by a mere act of will. There is, however, a social sense that prompts "the self to bethink itself of its social essence and to realize itself by not trying too desperately for self-realization."[3] In the end, despite Niebuhr's great influence on American thought, it appears that Wilson Carey McWilliams is correct in asserting that his basic political ideas are largely the same as those of the liberals whom he criticizes.[4]

Niebuhr approached politics from a theological orientation; other modern writers have found insights from psychology. Harold D. Lasswell, for example, educated in both political science and psychoanalysis, applied Freudianism to politics in his work *Psychopathology and Politics* (1930). He identified political actors by their personality types and concluded that, since they were shaped by their psychological backgrounds, their actions were predictable. Lasswell accepted the findings of sociologists Gaetano Mosca, Vilfredo Pareto, and Robert Michels in Europe that all groups are led by elites and thus argued that democracy consists not of rule by the people but rather of rule by an elite chosen by the people to insure restrictions upon the rulers.[5] He considered equality to exist along with elite rule if "elite recruitment is based on values to which there is equal access."[6]

Some of the greatest insights arising from the application of psychoanalysis to politics are to be found in the work of Erich Fromm. In *Escape from Freedom* (1940), *The Sane Society* (1955), and numerous other writings, he developed the theme of alienation within modern industrial society resulting from depersonalization and a treatment of persons as objects and commodities. Such alienation causes many persons to seek an "escape from freedom" in destructive activity, extreme conformity, or the acceptance of authoritarianism. He noted a tendency to judge persons by their adjustment to society, not by whether they were right or wrong. Many social scientists and therapists define "mental health" by just such an adjustment, but Fromm argued that societies may themselves be sick and that adjustment to such societies cannot be logically the criterion of mental health. A healthy society would be one in which human beings develop in accordance with the laws of their own nature, spontaneously relating to physical things by voluntary and creative work, and to other human beings by love.

Fromm considered many modern institutions to be corrupting, and he called for human beings to be true to themselves and their own authority, and not to be subjected to the authority of others. He advocated a political system combining both centralized and decentralized units, with citizens participating in decisions that affect them and workers participating in management. Meaningful worker participation would require that all have a stake in the final product of their labor and that they be fully informed of the conditions affecting them. The same principle would apply to political life, with citizens prescribing the functioning of their own institutions and relying upon discussion in small local groups of 500 or fewer. Such "town meetings" across the nation would constitute collectively a "House of Commons," and another house could be formed consisting of representatives elected from the whole country. Fromm would provide also for a nationally elected executive and for new forms of education.[7] Although Fromm's rather utopian scheme is interesting, his greatest value lies in his description of the sickness of societies dominated by corporate industrialism.

Walt Anderson has taken an idea formulated by the late psychol-

ogist Abraham H. Maslow and related it to politics in a highly
significant fashion, especially in relation to considerations of sane
versus insane societies. Maslow thought of the person with sound
mental health as being "self-actualizing." He said that although most
sociologists and anthropologists would take it hard, self-actualizing
persons transcend themselves and their culture to become a little
more of their species and a little less of their local group. Anderson
noted that political scientists might also take it hard because that idea
might well undermine traditional political notions of obligation and
authority.[8] Self-actualized persons, according to Anderson, simply
outgrow much of what they have been taught and grow beyond the
confines of their social and political institutions. Of course Thoreau
was saying the same thing from a different perspective a century
before, but Maslow and Anderson have added a psychological dimension to the argument.

Sociologist David Riesman and others have suggested a similar
formulation in their notion of the "autonomous" personality type.[9]
Although self-actualizing or autonomous persons may choose to be
thoroughly conventional in daily behavior and not rebels at all, they
are capable of unconventionality and even of rebellion should conditions warrant. Their attitude toward social institutions is one of
tolerance, not firm acceptance, and their conventionality would be
thrust off immediately in the event that it became inconvenient or
too costly for them to maintain.

Anderson is correct in identifying the revolutionary potential of
an idea such as that of the self-actualizing person. If it is accurate, he
said, it means that many of society's strongest and wisest members
are within society in a manner fundamentally different from other
members. Their rebellion, if it occurs, results not from deprivation as
the Marxist would assume, nor from personal pathology, as asserted
by Freud, but from rational choice. Society's healthiest members
would therefore present the greatest potential for radical action
although not necessarily the greatest likelihood of such action.[10]

Maslow, Anderson, Riesman, and Fromm present stimulating
ideas regarding the nature of society and the relationship to society
of the individual personality. At issue, of course, is the definition of
"mental health." Critics such as psychiatrist Thomas Szasz have
contended that societies define "insanity" and "mental health" in
political, not scientific, ways. Szasz has argued that modern psychiatry frequently serves the state in precisely the same manner as do
police and correctional agencies by enforcing conformity to social
goals, and that the medical model is simply inappropriate when used
to define mental states.[11]

The Conservative Critique of Modern Political Assumptions

At the same time that many began to turn their attention to the conditions of modern life, the development of the wartime state and its continuance because of the cold war brought further concern.[12] The modern state and the modern corporation increased in power at an unprecedented rate, and militarization came to be accepted as a part of American life. According to historian Arthur Ekirch, few Americans realize the "extent to which military influence and control [has] penetrated what would normally have been regarded as exclusively civilian responsibilities and institutions."[13] With the adoption of peacetime military conscription and what Ekirch has called the "garrison state" came governmental propaganda that individual sacrifice was a good in itself and that any service, so long as it was to the state, constituted a democratic privilege.[14]

Traditionally, of course, American political thought has considered the state to be the servant of the people. The emphasis in the cold war era upon duty to the state rather than upon the rights of the people was in direct contradiction to the thought of most of the Founding Fathers and would have been branded by Thomas Jefferson as a dangerous subversion of American principles. Nevertheless, even the bulk of the liberal community accepted the argument, and it went without question, from mainstream political elements at least, until the downfall of Richard Nixon. Liberals and conservatives alike, for example, praised John Kennedy's famous statement in his Inaugural Address: "Ask not what your country can do for you, ask what you can do for your country."

The growth in governmental and nongovernmental power encouraged some scholarly attention to pacifism and anarchism as the years progressed, but relatively little. The growth of power, especially as applied to liberal programs, did however stimulate questions from the mainstream as to the role of government. More penetrating questions came from a vocal conservative movement.

In 1944 Friedrich A. Hayek published his enormously popular *Road to Serfdom.* Hayek was an Austrian economist who was then a British citizen and who later joined the faculty of the University of Chicago. He called himself a liberal of the nineteenth century and charged that economic planning brought with it an inevitable loss of human freedom. His argument was reminiscent of that of Herbert Hoover; all forms of collectivism, he believed, brought tyranny by ignoring the ends of individual citizens.

The essence of Hayek's position was that a plan, in order to be effective, had to be carried through to completion. In order to carry it through to completion, it had to be placed beyond the reach of popular control. If the plan were beyond control, the people no longer ruled; the planner would be supreme. As Hayek saw it, governmental power had grown, and the power of the individual had lessened. He believed that as a rule it was well-meaning reformers who brought about this turn toward collectivism and paved the road to serfdom. He considered individual choice in the marketplace to be the basis for freedom and did not admit any degree of restriction on that freedom by nongovernmental factors. Historically, of course, there is no necessary incompatibility between democracy and socialism and no necessary correlation between capitalism and democracy. In fact, the Anglo-American traditions of popular government predate American or English capitalism. Nevertheless Hayek presented a sophisticated and tightly reasoned argument, and he did identify some of the potential for danger inherent in governmental economic planning.

Hayek's book attracted the immediate attention of American conservatives, most of whom failed to recognize the complexity of his thought and interpreted him as calling purely for laissez faire. For example, he wrote that an extensive system of social services is compatible with economic competition if the system of services is properly organized.[15] He said that freedom is endangered only if a society attempts to provide its citizens with a given level of comfort or to insure the position of a person or group when compared with others. If there were genuinely insurable risks, he conceded, there were strong arguments to support "comprehensive systems of social insurance."[16] Because as a whole the conservatives of the 1940s strongly opposed such programs, they appeared to have been attracted more to Hayek's title than to the thorough digestion of his thought; it is worthy of note in this connection that *Reader's Digest* condensed his book for popular consumption.

The Road to Serfdom stimulated two rejoinders, Herman Finer's *Road to Reaction* and Barbara Wootton's *Freedom Under Planning*, both published in 1945. Finer pointed out some difficulties in Hayek's book but relied mainly upon bitter denunciation. Wootton's book is a much more incisive retort, alleging that freedom and planning are indeed compatible, but admitting that the process does involve some danger. There were probably more points of agreement between Hayek and Wootton than either would have recognized or admitted.

Hayek paved the way for the New Conservative movement that Peter Viereck began at the end of the 1940s, a movement that included such figures as Russell Kirk, Clinton Rossiter, and a variety of writers, not all of whom would agree on anything other than major points. Viereck's study of Metternich, *Conservatism Revisited* (1949), dealt with order and the preservation of humane values. In the main Viereck followed classic conservative thought, but he welcomed the liberal social conscience and admitted that the values that he sought to conserve were liberal values. Like the liberals, he favored change but stressed that it must be evolutionary, not revolutionary. As a true conservative, however, he had a low estimate of human nature and a reverence for tradition. Nevertheless, he cautioned conservatives against blind opposition to the programs that originated in the New Deal because those programs fit his definition of evolutionary change and prevented more revolutionary measures. Viereck strongly attacked right-wing extremism, which he contended arose from populistic influences; he applauded the defeat of Senator Joseph McCarthy, the self-proclaimed defender of democracy against communism in the 1950s, and he also rejected the close association with the business community that characterized many conservatives. Although as a conservative he emphasized a class hierarchy, many modern liberals share his concern with the quality of life and with humane values.[17] Viereck's writings are essentially moderate and witty statements whose benign tone fits well with modern liberalism.

Russell Kirk, on the other hand, wrote with no trace of moderation. Clinton Rossiter, himself a conservative, described Kirk as a man who had lost patience with developments in America in every field from art to politics. In his zeal to return to classic conservative thought, he said, Kirk sounded like a radical by attacking what for better or worse had become the American way of life. He had the sound of a man born a century and a half too late and in the wrong country.[18] And so he had.

Kirk outlined his approach in *The Conservative Mind* (1953), stressing his convictions that civilized society requires order and classes and that a divine intent rules all. Human beings, he contended, are more emotional than reasonable and must therefore be controlled. Moreover, property and freedom are inseparably connected, and changes are more likely to be for the worse than for the better. Kirk was frankly drawn to the past and would restore it and its aristocracy rather than turning to the leaders of modern business. Good government was his goal and popular government his fear. His temperament is illustrated by the title of his 1963 book *Confessions of a Bohemian Tory*. So great was his enthusiasm for hierarchy that even such things as poverty and ignorance he saw not as evils, but as "either indifferent, or else . . . occasions for positive virtue, if accepted with a contrite heart."[19] He favored the economic policies of the nineteenth-century advocates of laissez faire but he abhorred their individualism and their rejection of tradition as a guide. His doctrines, like his temperament, seem misplaced and irrelevant in modern America.

Willmoore Kendall, a political scientist, presented a different form of conservatism. He denied that conservatism was wedded to aristocracy or that it was hostile to change as such, although he admitted its opposition to certain kinds of changes. He also denied that conservatism was against governmental power or that it was allied with free enterprise. Instead, he argued, conservatism was political loyalty to the institutions and practices devised by the Founding Fathers in the Philadelphia Convention.[20] He opposed liberal programs because he contended that they were at variance with those laid down by the Founding Fathers. Congress he saw as representing a form of democracy and providing a stability of which he approved; the power of the President, on the other hand, represented a populistic and innovative strain that he opposed. Kendall argued that all societies had an orthodoxy that they would not and could not permit to be attacked. American society, therefore, should protect its orthodoxy, by frankly authoritarian and nonlibertarian means if necessary. The bulk of his writing generates the clear impression that the Constitution's protections of liberty are its most expendable parts.

Kendall scorned the pursuit of self-interest, which he thought to be the foundation of modern liberalism that followed Thomas Hobbes and John Locke, and called for attention to duty. There is a higher law that should dominate the actions of humanity, and that higher law, not contract theory or consent of the governed, should determine national policies, Kendall believed. He denied that the higher law was represented by majority opinion. His conclusions are starkly at variance with those of Viereck. Viereck, for example, supported Joseph McCarthy's ultimate censure by the Senate and the Supreme Court's efforts to end racial segregation; Kendall opposed both. In his enthusiasm for orthodoxy Kendall came close to embracing a stifling conformity. In his efforts to oppose communism he contradicted his own basic argument, contending that the consensus of the American people did not favor an open society and therefore that they were justified in suppressing deviant political opinion.[21] It would appear that higher law is appropriate when it supports Kendall's position, but that public opinion may be the criterion of truth if it provides stronger support, despite the fact that his entire argument denies the validity of public opinion as a justification for political action. One of Kendall's most prominent characteristics was the conviction that his opinion constituted the Truth; in such circumstances, any justification may appear to be appropriate without regard to consistency.

As discussed earlier, much of what may pass for conservatism in the American tradition is really "conservative" only in contrast to the dominant liberalism. Figures such as John Adams, Alexander Hamilton, John Quincy Adams, John C. Calhoun, E. L. Godkin, and William Graham Sumner may be identified with American conservatism, along with two more members of the Adams family active as historians and social thinkers near the turn of the century, the brothers Henry and Brooks Adams. During the 1920s the Neo-humanist thought of the elitist literary critics Paul Elmer Moore and Irving Babbitt also contributed to conservative thought in America. In varying degrees, they all were suspicious of democracy and equalitarianism, preferring an ordered society with an identifiable aristocracy.

Essentially modern conservatism in the United States follows one of two directions. One is that charted by the Manchester liberals of the nineteenth century, who were identified with laissez-faire individualism and minimal government. Modern versions of their doctrines are more or less accepted by such diverse representatives as Hayek, Milton Friedman, Barry Goldwater, and Ayn Rand. The other direction is taken by a group that rejects such individualism and places society and tradition at the point of concern. This group also includes a great variety of thinkers, such as Walter Lippmann and William F. Buckley, Jr., in addition to Viereck, Kirk, and Kendall. It tends to have more in common with classical conservatism than has the individualist group.

Of course, not all conservative political thinkers fit neatly into either of these categories. One such theorist is Robert Nozick, although his work bears some resemblance to that of the individualist school. Nozick is one of the few able and articulate writers among a large number representing wide variation in detail who may be called right-wing individualist anarchists. In his work *Anarchy, State, and Utopia* (1974), Nozick showed himself as hostile to the state, which he assumed to be the greatest violator of individual rights. Working from a theory of individual rights, he argued that persons should be treated as ends, not as resources for others, and that they can arrive at their potential only when their rights are protected and respected. Thus he favored a minimal state, one that exists only to protect rights. Unfortunately, he treated rights in so restricted a fashion that what emerged was the protection of a virtually unqualified right to property, and nothing else.

George Kateb in a superb essay demonstrated the tragic narrowness of Nozick's approach.[22] Kateb conceded that there should be a growing fear of the state in America, and it should truly be fear, not annoyance or irritation. The state is all pervasive and it has clearly shown that there is no crime of which it is incapable. We are not yet slaves, he said, but we are progressively less free as the state encroaches more and more. Because of Richard Nixon's appointments to the bench, the Supreme Court has defaulted in its task to protect the citizen so that only the theorist remains to awaken the people or to sharpen their willingness to resist. Kateb called for a new Tom Paine but wrote sadly that Nozick not only failed to fulfill the role but that he increased the dangers. The "terrible distortion" that destroyed the book's usefulness in defending limited government was Nozick's definition of rights as nothing but the right to property. As Kateb pointed out, an unqualified right to property in most circumstances leads directly to the degradation of huge numbers of persons who would have a theoretical right to property, but who in fact own no property.

Nozick denied that property brought power, and he argued for unlimited acquisition, assuming that there were no fraud or force. He stressed that human beings have a duty to respect others but said that there existed no duty to relieve the distress of others. Arguing as if the great power of the modern state resulted from its effort to redistribute property to achieve economic equality, he wrote that if free individuals living in a state of nature today were to refound a state, they would do it solely to protect their property and in such a manner that it did not threaten their right to property. As Kateb made clear, much property is created by the state itself and would not have existed in a state of nature. Moreover, Kateb felt that there is a duty to relieve distress, especially if it can be done at little or no inconvenience. Finally, according to Kateb, it is simply wrong to credit efforts to transfer property from the wealthy to the poor as the cause of the growth in state power. The swollen state, he said, results from the corporate empire, with its subsidies to business and industry and its unimaginably large sums spent on armaments.

Kateb's most telling point goes beyond questions of fact or interpretation to deal with consequences. Realizing that the state's absence would have been too dangerous for property, Nozick argued for a minimal state, although he appears to have preferred no state. The state would be minimal in that it would exist only to protect property, but, according to Kateb, this minimal function might involve "a vast state apparatus if it was required to repress a numerous discontented mass that felt itself neglected or exploited." The job would be minimal, but the powers required to perform the job might be great. "The night watchman state can be a police state," and Nozick's principles would not prevent it.[23]

Leftist Thought and Movements for Reform

Kateb noted that Nozick could not be the new Tom Paine, but felt that someone of his brilliance was needed. Certainly the American left, throughout the twentieth century at least, has been trying to fulfill the role of a Tom Paine. One who tried was Scott Nearing, born in 1883 and still alive and well in 1977. He studied with economist Simon Patten, whose influence he acknowledged grate-fully, and he devoured works by Tolstoy, George Bernard Shaw, John Ruskin, Henry George, and Edward Bellamy.[24] He had been a parishioner in the church of Russell Conwell, of "Acres of Diamonds" fame, but resigned in disgust, convinced that the Christian church was an instrument of corruption throughout all of Western civiliza-tion.[25] He was fired from various teaching positions because of his radicalism and was prosecuted during World War I for his opposition to the war, which he termed "the great madness" in a pamphlet by that name. Nearing was acquitted by a jury although he admitted having written the pamphlet and although the Rand School of Social Science was found guilty of having published it and was fined! Morris Hillquit, in *The Trial of Scott Nearing and the American Socialist Society*, said that the transcript of the trial was extraordinarily valuable not only for its lucid explanation of socialism, but because it was an authentic record of an American political trial.

Nearing was very popular as a debater, speaking all over the country and even appearing on nationwide radio broadcasts in the 1930s. Although once a Communist party member, he broke with the party because of its efforts to control his individualism; he condemned censorship, brutality, and repression in both socialist and capitalist countries. Eventually he retired to a simple rural life and extended his pacifist principles to embrace vegetarianism because he thought that all creatures had a right to live and not to be forced to feed or to serve others.

Nearing wrote that his main concerns were for the human race and for the provision of a good life for all. He did not oppose technology, but he urged that it be used only for good, not for evil.[26] Nearing called openly for radicalism, saying that reformers or social workers were like those who would provide ambulance service at the bottom of a dangerous cliff from which persons frequently fell, whereas radicals were those who would instead build a fence at the top to prevent anyone from falling. Similarly, he compared the abandonment of cannibalism and slavery to the ultimate abandon-ment of capitalism in favor of socialism.[27] As an intense individualist Nearing was not an orthodox Marxist; he criticized the tendency in

Marxism to suppress individuality and was strongly opposed to violence. He was not typical of the left but is worthy of note because of his long role as an abrasive critic of the system and one whose experience ranged from urban activism to rural retreat in the manner of Thoreau.

Most analysts argue that modern liberalism contains two distinct schools: the Old Left and the New. Furthermore, they maintain that the Old Left was more or less destroyed during the cold war hysteria of the 1940s and 1950s, and that the development of the New Left in the late 1950s and early 1960s was spontaneous and original. There is evidence, however, that there were strains of continuity and that much of the New Left had roots in the Old.[28] The Old Left was largely Marxist. In the 1940s Marxist groups were split by internal disputes and rapidly lost their influence; the Trotskyites, who followed the doctrines of the exiled Russian Leon Trotsky, almost disappeared. Many intellectuals who had been Marxists or sympathetic to Marxism rejected their Marxist past, some to become conservatives.

In the late 1950s pacifist groups formed, following such leaders as A. J. Muste, David Dellinger, and Bayard Rustin, who had been active for years. During World War II the radical pacifists had not been absorbed as had the Marxists into a defense of the system, and they had remained forceful social critics, forming a bond of continuity between the Old Left and the New. Rosa Parks, whose refusal to give up her seat on a bus to a white man in December 1955 led to the Montgomery, Alabama, bus boycott, had attended an institute on nonviolence at the Highlander Folk School that had been established in Tennessee in the late 1930s. Such magazines as Dwight Macdonald's *Politics*, Dave Dellinger's *Alternative*, Dorothy Day's *Catholic Worker*, and A. J. Muste's *Fellowship* served to transmit many radical ideas to the new generation; the demise of the Communist party should not obscure the importance of the radical pacifists and other leftist groups to subsequent leftist developments.[29]

By the 1950s most political scientists had come to accept pluralism as the most accurate description of the workings of American society (see p. 154, footnote 14). Pluralism substituted the group for the individual as the basic unit of democratic politics, and it viewed public policy as the result of competition between organized interests, with the government serving largely as a broker or a referee although often acting itself as an interest group. In 1956 a sociologist, the late C. Wright Mills, published *The Power Elite*, which described society instead as dominated by an elite that controlled the major interests. Mills expressed his indignation at modern society in all his writings and called upon the young to express their outrage and to be less courteous. His was the opening attack of a movement that soon was to become the New Left.

In 1962 the New Left produced its most significant document, the Port Huron Statement by Thomas Hayden; the statement heralded the founding of the Students for a Democratic Society.[30] It proclaimed the person to be "infinitely precious and possessed of unfulfilled capacities for reason, freedom, and love," and it opposed "the depersonalization that reduces human beings to the status of things." It called for a replacement of power rooted in possession, privilege, or circumstance by "power and uniqueness rooted in love, reflectiveness, reason, and creativity." A key principle was "the establishment of a democracy of individual participation, governed by two central aims: that the individual share in those social decisions determining the quality and direction of his life; that society be organized to encourage independence in men and provide the media for their participation." Participatory democracy was to provide a political life based on several root principles: among them

> that decision-making of basic social consequence be carried on by public groupings; that politics be seen positively, as the art of collectively creating an acceptable pattern of social relations; that politics has the function of bringing people out of isolation and into community; . . . that work should involve incentives worthier than money or survival . . . [and] that the economy itself is of such social importance that its major resources and means of production should be open to democratic participation and subject to democratic social regulation.

The statement also proclaimed violence to be abhorrent because generally it would require the person or group toward which the violence was directed to be transformed into a depersonalized object of hate. It urged that the means and institutions of violence be abolished and that institutions of non-violence be developed.

Hayden suggested that the university was the proper forum for action to begin the process of creating a more open, just, and humane society. He was a keen critic of the gap between professed values and reality. Although he appears to have been influenced by Fromm and Mills, among others, the Port Huron Statement and other of his writings display considerable originality and incisive thought.

The civil rights movement came to fruition during the years of the New Left. Although there were similarities among the movements and they were related, the civil rights movement was independent of the New Left and was the culmination of years of independent activism. Martin Luther King, Jr., was its most important theoretician, and his policy of nonviolence indelibly marked the entire movement. King had studied Gandhi, Thoreau, and the radical pacifists of the 1940s and applied their tactics effectively. His influence is significant far beyond the civil rights movement, as is illustrated by his receipt of the Nobel Peace Prize. He earned a secure place among the contributors to Christian pacifist thought, and his success in applying direct nonviolent action makes his achievements more than theoretical.

One of King's best-known works, his "Letter from Birmingham Jail," is also one that is most valuable as a concise reflection of his thought.[31] King prepared the letter in response to criticism of his tactics by a group of clergymen. In it he said that he came to Birmingham because injustice was there and noted that the clergymen, although deploring the demonstrations that had taken place for civil rights under his leadership, had failed to express concern for the conditions that had brought the demonstrations about. He explained his devotion to nonviolent, direct action, which was to be used when there was no alternative available for the peaceful pursuit of justice, and outlined four basic steps that were required of any nonviolent campaign. They began with the collection of facts to ascertain that injustices existed and proceeded to negotiation, self-purification, and then direct action itself.

Direct action, or civil disobedience, the peaceful disobeying of unjust laws, was the cause of the greatest concern. King explained that the purpose of direct action was simply to force the community to negotiate the issues when it had previously refused to do so. Blacks had waited more than 300 years on these shores and were still being told to wait. The time, he said, had come.

King stressed that he continued to advocate obedience to law; it was only unjust laws that should be broken. Just laws he defined as those that are consistent with the moral law or the law of God, and unjust laws are those out of harmony with moral law. He said further that any law that uplifts the human personality is just and any that degrades it is unjust. He therefore could urge obedience to the desegregation decision of the Supreme Court while advocating disobedience to any segregation ordinance. As concrete examples, he said that a law is unjust if it is inflicted upon a minority that is not permitted to vote, or if it compels a minority to obey but does not place the same restrictions upon the majority. King cautioned that the important fact is not the law, but justice; to obey an immoral law is legal, but wrong. His tactics were fully consistent with those of classic pacifism and civil disobedience. He warned against evading or defying the law, saying that such a course could lead to disorder and anarchy. The person who breaks an unjust law should do so openly, in a spirit of love, and with a clear willingness to accept the penalty.

King was consistent in emphasizing nonviolence and in urging organization. He was frank to question the system itself, whether it enforced segregation at home or inflicted violence on others abroad. He has earned an honored place in American political thought and also greatly affected action by encouraging civil disobedience and black self-esteem. Inevitably, so forceful a leader will have an impact upon other elements as well. King was not a militant, but his successes made it likely that some who followed in his footsteps, but rejected his thought and doctrines, would be.

One of the most gifted of the black militants was Malcolm X, whose organizational skills and inflammatory rhetoric catapulted him to early prominence. He greatly influenced black radical thought and contributed many of the ideas that found activist advocates in the Black Panther party. Although the black militant movement is largely scattered, many of its ideas have outlived it. Malcolm himself was assassinated after having left the Black Muslim movement, but not before he succeeded in founding a short-lived Organization of Afro-American Unity and in preparing much of the theoretical groundwork for black revolutionaries. He called for black nationalism and for violence, when necessary. He outlined economic and social doctrines that owed much to Marx. Central to his teaching was the assertion that power can be checked only by power.

Malcolm was well known for his belief that whites were the common enemy of blacks, and a common oppressor. It was no more wrong to be violent in defending blacks than it was to be forced into wars to defend America with violence. All revolutions were bloody, and he called for revolution. His beliefs are summed up in his injunctions to "be intelligent. Be peaceful, be courteous, obey the law, respect everyone; but if someone puts his hand on you, send him to the cemetery."[32]

Not long before his death, Malcolm traveled extensively in Africa and the Middle East. The travels broadened his views, made them more secular, and added an international dimension. They did not eliminate his insistence that violence was necessary. In his view, there could be no true peace without freedom. In response to allegations that he had changed, he asked how it was that a white man could expect a black man to change unless the white man himself had changed. He continued to call for violent revolution, but he insisted that he was not "un-American," or anti-American; he only opposed certain actions that America had taken and was taking. As he noted:

> It's true I'm a Moslem and I believe in brotherhood and I believe in the brotherhood of all men. But my religion doesn't make me a fool. My religion makes me be against all forms of racism. It keeps me from judging any man by the color of his skin. It teaches me to judge him by his deeds and his conscious behavior. And it teaches me to be for the

rights of all human beings, but especially the Afro-American human being, because my religion is a natural religion, and the first law of nature is self-preservation.[33]

His message, therefore, remained violent, but he had come to speak of brotherhood, which introduced a strong note of hope. Not only those who study black politics in America, but all who would understand American political thought and American social conditions would do well to read the *Autobiography of Malcolm X* (1965).

Like the movement for black rights the New Left too developed militant factions. Nevertheless, it contributed greatly to nonviolent thought and to the application of the techniques of nonviolence. It produced some superb social criticism. Charles A. Reich, for example, in his 1970 book *The Greening of America: How the Youth Revolution Is Trying to Make America Livable*, caught the romantic flavor of the New Left and contended that the movement was bringing about what he termed "Consciousness III," which was to result in a new world based upon the principles of love and humanity. His conclusions were romantic, as was the New Left itself, and were justly criticized as wild exaggerations and wishful thinking. But his documentation of modern industrial societies as "the corporate state," a huge corporation that proceeds relentlessly on totally uncontrolled by the government or any other agency or combination of agencies, was unusually perceptive.

The New Left owed much also to the writings of Herbert Marcuse. Marcuse's major books are *Eros and Civilization* (1955), *Soviet Marxism* (1958), *One-Dimensional Man* (1964), *An Essay on Liberation* (1969), and *Counter-Revolution and Revolt* (1972). Marcuse, like Fromm and Lasswell, used Freudian principles in an attempt to gain insights into politics and society. He granted that any social system involves some repression, but his goal was to eliminate what he called "surplus repression," or repression beyond that necessary to maintain the fabric of society. Because of its warping effects upon the individual, Marcuse argued that modern industrialism is essentially evil, both in the United States and in the Soviet Union. The latter, he contended, is worse in practice than the United States, but it has greater potential for good. Because neither system can be corrected peacefully, revolution may be justified.

Marcuse's attitude toward violence is not absolute. He argued that nothing can justify indiscriminate terror, cruelty, or arbitrary violence, while maintaining that some violence may be justified historically. He appears to have believed that the radicalization of American youth in the 1960s was a hopeful sign that a revolutionary situation might have been developing, but the essential ingredient would be workers, not students. The Establishment, he contended, works to prevent the development of revolution. By gearing its policies and practices to the development of false wants and the fulfillment of false needs, its artificial products produce artificial attitudes and habits. In such an artificial world sexuality is weakened and gratification comes through the satisfaction of false appetites, warping erotic impulses and creating a false sense of satisfaction and approval of the system. Even the language practices that the Establishment encourages are repressive and prevent true understanding:

> The acronym NATO no longer calls to mind nations on the North Atlantic, as the full title does, thereby making it less likely that the membership of Turkey and Greece will be questioned; AEC is just another administrative agency; USSR abbreviates both Socialism and Soviet; AFL-CIO eclipses the radical political differences that once divided the two groups.[34]

In the long run, however, Marcuse was optimistic that "the political dimension can no longer be divorced from the aesthetic, reason from sensibility, the gesture of the barricade from that of love."[35]

So convinced was Marcuse of the repression of the modern industrial state that he considered even that characteristic most praised by libertarians, tolerance, to be repressive. In his essay "Repressive Tolerance" he argued that true tolerance "would call for intolerance toward prevailing policies, attitudes, opinions, and the extension of tolerance to policies, attitudes, and opinions which are outlawed or suppressed."[36] As George Kateb has written, Marcuse's theory of toleration is the most notorious part of his work, both because he interprets the system's tolerance as a covert form of manipulation and because he "re-designates apparent intolerance as real tolerance." Kateb suggested that although Marcuse's notion is laughable as a pure theory of toleration and deserves the abuse that it has received, Marcuse has disclosed his true intention, which is not to justify tolerance at all, but to provide "a moral justifiability of revolution against a democratic political order he does not really think democratic."[37]

In effect, Marcuse maintained that love can replace the restraining influence of institutions. In a utopian state institutional checks would be unnecessary, as would the political process itself. Like many others, he produced telling criticisms of the present order. His romantic prescriptions, however, are sufficiently vague and at times frightening, as in the case of "repressive tolerance," that it would be well to think twice before surrendering the hard-won institutional safeguards that do exist, however inadequate they may be.

During the years in which the New Left and the civil rights movements were prominent in the United States, another movement developed, that for women's rights. Women had made very little headway since the adoption of the Nineteenth Amendment over four decades before, and discrimination against women in employment and other matters was causing intense indignation among many women and others interested in equality for all citizens. In June 1966 a large number of concerned women met in Washington, D.C.; the result was the formation of the National Organization for Women (NOW). The first act of that group was to send telegrams to the Equal Employment Opportunity Commissioners in the states protesting their lack of action against sex-segregated want ads.

The following year at its second national conference in November 1967, NOW adopted a Women's Bill of Rights. Its eight demands were: (1) an equal rights amendment to the Constitution, (2) enforcement of laws banning sex discrimination in employment, (3) maternity leave rights in employment and in social security benefits, (4) tax deductions for home and child care expenses for working parents, (5) child care centers, (6) equal and unsegregated education, (7) equal job-training opportunities and allowances for women living in poverty, and (8) recognition of the right of women to control their reproductive lives.[38]

As with most political movements, there were numerous splits, not only into moderate and radical groups, but within those factions as well. On the extreme were groups such as WITCH (Women's International Terrorist Conspiracy from Hell) and the militant lesbian group SCUM (Society for Cutting Up Men), which looked forward to the day in which it would be possible to have an all-female world with reproduction by parthenogenesis. Unfortunately, because of publicity from those hostile to the movement, some have interpreted such extremist splinter groups to be representative of what they term "women's lib" in general, and have so characterized the entire effort to bring about equal rights.

The equal rights movement has both theoretical and practical accomplishments to its credit. Movement publications have flourished, including, notably, *Ms.* magazine, which has served to increase public sensitivity to the rights of women. Some groups have adopted socialist principles, some have gone beyond into forms of radical feminism, but most prominent are the moderates working to better the position of women within the present system. Among the practical accomplishments have been the election of women to significant political office, including governorships and several seats in Congress. There had been occasional women members of Congress for the past few decades, but usually they arrived at their positions by being elected to succeed their husbands who died in office. The new breed of women elected to the House of Representatives includes such outstanding current or former members as Patsy Mink of Hawaii, Shirley Chisholm of New York, Yvonne Burke of California, Elizabeth Holtzman of New York, and Barbara Jordan of Texas.

Largely because of the efforts of Representative Martha Griffiths of Michigan, a long-time member of the House (now retired), the Congress proposed the Equal Rights Amendment in March 1972. It appeared for a time as if there would be little difficulty in achieving ratification by the necessary thirty-eight states, but concerted action by right-wing political groups and fundamentalist religious organizations has so distorted popular understanding of the proposed Twenty-seventh Amendment that several states have refused to ratify. The wording, "Equality of rights under the law shall not be denied or abridged by the United States or by any State on account of sex," appears to be clear and simple, yet such well-financed opponents as Phyllis Schlafly, the John Birch Society, the Ku Klux Klan, and the Christian Crusade have managed to convince many that it would bring bisexual restrooms, force all women to work, and legalize homosexual marriages. The fate of the amendment is in doubt, a situation that demonstrates the power of a determined minority to appeal to the fears and prejudices of the people.

In legal terms the movement for black rights has had greater success than the women's movement, partly because constitutional amendments protecting black rights (the Thirteenth, Fourteenth, and Fifteenth) already existed. The civil rights legislation of 1964 and 1965 brought great changes in some respects, building upon the Supreme Court's *Brown* v. *Board of Education of Topeka* ruling in 1954. The black movement as a whole has changed American life and brought forth prominent yet diverse spokesmen who have taken their messages to the American people.

Apart from organized movements the last two decades have seen insightful work in many fields and from many quarters that have relevance to politics and political life. Hannah Arendt has called attention to "the banality of evil," the fact that evil acts are often committed by "nice" people with little or no recognition of their responsibility.[39] Ivan Illich has questioned the entire structure of public education in the same manner in which Szasz criticized the role of psychiatry and psychiatrists.[40] Blacks, Chicanos, American Indians, pacifists, feminists, anarchists, and others are publicizing their views and forcing others to take note. It has been a time of ferment, yet a time in which the dominant themes have been to encourage quiescence and to deny that changes are necessary. The past decade witnessed the election of Richard Nixon and Spiro Agnew to office because of their divisive appeals that they contended were directed to a "silent majority." Along with the ferment came an increasing growth of the state and official repression emanating mainly from the executive branch but often supported, if only passively, by Congress. The downfall of Nixon and Agnew was fortunate for the long-term health of the polity, but it does not prove that a healthy state exists. Nixon was a creature of the system, and his record was open before he was elected.

Saul Alinsky has demonstrated that the public has power if it is organized. Alinsky for years was a community organizer and had enormous success in assisting minorities in righting wrongs. He called for irreverence, for an understanding of the forces with which one must contend, for a use of the opponent's own strength against him (which his opponents described as Alinsky-style mass jujitsu), and for flexibility. Above all, he urged understanding, an open society, and organization. Hatred should be reserved for situations, and people should be seen "not as sellouts and betrayers of moral principles, but as the results of ongoing processes."[41] He pointed out the differences between "haves" and "have nots," and the shifts that generally come when one is converted to the other. He downgraded ideologies, pointing out the changes that have come to both the Soviet Union and the United States as they moved from "have not" to "have" status.[42]

Alinsky wrote that "we must accept open-ended systems of ethics and values, not only to meet the constantly changing conditions but also to keep changing ourselves, in order to survive in the fluid society that lies ahead of us. Such systems must be workable in the world *as it is*." Moreover, the people must be convinced that if they find a way to join together they need not simply accept their fate, but can have the power to shape their world.[43] In his Farewell Address in January 1961, President Eisenhower warned: "In the councils of government we must guard against the acquisition of unwarranted influence, whether sought or unsought, by the military-industrial complex. . . . We must never let the weight of this combination endanger our liberties or democratic processes. We should take nothing for granted." The abuse of power by Eisenhower's successors that has been responsible for the resignation of a President and systematic assaults on the principles of the Constitution illustrates the truth of his words and demonstrates that the situation against which he warned was not fanciful. Alinsky's example demonstrates that the people do have the power to counter such assaults, if they understand, organize, and act.

There is a point at which political philosophy and political action meet. If the philosophy is weak, the actions will be uncontrolled. A strengthening of political philosophy could well be the most practical action possible today.

NOTES

1. Reinhold Niebuhr, *Moral Man and Immoral Society* (New York: Scribner's, 1960), p. 48 (originally published in 1932).

2. Reinhold Niebuhr, *The Children of Light and the Children of Darkness* (New York: Scribner's, 1960), pp. 9–12 (originally published in 1944).

3. Reinhold Niebuhr, *Man's Nature and His Communities* (New York: Scribner's, 1965), pp. 124–125.

4. See "Reinhold Niebuhr: New Orthodoxy for Old Liberalism," *American Political Science Review* 56 (December 1962), 874–885.

5. Harold D. Lasswell and Abraham Kaplan, *Power and Society* (New Haven, Conn.: Yale University Press, 1950), p. 202.

6. Ibid., p. 225.

7. Erich Fromm, *The Sane Society* (New York: Rinehart, 1955), pp. 321–348; for a discussion of dehumanization see Lewis Yablonsky, *Robopaths* (Baltimore: Penguin, 1972).

8. Walt Anderson, *Politics and the New Humanism* (Pacific Palisades, Cal.: Goodyear, 1973), p. 39.

9. See *The Lonely Crowd* (New Haven, Conn.: Yale University Press, 1961), part 3.

10. Anderson, *Politics*, pp. 40–45.

11. See, for example, Thomas Szasz, *Law, Liberty and Psychiatry* (New York: Macmillan, 1963).

12. For an excellent brief treatment of the immediate post–World War II years, see Herbert Agar, *The Price of Power* (Chicago: University of Chicago Press, 1957).

13. Arthur A. Ekirch, Jr., *The Decline of American Liberalism* (New York: Atheneum, 1971), p. 325.

14. Ibid., pp. 326–332.

15. Friedrich A. Hayek, *The Road to Serfdom* (Chicago: University of Chicago Press, 1957), p. 37.

16. Ibid., pp. 119–120.

17. See the revised and enlarged edition of *Conservatism Revisited* (New York: Free Press, 1962), which examines the developments within the New Conservative movement.

18. Clinton Rossiter, *Conservatism in America* (New York: Knopf, 1962), pp. 221–222.

19. Russell Kirk, *A Program for Conservatives* (Chicago: Henry Regnery, 1954), p. 177.

20. Willmoore Kendall, *The Conservative Affirmation* (Chicago: Henry Regnery, 1963), pp. ix–xi.

21. Ibid., pp. 74–98.

22. "The Night Watchman State," *The American Scholar* 45, no. 1 (Winter 1975–1976), 816–826; see also Douglas Rae's critical review in *The American Political Science Review* 70 (December 1976), 1289–1291.

23. Ibid., 825.

24. Scott Nearing, *The Making of a Radical: A Political Autobiography* (New York: Harper & Row, 1972), pp. 21–29.

25. Ibid., pp. 32–34.

26. Ibid., pp. 255–256.

27. Ibid., pp. 24 and 125.

28. See Penina Migdal Glazer, "From the Old Left to the New: Radical Criticism in the 1940's," *The American Quarterly* 24, no. 5 (December 1972), 584–603.

29. Ibid.

30. See selections from the Port Huron Statement in Loren Baritz, ed., *The*

American Left (New York: Basic Books, 1971), pp. 389–397; quotations are from pp. 392–393, and 394.

31. "Letter from Birmingham Jail—April 16, 1963," in his *Why We Can't Wait* (New York: Harper & Row, 1963).

32. "Message to the Grass Roots," in *Malcolm X Speaks* (New York: Merit Publishers, 1965); reprinted in Richard P. Young, ed., *Roots of Rebellion* (New York: Harper & Row, 1970), pp. 347–357; the quotation is on p. 354.

33. From *Two Speeches by Malcolm X* (New York: Merit, 1969); reprinted in ibid., pp. 358–369; the quotation is on p. 364. See also the "Statement of Basic Aims and Objectives of the Organization of Afro-American Unity," in George Breitman, ed., *The Last Year of Malcolm X: The Evolution of a Revolutionary* (New York: Merit, 1967), pp. 105–111.

34. Herbert Marcuse, *One-Dimensional Man* (Boston: Beacon, 1964), p. 94.

35. *Counter-Revolution and Revolt* (Boston: Beacon, 1972), p. 130.

36. In Robert Paul Wolff, Barrington Moore, Jr, and Herbert Marcuse, *A Critique of Pure Tolerance* (Boston: Beacon, 1965), p. 81.

37. George Kateb, "The Political Thought of Herbert Marcuse," in *Perspectives on Political Philosophy* vol. 3, James V. Downton, Jr., and David K. Hart, eds. (Hinsdale, Ill.: Dryden, 1973), pp. 411–437; the quotations are from p. 436.

38. See Barbara Deckard, *The Women's Movement* (New York: Harper & Row, 1975), pp. 329–331.

39. *Eichmann in Jerusalem: A Report on the Banality of Evil* (New York: Viking, 1963); Arendt's works are among the most perceptive in modern political literature, and they all may be read with profit. The best reflection of her thought in general is probably *The Human Condition* (Chicago: University of Chicago Press, 1958).

40. *Deschooling Society* (New York: Harper & Row, 1971).

41. Saul D. Alinsky, "Introduction" to *Reveille for Radicals* (New York: Vintage, 1969); quotation is from p. x.

42. Ibid., p. 228.

43. Ibid., pp. 207–209; quotation is from p. 207.

ADDITIONAL READINGS

Berrigan, Philip. *Prison Journal of a Priest Revolutionary.* New York: Holt, Rinehart and Winston, 1970.

Brecht, Arnold. *Political Theory: The Foundations of Twentieth Century Political Thought.* Princeton, N.J.: Princeton University Press, 1959.

Buckley, William F., Jr., ed. *American Conservative Thought in the Twentieth Century.* Indianapolis: Bobbs-Merrill, 1970.

Carmichael, Stokeley, and Charles V. Hamilton. *Black Power: The Politics of Liberation in America* New York: Vintage, 1967.

Charlesworth, James C., ed. *Contemporary Political Analysis.* New York: Free Press, 1967.

Clarke, John H., ed. *Malcolm X—The Man and His Times.* New York: Macmillan, 1969.

Cleaver, Eldridge. *Soul on Ice.* New York: McGraw-Hill, 1968.

Coffin, Tristam. *The Armed Society: Militarism in Modern America.* Baltimore: Penguin, 1968.

Cohen, Carl. *Civil Disobedience: Conscience, Tactics, and the Law.* New York: Columbia University Press, 1971.

Coker, Francis W. "Some Present-Day Critics of Liberalism." *American Political Science Review* XLVII (March 1953).

Connally, William E., and Glen Gordon, eds. *Social Structure and Political Theory.* Lexington, Mass.: D. C. Heath, 1974.

Dahl, Robert. *After the Revolution? Authority in a Good Society.* New Haven, Conn.: Yale University Press, 1970.

Dolbeare, Kenneth M. and Patricia. *American Ideologies, The Competing Political Beliefs of the 1970s.* 2nd ed. Chicago: Markham, 1973.

Douglas, William O. *Points of Rebellion.* New York: Vintage, 1970.

Fusfeld, Daniel R. "The Rise of the Corporate State in America." *Journal of Economic Issues* VI (March 1972).

Germino, Dante. *Beyond Ideology: The Revival of Political Theory.* New York: Harper & Row, 1967.

Gould, James A., and Vincent V. Thursby, eds. *Contemporary Political Thought.* New York: Holt, Rinehart and Winston, 1969.

Harrington, Michael. *The Accidental Century.* New York: Macmillan, 1969.

Hayden, Thomas. *Trial.* New York: Holt, Rinehart and Winston, 1970.

Howe, Irving, ed. *The Radical Papers.* Garden City, N.Y.: Doubleday, 1966.

Janis, Irving L. *Victims of Groupthink.* Boston: Houghton Mifflin, 1972.

Kariel, Henry S. *Open Systems: Arenas for Political Action.* Itasca, Ill.: Peacock, 1969.

Matson, Floyd W. *The Broken Image.* New York: Braziller, 1964.

Meier, August, Elliott Rudwick, and Francis L. Broderick, eds. *Black Protest Thought in the Twentieth Century.* 2nd ed. Indianapolis: Bobbs-Merrill, 1971.

Meyer, Frank S., ed. *What Is Conservatism?* New York: Holt, Rinehart and Winston, 1965.

Morgenthau, Hans J. *The Purpose of American Politics.* New York: Vintage, 1960.

Reid, Herbert G. "Morris Cohen's Case for Liberalism." *Review of Politics* XXXIII (October 1971).

―――, and Ernest J. Yanarella. "Toward a Post-Modern Theory of American Political Science and Culture: Perspectives from Critical Marxism and Phenomenology." *Cultural Hermerreutics* II (1974).

Riemer, Neal. *The Revival of Democratic Theory.* New York: Appleton-Century-Crofts, 1962.

Riesman, David, et al. *The Lonely Crowd.* New Haven, Conn.: Yale University Press, 1950.

Roelofs, H. Mark. *Ideology and Myth in American Politics: A Critique of a National Political Mind.* Boston: Little, Brown, 1976.

Roosevelt, James, ed. *The Liberal Papers.* Garden City, N.Y.: Doubleday, 1962.

Rosenstone, Robert A., ed. *Protest From the Right.* Beverly Hills, Calif.: Glencoe, 1968.

Skidmore, Max J., ed. *Word Politics: Essays on Language and Politics.* Palo Alto, Calif.: James E. Freel and Associates, 1972.

Spitz, David. *Patterns of Anti-Democratic Thought*. New York: Macmillan, 1949.

Stolz, Matthew F., ed. *Politics of the New Left*. Beverly Hills, Calif.: Glencoe, 1968.

Tiger, Lionel, and Robin Fox. *The Imperial Animal*. New York: Delta, 1971.

Whyte, William H. *The Organization Man*. Garden City, N.Y.: Anchor Books, 1957.

Wolin, Sheldon. "Political Theory as a Vocation." *American Political Science Review* LXII (December 1969).

Index

Abolitionist movement, 135–137, 149–153
"Acres of Diamonds" speeches, 163–164
Adams, Abigail, 47–48, 134
Adams, Brooks, 235
Adams, Charles Francis, 49n
Adams, Henry, 235
Adams, John, 38, 42, 55, 88
  mixed-government theories of, 82
  as President, 79, 80, 83
  on women, 48
Adams, John Quincy, 137
Addams, Jane, 190
Agar, Herbert, 247n
"Age of Reason, The" (Paine), 45
Agnew, Spiro T., 245–246
Agrarianism, 91, 212
Agrarian Justice (Paine), 45, 91
Albany Plan of Union, 39
Alien and Sedition Acts (1798), 79, 80, 83
Alienation, 229
Alinsky, Saul, 246
American Federation of Labor (AFL), 195–196
Americanism. See Nationalism
American Revolution, 38–39
Anarchism, 151, 174, 176–177, 235
  Thoreau and, 115–116
Anderson, Thornton, 49n
Anderson, Walt, 229–230
Andrews, John B., 189
Anglican Church, 6, 9–10, 18, 19, 31
Anti-Semitism, 219
Arendt, Hannah, 71–73, 84n, 245
Arieli, Yehoshua, 118n

Aristocracy, 60
  Jacksonianism and, 96, 97, 99
  modern conservatism and, 233–235
  Taylor on Adams's, 82
  See also Elites
Aristotle, 1, 2, 4, 5
Arnold, Thurman, 217, 218
Articles of Confederation, 55–61
Augustine, St., 3–4
Autonomous personality type, 230

Babbitt, Irving, 235
Bailyn, Bernard, 64n
Baldwin, Roger, 190
Ballou, Adin, 177
Bancroft, George, 100
Bank of the United States, 77–78, 87, 97–98, 123
Banneker, Benjamin, 74–75
Banzhaf, John, III, 222–223
Barton, Bruce, 199
Beard, Charles A., 62–64, 187
Beitzinger, A. J., 27, 31, 34n, 85n
Bell, Daniel, 175, 192n, 224n
Bellamy, Edward, 170
Bellamy, Rev. Francis, 178
Berger, Victor, 196
Berle, Adolph A., 211
Berns, Walter, 198
Bestor, Arthur, Jr., 119n
Biddle, Nicholas, 97–98
Bigelow, John, 48n
Bill of Rights (first ten amendments to the Constitution), 59, 76–77, 81
  See also specific amendments
Bills of rights, 22

Northeast Ordinance of 1787, 56–57
  Virginia, 53
Blacks, 40
  enfranchisement of, 53
  Jefferson on, 73–75
  proslavery theories of inferiority of,
    144–146
  See also Civil rights movement;
    Segregation, racial; Slavery
Bliss, William Dwight Porter, 178
Boas, Franz, 199
Body of Liberties, 25–26
Boston *Gazette*, 1775 debates in, 41–42
Boucher, Jonathan, 42
Bourne, Randolph, 191
Bradford, William, 17
Brandeis, Louis, 217
Brewster, William, 10, 17
Brisbane, Albert, 108–109
Brissenden, Paul F., 205*n*
British constitution, 39, 42, 43
Brook Farm, 107–109
Browder, Earl, 221
Brown, John, 117, 137, 152
Browne, Robert, 9
Brownson, Orestes, 112–114
Bryan, William Jennings, 200
Buck v. *Bell*, 198, 216
Burgess, John W., 127, 128
Bushnell, Horace, 178

Calhoun, John C., 126, 135, 139–143
Calvin, John, 8, 9
Calvinism, 6, 8–10, 15*n*, 104, 161
  See also Puritanism
Cambridge Platform, 20–21
Capitalism, 142, 165, 203, 213, 214
  See also Industrialism
Cardozo, Benjamin, 217
Carlton, Frank T., 101*n*, 102*n*
Carnegie, Andrew, 164–165
Cartwright, Samuel A., 144
Carver, John, 17
Central government, 77
  Articles of Confederation and, 55–58
  Constitutional convention and, 58–60
  See also Federalists; National power
Checks and balances, 53, 54, 62
Chesterton, G. K., 15*n*
Christian political thought, 3–6
Christian socialists (Social Gospel),
    177–179
Church, the
  in Christian thought, 3–5
  Lutheran view of, 7, 8
  separation of state and, 9, 28
  Wise on, 32
  See also specific churches

Church membership, 8, 19–21, 25
Church of England. *See* Anglican
    Church
Cicero, 2
Cities, 70, 75
City of God, The (St. Augustine), 3
City-state (polis), 2
Civil disobedience, 240, 241
Civil rights movement
  1950s–1960s, 114, 239–241, 245
  in post-Reconstruction period,
    179–184
Civil War, 126, 137–138, 156
Clarke, John Henrik, 205
Class, economic, 89, 141–142
Class conflict, 89, 179, 222
Clergy, 95
Cold war, 131, 223, 231
Colonial America
  European consciousness in, 36–37
  loyalist position in, 42–43
  parliamentary authority over, 39–42
  political writers in, 39–46
  secularization of politics in, 31–33
  See also New England colonies; *and
    specific colonies*
Commons, John R., 91, 101*n*, 102*n*, 162
Common Sense (Paine), 43–45
Communist party, 221
Compact. *See* Covenant, concept of
Concurrent   majority,   principle   of,
    140–143
Congregationalists, 10
  in colonial New England, 18–20, 25
  local-control principle of, 18, 19
  Wise's defense of, 32
Congress, United States
  judicial review of acts of, 122
  national power and, 124
  women in, 244–245
Connecticut, colonial, 24, 25, 52
Conscience, freedom of, 28–30, 52
  See also Religious freedom
Consent, principle of, 2–3, 10, 13, 60, 81
  in colonial New England, 19, 22
  prerevolutionary writers on, 40–42
Conservatism
  early republic and, 67–68, 70
  Hayek's, 231–232
  in Jacksonian period, 88–89
  Kendall's, 234–235
  Kirk's, 233–234
  modern, 226–227, 231–236
  Nozick's, 235–236
  Social Darwinism and, 160
  stake-in-society theory of, 89
Constitution, United States, 58–64
  economic interpretation of, 62–64

Founding Fathers and, 67, 69
loose construction of, 121–122
national power and, 122–125
parties and, 61–62
pragmatist interpretation of, 215–216
ratification of, 59, 61
slavery and, 69, 89, 151
strict construction of, 71, 77–78, 121–122
See also Bill of Rights; Judicial review; *and specific amendments*
Constitutional convention (1787), 58–60
Constitutionalism, 2, 51, 67–69
Constitutions (written), 22
precedents for, 52
state, 52–55, 88, 89
See also British constitution
Continental Congress, 55
Contract, concept of, 81, 109
Congregational principle and, 19
Hobbes's view of, 11
Locke's view of, 13
prerevolutionary writers' views on, 41–44
See also Covenant, concept of
Conventions, nominating, 97
Conwell, Russell H., 163–164, 237
Cooper, James Fenimore, 99–100
Corporations, 211
Corwin, Edward S., 64*n*
Cotton, John, 19–22, 26–28, 30
Coughlin, Rev. Charles, 219
Covenant (compact), concept of in colonial New England, 21–23, 25
in Hebrew thought, 3
See also Contract, concept of
Crisis, The (Paine), 45
Croly, Herbert, 188
Cromwell, Oliver, 10

Dahl, Robert A., 154*n*
D'Arcy, Martin, 15*n*
Darwin, Charles, 157, 158
Davidson, Donald, 212
DeBow, James D. B., 144
Debs, Eugene V., 175, 216
Debtors, 57, 59
Deckard, Barbara, 102*n*, 192*n*, 248*n*
Declaration of Independence, 46–48, 55
Constitution and, 62–63
slavery issue and, 143, 145, 147–150
DeLeon, Daniel, 175
Democracy
Brownson's view of, 113, 114
colonial New England and, 17–26
colonial Pennsylvania and West Jersey and, 30–31

Cotton on, 20
Founding Fathers and, 68
Jacksonian. *See* Jacksonianism
Lippmann's view of, 201–202
Mencken's view of, 200
Niebuhr's view of, 228
participatory, 72, 239
Tocqueville's views on, 98–99
war and, 130
Wise on, 32
Democratic-Republican clubs, 83, 87
Dennis, Lawrence, 220
Dewey, John, 168, 187, 214–215, 227
Dickinson, John, 40–41
Direct nonviolent action, 240–241
Disposers, 52
Dissent in New England colonies, 26–29
Divine law, 3–5
Divine right of kings, 6
Dos Passos, John, 197
Douglas, Stephen A., 139, 147–148
Douglass, Frederick, 151–152
Du Bois, W. E. B., 182–184, 204–205
Dulany, Daniel, 40

East, Edwin, 198
Economic Interpretation of the Constitution of the United States, An (Beard), 62–64
Economic planning, 231–232
Education, "state guardianship" over, 92–93
Eisenhower, Dwight D., 246
Ekirch, Arthur, 231
Elections
in colonial New England, 18, 25, 28
Paine on, 44
See also Franchise
Eleventh Amendment, 76
Eliot, John, 29–30
Elites, 220, 229
See also Aristocracy
Elliot, Jonathan, 84*n*
Ellis, Charles Mayo, 105–106
Emancipation Proclamation, 149
Emerson, Ralph Waldo, 105–107, 109–110, 115, 116
England
Calvinism (Puritanism) in, 9–11
Montesquieu on, 13–14
See also Parliament
English constitution, 39, 42, 43
English king, prerevolutionary writers' views on, 41–43
Equalitarianism, 21
Equality, Social Darwinism and, 158
Equal Rights Amendment, 244, 245
Equity (journal), 177
Eugenics, 197–199

Executive branch, 62, 53, 97
  See also Checks and balances; Judicial
  review; President, the; Separation
  of powers

Farmer-labor parties, 168
Farrell, James T., 197
Fascism, 219, 220
Federal government. *See* Central gov-
  ernment; Federalists; National
  power
Federalist, The, 61, 62, 68
Federalists, 40, 57–62, 70, 77–80, 83,
  123
  See also Hamilton, Alexander
Field, Stephen, 163
Filmer, Robert, 42
Finer, Herman, 232
First Amendment, 146
Fitzgerald, F. Scott, 199
Fitzhugh, George, 139, 142, 144–147
Fletcher v. *Peck*, 122
Foner, Philip S., 49n
Fourier, Charles, 108–109
Fourteenth Amendment, 127, 179
Franchise, 53, 88, 97
  See also Women's suffrage
Francis, Convers, 109
Frank, Jerome, 217
Frankfurter, Felix, 197
Franklin, Benjamin, 39, 55
Franklin, John Hope, 192n
Fremont, John C., 154n
Fromm, Erich, 229
Frontier thesis, Turner's, 128
Fuller, Margaret, 106, 107, 111–112
Fundamental Orders of Connecticut,
  24, 25, 52
Funding Act (1790), 77

Gabriel, Ralph Henry, 119n, 166, 167,
  171n, 179, 192n
Gandhi, Mohandas, 114
Garrison, William Lloyd, 137, 150–152
Garvey, Marcus, 204–205
Gelasius I, Pope, 4
General Court, in colonial New En-
  gland, 18, 21, 25
George, Henry, 168–170
Georgia, 135
Gladden, Washington, 177–178
Glazer, Penina Migdal, 247n
Gliddon, George R., 144
Gobineau, Count Joseph Arthur de,
  144–145
Godkin, E. L., 162, 163
Gospel of Wealth, 163–166
Government

central. *See* Central government
conservative critiques of, 231–236
Garrison's view of, 151
Hobbesian view of, 11–12
Lincoln's attitude toward, 148–149
local, 18, 44, 71–73
Paine's views on, 44
Thoreau's views on, 115–117
Ward's views on, 166
  See also State, the
Governors in colonial America, 18, 25,
  28, 53
Grangers, 167–168
Great Depression, 131, 208, 223
Greek thought, 1–3
Griffiths, Martha, 245
Grimes, Alan P., 48n, 85, 119n, 140,
  146, 157–158
Gronlund, Laurence, 175
Guttman, Allen, 84n

Halfway Covenant, 21
Hallowell, John H., 15n
Hamilton, Alexander, 60
  Bank of the United States and, 77, 78
  early writings, 41, 42
  Federalist articles, 61
  on implied powers, 78
  Jefferson compared to, 70, 75–76
  political philosophy of, 75–76
Hamiltonianism, 70, 83, 123
Hammond, J. H., 139
Harding, Warren G., 198
Harper, William, 143–144
Harrington, James, 12
Hawthorne, Nathaniel, 107, 108
Hayden, Thomas, 239
Hayek, Friedrich A., 231–232
Haymarket incident (1886), 176
Hayne, Robert, 124
Haywood, "Big Bill," 190
Hebrew thought, 3
Helper, Hinton Rowan, 147
Hemingway, Ernest, 199–200
Henry, Patrick, 61
Herron, George D., 178–179
Hillquit, Morris, 237
Hobbes, Thomas, 11–13, 15n
Hobbesian views, 69, 113, 140, 146, 220
  of prerevolutionary writers, 42, 43
Hofstadter, Richard, 69, 140–142, 149,
  160, 161, 192n, 223n, 224n
Hoig, Stan, 192n
Holmes, George Frederick, 145
Holmes, Oliver Wendell, 198, 215–217
Hooker, Richard, 12
Hooker, Thomas, 24–25, 33n
Hoover, Herbert, 209–211, 213

Hopkins, Mark, 163
Huntington, Bishop F. D., 178
Hutchinson, Anne, 26–27
Hutchinson, Thomas, 53
Hylton v. *United States*, 122

Illich, Ivan, 245
Immigration Act (1924), 198
Imperialism, 129, 188–189
Implied powers, doctrine of, 78
Income tax, 44
Indians, 47, 175
   Jefferson on, 73
   in New England colonies, 28–30
Individualism, 67, 113, 178
   Declaration of Independence and, 46
   Hoover's, 209, 210
   modern conservatism and, 235
   Paine's, 45
   Transcendentalism and, 104, 107–110
Individual rights, 141
   in Greek and Roman thought, 1–3
   Hobbes's and Locke's views on, 12–13
   Lutheranism and, 7–8
   See also Rights of man
Industrialism, 106, 146, 156–157, 170
   Hamilton and, 75
   Hoover and, 209–211
   Progressives and, 187–188
   See also Capitalism
Industrial Workers of the World (IWW),
   196
Inequality, Winthrop on, 19
Inheritance tax, 44
Initiative, 30
Instrumentalism, 214–215
Interposition, 80
Ireton, Gen., 10, 11
Iroquois League, 30

Jackson, Andrew, 96–98, 123–124
Jacksonianism, 87–90, 96–98, 114
   contemporary analyses of, 98–101
Jacobson, J. Mark, 42
Jaffa, Harry V., 154n
James, William, 187, 202, 214–215
Jay, John, 61
Jefferson, Thomas, 14, 57, 94, 122, 123
   on blacks, 73–75
   Declaration of Independence and,
      46–47, 135
   Hamilton compared to, 70, 75–76
   Hamiltonian program opposed by,
      78–79
   Madison and, 81
   political philosophy of, 70–75
   as President, 80, 83
   on Virginia constitution, 54

ward ("small republic") system pro-
   posed by, 71–73
on women, 73
Jeffersonianism, 80–84, 96, 110
Johnson Act (1921), 198
Jones, Jesse H., 177
Joughin, G. Louis, 206n
Journalism in Progressive period, 185
Judeo-Christian thought, 3–6
Judicial review, 2, 14, 51, 52, 62, 80, 87
   national power and, 122
   Otis and, 40
Jungle, The (Sinclair), 186
Jurisprudence, pragmatic, 215–218

Kaplan, Abraham, 247n
Kateb, George, 235–236, 243
Kelley, Florence, 189
Kendall, Willmoore, 234–235
Kennedy, John F., 231
Kent, Chancellor James, 88
Kentucky and Virginia Resolutions
   (1798 and 1799), 79–80
Key, V. O., Jr., 206n
King, Martin Luther, Jr., 114, 239–241
Kirk, Russell, 232–234
Knox, Henry, 78
Koch, Adrienne, 49n, 71, 84n, 85n
Ku Klux Klan, 197, 204, 205

Labor unions, 93, 203, 204
Lafayette, Gen. marquis de, 94
La Follette, Robert M., 202
Laissez faire, principle of, 14, 158, 159,
   187–188
Land values, George's views on,
   168–169
Lare, James, 200–201, 206n
Lash, Joseph P., 206n
Laslett, Peter, 16n
Lasswell, Harold D., 228–229, 247n
Law(s)
   in Christian thought, 3–6
   codification of, 25
   divine, 3–5
   in Greek and Roman thought, 1–3
   in Hebrew thought, 3
   Locke's view of, 12, 13
   natural. *See* Natural law
   state, judicial review of, 122
   See also Jurisprudence, pragmatic
Leach, Richard, 14, 49n, 84n, 101n, 119n
Leftist thought
   modern, 237–239
   See also Marxism; Socialism
Legal realism, 217
Legislature
   in colonial New England, 18, 25, 28

judicial review of. See Judicial review
Otis on, 39–40
in state constitutions, 53, 54
See also Checks and balances; Congress, United States; Parliament; Separation of powers
Lens, Sidney, 137
Leonard, Daniel, 42
Lerner, Ralph, 154n
Levellers, 10
Leviathan, The (Hobbes), 11
Levy, Leonard W., 84n
Lewis, Sinclair, 200, 220
Liberalism (liberals), 13
in early republic, 67, 68, 70
Hobbes and, 11
modern, 226–227
Viereck and, 233
Liberator, The (abolitionist newspaper), 137, 150, 151
Liberty, Puritan views on, 22–26
Lieber, Francis, 100–101, 126–127
Lilburne, John, 10
Lincoln, Abraham, 124, 126
slavery issue and, 136, 138, 147–149, 152
Lippmann, Walter, 200–202
Literature, political statements in (1920s), 199–202
Lloyd, Henry Demarest, 185
Local government, 18, 44, 71–73
Localism, 18, 21
Locke, John, 12–13, 46, 81
Otis and, 39, 40
Long, Huey, 219
Lovejoy, Elijah, 136–137
Loyalty, philosophy of, 186
Luther, Martin, 6–8
Lynching, 203
Lynd, Helen, 196
Lynd, Robert, 196
Lynd, Staughton, 176

McCarthy, Joseph, 233, 234
McCulloch v. Maryland, 87, 122–123
McDougall, William, 197–198
McGaughey, Mary Donna, 49n
McWilliams, Wilson Carey, 228
Madison, James, 60, 61, 76, 77, 79–81, 87, 88
Magistrates in colonial New England, 18, 21, 23–25
Majority, concurrent, 140–143
Majority rule, 201
See also Democracy
Malcolm X, 241–242
Man, Henri de, 196
Manheim, Jarol B., 224n

Manifest Destiny, 128–129
Manufacturing, 75, 78
See also Industrialism
Marbury v. Madison, 40, 80
Marcuse, Herbert, 242–243
Maritain, Jacques, 15n
Marshall, John, 87, 88, 122–123
Martin v. Hunter's Lessee, 122
Marx, Karl, 140
Marxism, 175, 179, 220–222, 227, 237–238
Maryland, 55
Maslow, Abraham H., 230
Mason, A. T., 14, 15n, 49n, 57–58, 84n, 88, 101n, 119n, 134, 211, 223n
Mason, George, 61
Massachusetts, 18, 25–26, 134
Mather, Cotton, 32
Mayflower Compact, 17, 22
Mayhew, Jonathan, 32, 33, 36
Means, Gardiner C., 211
Mencken, H. L., 199, 200, 216
Mental health, 229, 230
Middle Ages, 4–7
Middle-class values, Social Darwinism and, 161, 162
Miller, Perry, 24, 33n, 34n, 111, 118n, 171n
Mills, C. Wright, 238–239
Mirkin, Harris, 49n, 65n
Missouri Compromise, 135, 136
Monroe, James, 88
Montesquieu, Baron de, 13–14, 81
Moore, Paul Elmer, 235
Morgan, Edmund M., 206n
Morgan, Edmund S., 33n, 34n
Morgan, Lewis Henry, 167
Most, Johann, 176
Muckrakers, 185–186
Muste, A. J., 238

Nader, Ralph, 222
Nation, The (periodical), 162, 163
National American Suffrage Association, 168
National Association for the Advancement of Colored People (NAACP), 182
National Bank. See Bank of the United States
Nationalism, 112, 121, 127–131, 170
National Organization for Women (NOW), 244
National power, growth and consolidation of, 121–127
Naturalistic determinism, 166, 167
See also Social Darwinism
Natural law, 11, 217

Declaration of Independence and, 46,
  47
 in Greek and Roman thought, 2
 Jefferson and, 71
 Otis on, 39
 prerevolutionary writers' view of, 39,
  40
 Social Darwinism and, 158, 178
Natural rights, 32, 33, 43, 100, 143, 145,
  175-176
 Hamilton on, 41
 See also Rights of man
Nature, 11-12
Nearing, Scott, 237-238
Nevins, Allan, 138, 141, 153*n*
New Conservative movement, 232-233
New Deal, 167, 202, 208-209, 211,
  213-223, 233
 critiques of, 218-223
 pragmatism and, 214-218
New England colonies
 democratic tendencies in, 17-26
 dissent in, 26-29
 Indians in, 28-30
 See also specific colonies
New Left, 238, 239, 242
New York State, 93
Niebuhr, Reinhold, 227-228
Ninth Amendment, 77
Nixon, Richard M., 245-246
Nonviolence, 239
Nonviolent resistance, 117
Northwest Ordinance of 1787, 56-57
Notes on the State of Virginia (Jefferson), 54,
  73
Nott, Josiah C., 144
Noyes, John Humphrey, 151
Nozick, Robert, 235-237
Nullification of federal acts by states,
  79-80

Obedience to state authority, 9, 12, 43,
  115
 in Christian (pre-Reformation)
  thought, 3-5
Oceana (Harrington), 12
Oligarchy, 19-21
O'Sullivan, John Lewis, 114
Othello (pseudonym), 90
Otis, James, 39, 40
Overton, Richard, 10

Paine, Thomas, 43-46, 83, 91
Parliament, 10, 14, 39, 40
 authority over American colonies,
  39-42
Parrington, Vernon L., 20, 21, 24, 33*n*,
  34*n*, 49*n*, 70, 110, 118*n*, 150

on Lieber, 126-127
Participation, political, 69, 72
 See also Franchise
Participatory democracy, 72, 239
Parties, 61-62, 97
 See also specific parties
Paterson, William, 60
Peabody, Elizabeth, 108
Peirce, Charles S., 187, 214
Pennsylvania, 30-31, 55
Phillips, David Graham, 186
Phillips, Wendell, 151
Philosophy in Progressive period,
  186-187
Physiocrats, 14
Pilgrims, 17-18
Planning, economic, 231-232
Plantation Agreement at Providence, 52
Plato, 1, 2
Plessy v. *Ferguson*, 179
Pluralism, 140, 141, 202, 238
Plymouth Colony, 17-18
Political participation, 69, 72
 See also Franchise
Populists, 184-185
Porter, Noah, 159
Port Huron Statement, 239
Pound, Roscoe, 217
Poverty, Paine's proposals for elimina-
  tion of, 44, 45
Powell, Adam Clayton, Jr., 205
Power
 fear of, in early republic, 67, 68, 71
 Puritan view of limitations of, 21-22
 state constitutions' view of, 54
Pragmatism, 187, 214-218
Predestination, Calvinist view of, 8
Presbyterians, 10, 18, 20
 See also Puritanism
President, the, 61, 141
 See also Executive branch
Pritchett, C. Herman, 198
Progress and Poverty (George), 168-169
Progressive period, 171, 184-189
Prohibition, 195
Property (property rights), 3, 57, 61
 Founding Fathers and, 69, 70, 81
 Locke's view of, 12
 Nozick's conservatism and, 235, 236
 Skidmore's views on, 91-92
 Social Darwinism and, 161, 163-165
 as voting requirement, 53, 88
Protestant Reformation, 6-11
Psychoanalysis, 228, 229
Psychology, 228-230
Pufendorf, Samuel, 32
Puritanism (Puritans), 200
 in England, 9-10

Indians and, 29–30
intolerance of, 20, 21, 25–27
liberty and, 22–26
limitations of power and, 21–22
in New England colonies, 17–30
Williams's criticism of, 27–29

Quakers, 30–31, 134

Racial segregation, 179, 190, 212
Racism, 37, 197–99, 203
Rae, Douglas, 247*n*
Rainboro, Col., 11
Randolph, A. Philip, 202–203
Randolph, Edmund, 78
Randolph, John, 88
Ransom, John Crowe, 211–212
Rauschenbusch, Walter, 179
Reason (rationality)
    law of. *See* Natural law
    Transcendentalism and, 105, 106
Rebellion, right of (right of revolution),
    11, 13, 46
Recall, 30
"Red scare" (1920s), 195, 196
Referendum, 30
Reformation, Protestant, 6–11
Reform movements, 167–171
Reich, Charles A., 242
Religion
    socialism   and   (Social   Gospel),
        177–179
    Transcendentalism and, 105, 106
    wealth and, 163–165
    See also Church, the; *and specific religions*
Religious freedom, Williams's views on,
    28–29
Religious intolerance in colonial New
    England, 20, 21, 25–27
Rent, George's proposed single tax on,
    169
Repression, Marcuse's theory of, 242,
    243
Republicanism, 21, 69, 71
Revolution, 3, 32
    right of, 11, 13, 46
Rhode Island, 28, 52, 57, 90
Ribuffo, Leo, 224*n*
Ricardo, David, 169
Riesman, David, 230
Rights. *See* Bills of rights; Individual
    rights; Natural rights; Property;
    Rights of man
Rights of man (human rights), 70
    prerevolutionary writers' views on,
        38, 40, 43, 48
    slavery and, 133, 134, 143, 145,
        147–148

See also Bill of Rights; Bills of rights;
    Natural rights
Rights of Man, The (Paine), 45
Ripley, George, 105–107
Road to Serfdom, The (Hayek), 231–232
Roane, Spencer, 122
Roche, John P., 137
Rockefeller, John D., 165
Roman Catholicism, 113
Roman political thought, 2–3
Romantic movement, 104
Roosevelt, Franklin D., 167, 208, 213
Roosevelt, Theodore, 185, 188, 189
Rossiter, Clinton, 33*n*, 200–201, 206*n*,
    233
Rousseau, Jean-Jacques, 83
Royce, Josiah, 186–187
Rubin, Louis D., Jr., 223*n*
Russett, Cynthia Eagle, 171
Ryle, Gilbert, 15*n*

Sacco, Nicola, 196–197
Santayana, George, 202
Schlesinger, Arthur, Jr., 138–139
Scholasticism, 4
Science, 215, 227, 228
Scopes Trial (1925), 200, 201
Scott, Dred, 136
Seabury, Samuel, 41, 42
Secularization of politics, 31–33
Segregation, racial, 179, 190, 212
Self-actualization, 230
Separation of powers, 13–14, 53, 60, 61
Separatism, 9–10, 17
    See also Congregationalists
Sewall, Samuel, 29
Shays's Rebellion (1786), 57, 58
Sibley, Mulford Q., 12, 15*n*, 16*n*
Sinclair, Upton, 165, 185–186, 197
Single tax, George's proposal for,
    169–170
Skidmore, Max J., 193*n*, 205*n*, 223*n*
Skidmore, Thomas, 91–93
Slavery, 29, 30, 47, 69, 110, 116, 125,
    133–153
    Calhoun's position on, 135, 139, 143
    Constitution and, 69, 89, 151
    economic issues and, 137–138
    Fitzhugh's position on, 142, 144–147
    in Jacksonian period, 89–90
    Lincoln and, 136, 138, 147–149, 152
    moderate position on, 147–149
    as moral issue, 138–139
    Northwest   Ordinance   and,   57,
        134–135
    rights of man (natural rights) and,
        133, 134, 143, 145, 147–148
    Southern position on, 139–147

in territories, 134–136
"wage slavery" of workers compared to, 142–146
Frances Wright and, 94
See also Abolitionist movement
Slave uprisings, 135–136
Smith, Adam, 14
Smith, Rev. Gerald L. K., 219
Social Contract. *See* Contract, concept of
Social Darwinism, 129–130, 157–167
meliorist, 166–167
Spencer and, 157–159, 161, 162
Sumner and, 159–161, 163, 166
wealth and, 163–165
Social Gospel, 177–179
Socialism, 108–109, 174–179, 186, 203, 214, 237
Bellamy's, 170, 171
democratic, 221–222
Social sciences, 159, 187
"Sociological" school of jurisprudence, 217
South Carolina, 90, 124, 135
Speech, freedom of, 26, 29
Spencer, Herbert, 157–159, 161, 162
Spooner, Lysander, 151–152, 176–177
Starr, Isadore, 192*n*
State, the
Bourne's analysis of, 191
Calvinist view of, 8, 9
in Christian thought, 3–5
Emerson's view of, 109–110
Gronlunder's socialism and, 175–176
obedience to. *See* Obedience to state authority
See also Government
State constitutions, 52–55, 89
State courts, Supreme Court's appellate power and, 122
State laws, Supreme court's judicial review of, 122
States' rights, 79–81
State taxes on federal agencies, 123
Steffens, Lincoln, 185
Stephens, Alexander H., 126, 138
Stoicism, 2, 3
Storing, Herbert, 182
Story, Joseph, 88
Stowe, Harriet Beecher, 137
Strauss, Leo, 15*n*
Students for a Democratic Society, 239
Sumner, William Graham, 159–161, 163, 166
Supreme Court
national power and, 122, 123
slavery and, 136, 138
See also Judicial review; *and specific cases*

Sweezy, Paul, 220–221
Synods, 20
Szasz, Thomas, 230

Taney, Roger, 136
Tarbell, Ida, 185
Tax(es)
George's single-tax proposal, 169–170
Hamilton and, 77
income, 44
Otis on, 39
Paine's views on, 44
regulatory vs. revenue, 40
without representation, 38, 40
state, on federal agencies, 123
Taylor, John, 79–83
Tenth Amendment, 77
Texas v. *White*, 126
Thayer, Webster, 197
Theocracy, 30
Thomas Aquinas, St., 4–6
Thomas, G. E., 48*n*
Thomas, Norman, 221–222
Thoreau, Henry David, 114–118, 230
Thorpe, Francis N., 64*n*
Tierney, Brian, 15*n*
Tipton, Diane, 85*n*, 131*n*
Tocqueville, Alexis de, 98–99
Tolerance, Marcuse's theory of, 243
Tolstoy, Leo, 168
Town meetings, 52
Townsend, Francis, 219
Transcendentalism, 104–115, 150, 177
Brook Farm and, 107–109
Brownson and, 112–113
Emerson and, 105–107, 109–110
individualism and, 104, 107–110
reason and, 105, 106
Whitman and, 112
Trotter, Monroe, 181–182
Tucker, Benjamin, 176, 177, 192*n*
Turner, Frederick Jackson, 128, 187
Tuskegee Institute, 180
Twain, Mark, 130, 162–163, 188–189
Twelve Southerners, 211–213
Twenty-seventh Amendment, 245
"Two swords," doctrine of, 4
Tyler, Alice Felt, 102*n*, 118
Tyrants, 5, 9

Unemployment, 196, 213
Unicameralism, 55
Unitarianism, 33, 104
Universal Negro Improvement Association, 204–205
Urban areas, 70, 75
Utilitarianism, 162

Utopian communities, 118
  Brook Farm, 107–109
  Wright's, 94–95

Vanzetti, Bartolomeo, 196–197
Veblen, Thorstein, 187
Vesey, Denmark, 135–136
Vestrymen in colonial Virginia, 31
Veto, presidential, 97, 124
Viereck, Peter, 232–234
Virginia
  Anglican Church in, 18, 19, 31
  colonial government of, 31, 37–38
  constitution of, 53, 54
Virginia Resolution, 79–80

Walker, David, 90
Walker, Quok, 134
Walzer, Michael, 15n
War, Bourne on, 191
Ward, Lester Frank, 166–167
Ward, Nathaniel, 25–26
Wards, Jefferson's system of, 71–73
Ware v. Hylton, 122
Warfield, Benjamin B., 15n
Warren, Josiah, 176, 177
Warren, Robert Penn, 212
Washington, Booker T., 180–183, 204
Washington, George, 76–78
Wealth, Social Darwinism and, 163–165
Webster, Daniel, 21, 88, 98, 124–126
West Jersey, 30, 31
Weyl, Walter, 188
Whiskey Rebellion, 77
Whitman, Walt, 112, 117
Whittemore, Robert, 95, 102n
Williams, Roger, 27–29, 36–37, 52
Williams, T. Harry, 224n
Wilson, James, 41

Wilson, Woodrow, 75, 131, 188–190
Wiltse, C. M., 142
Winthrop, John, 19, 23–27, 29
Wise, John, 32
Wish, Harvey, 33n, 34n, 102n, 144,
    154n, 172n, 192n, 205n, 206n
Wolin, Sheldon S., 15n
Women, 93, 95
  in Congress, 244–245
  Fuller on, 111–112
  Jefferson on, 73
  Puritan attitude toward, 27
Women's Bill of Rights, 244
Women's movement, 244–245
  late nineteenth century, 168
  in Progressive period, 189
Women's rights, 162
  Abigail Adams on, 47–48
  John Adams on, 48
  Fuller and, 111
  Paine's support of, 44
Women's suffrage, 53, 168, 189
Woodward, C. Vann, 179, 192n
Wootton, Barbara, 232
Work, Thoreau on, 115
Worker participation, 229
Workers
  Jacksonianism and, 96, 97
  slaves compared to, 142–146
  See also Class, economic; Labor unions
Workingman's party, 90–95
World War I, 131, 190
Wright, Frances, 93–95
Writs of Assistance Case (1761), 40

Yablonsky, Lewis, 247n

Zilversmith, Arthur, 153n
Zinn, Howard, 223n

About the Author

Max J. Skidmore is currently Head of the Department of Political Science at Southwest Missouri State University. He received his Ph.D. from the University of Minnesota, and specializes in American politics and political thought, and political rhetoric and symbolism. From 1965 to 1968 he was Director of American Studies and Associate Professor of Political Science at the University of Alabama. Earlier, he held various positions with the Department of Health, Education, and Welfare in Washington, D.C., including Administrative Assistant in the Office of the Commissioner of Social Security and Program Review Officer in the U.S. Office of Education. Among his publications are *Medicare and the American Rhetoric of Reconciliation*, University of Alabama Press, 1970, and *Word Politics: Essays on Language and Politics*, Freel, 1972. He is also co-author of *American Government: A Brief Introduction*, St. Martin's Press, 1974; 2nd edition, 1977.